At Home in the Himalayas

Also by Christina Noble
Over The High Passes: A Year in the Himalayas

AT HOME IN THE HIMALAYAS

Christina Noble

COLLINS · LONDON · 1991

William Collins Sons & Co. Ltd
London · Glasgow · Sydney · Auckland
Toronto · Johannesburg

CIP Data for this book is available from the British Library on request

ISBN 0 00 215380 7

First published in Great Britain in 1991

Copyright © Christina Noble 1991

Photoset in Linotron Meridien by
Rowland Phototypesetting Ltd
Bury St Edmunds, Suffolk
Printed and bound in Great Britain by
Hartnolls Limited, Bodmin, Cornwall

Contents

Foreword   ix

I THE BEGINNING

A Taste For the Hills   1

Manali   5

The First Summer   16

II FOOTLOOSE

Sial   31

Incomers   43

The Sisters   54

The Map   59

Confronting Death   63

The Last Footloose Trip   72

III EXPANSION

Home-making   77

Duff Dunbar   82

Zanskar   91

Motherhood   106

Children of Hadimba's Forest   116

Monsoon   129

The Accident   133

Chandrabhaga   138

Leaving Duff Dunbar   145

IV THE WEB

Enmeshed   151

Land   170

Professional Trekkers   184

Prini   195

Afterword: Today   200

Notes   205

Glossary   207

List of Illustrations

Between pages 52 *and* 53
Ploughing a field on the hillside above a village
Terraced cultivation
A house in Jugatsukh village
On the way to Hadimba's temple
Duff Dunbar
The veranda of Prini Ropa
Boura Singh and Tara
The carpenters, Sunk Ram and his brother
Sunita patterns Tara's hands with dye
Rahul and Tara taking a morning bath at Gulab Das's
Gungru, the *chaukidar*, and his wife
Karma
Taj and Chamba
Kranti, Dorze and Rahul on a picnic above Kothi

Between pages 132 *and* 133
A glacier on the way to the pass to Kugti
Prayer flags
A Gaddi shepherd and children
A Kullu basket for carrying hay
Stopping for *chang* with Dorze's mother and stepfather
A family camping expedition in Hampta *nala*
A stone-roofed village in Phojal *nala*
A Khampa woman in her tea-house
Chamba's mother welcomes him to Karsha
Masks and flower offerings on a *deota's rath*

Foreword

I have lived in Manali, at the head of Kullu valley in the Indian Himalayas, for nineteen years.

In the beginning I must have seemed like a hippie (or *hippini*, as the female is referred to in Kullu), though I didn't consider myself to be one. Nor was I concerned with improving myself, as advised by a Miss Isobel Savory in 1907:

> To roam about in the Himalayas in gypsy fashion, meeting with trifling adventures from time to time, is a complete change for an ordinary English girl; and it is easy to find every scope for developing self control and energy in many a 'tight corner'.

I was footloose, and simply enjoyed the idea of turning my back on the familiar, revelling in the journey, heedless of the end.

Then I became a businesswoman, organizing walking holidays, and some years later, with misgivings and fears, a wife, mother and householder. My life was like anyone else's, except that I was 7,000 feet up in the Himalayas. I don't think I tried to change things as the Memsahibs used to; I lacked their conviction. Our kitchen was far from European, and I didn't teach anyone to make bread or bake cakes – the tin-box oven we brought from Kashmir was soon used as a hens' nesting box. Our attempts to encourage adult literacy quickly petered out, and much of my early faith in Western medicine was dashed.

Over the years I taught very little; I learnt a lot. I absorbed unfamiliar values and new concepts. My Hindi isn't perfect, but it enabled me to become aware of the aspirations of the people I met, their different reactions to misfortune and suffering, their ideas of God, and the fetters that bind them in a network of relationships. Without some understanding of Hindi and without the experience of years in Kullu, I would never have appreciated the extent to which concepts are confined by language. As I found myself using turns of phrase which I wouldn't have used in English, I began unconsciously to absorb new ideas. Sometimes it has made writing difficult. For instance, I have found it hard to make it clear that in India niceties of rank are immediately evident in any conversation. And, though I combed large dictionaries, I failed to find English words to express either the behaviour or the significance of the *gaur*.

I don't want to give the impression that I felt myself to be in an alien world. I was provoked to write this book by the remark of a *Woman's Hour* interviewer. We were discussing the Gaddi shepherds. 'You make them sound really quite human,' she said, surprised. My friends in Kullu are friends by any yardstick. I like to think that absorbing different ways of thought sharpens your perception of other people's feelings and jolts your preconceptions. Not long ago someone said to me, 'You'll never understand the power of the *dush* [the spell which was attacking him at the time] because you weren't brought up among our gods.' It is true that I won't understand as well as if I had been born a *pahari*, but I understand better than I would if I hadn't spent nineteen years in the West Himalayas.

I wasn't the only one to be lured by the unfamiliar. During the years I have lived in Manali it has become more and more of a marketplace; not just for goods but also for opportunists. Locals and newcomers have had to learn new skills, to master the unfamiliar and to grasp opportunity. Some have been more successful than others.

I used to write many letters, particularly to my mother in Scotland. Their tone was always cheerful, busy and in control; if I had expressed doubts and fears from 9,000 miles away (the post took a week to ten days, and a telegram at least forty-eight hours), she would have worried. I knew she wanted reassurance, and at the same time I wanted her to have a vivid picture of my world and the people around me. From time to time I also wrote a diary, which reveals quite different moods.

1989

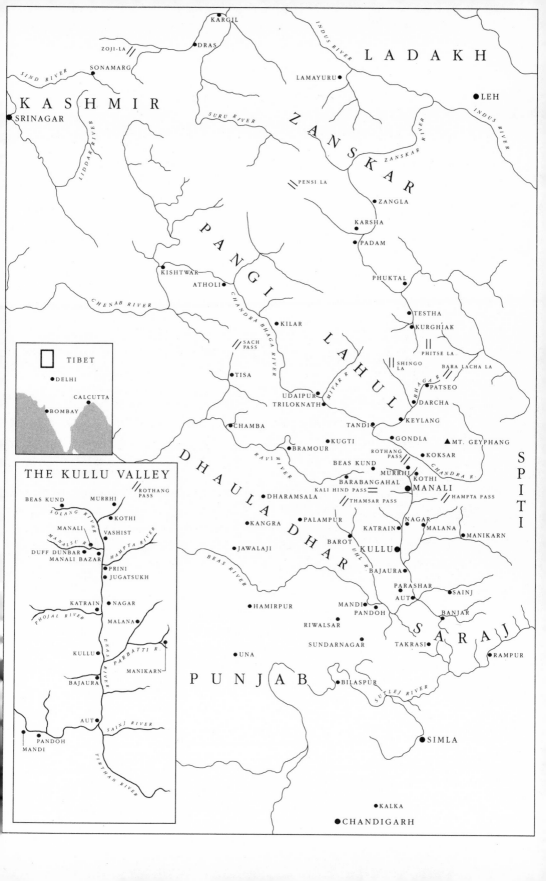

I
The Beginning

A Taste for the Hills

Letter to my mother from Manali, August 1970
We travelled by train from Delhi to Chandigarh and then on by
bus (nine hours) to Mandi. At Mandi, in the foothills, it was
uncertain whether the road was open: no buses were running
because of landslides in the gorge. In the end John and I had a lift
with some boys who had driven from Germany in a Volkswagen
van. But we wished we had waited for a bus. They were large,
with huge telephoto lenses and loud jokes. And their driving was
terrifying. The gorge was grey, muddy and inhospitable. Labourers
were at work; no bulldozers but Tibetans – men and women in
striped aprons, one wielding the spade, the other pulling on a rope
– their babies in bundles and baskets under the cliffs. In some
places landslides had fallen down the cliff-face on to the narrow
road; in others the road itself had fallen away, a hundred feet into
the swirling, silty river: frightening. The Germans thought it funny
to try to barge through the road blocks, showing off their four-
wheel drive, skidding and scattering shrieking labourers.

Out of the gorge we were in Kullu valley and the sky cleared.
After the flat, all-pervasive light of the plains, it was suddenly a
European, dappled light – alders and willows, pale greens. There
were thin, black cows; and threadbare pastures, army huts and
Tibetan shacks take up much of the grazing. There were apple
orchards and fields of unripe maize. The Beas river, wide and
rock-strewn, cuts through the bottom of the valley, fast, dirty and
forceful. Kullui women wear checked blankets, nose ornaments
and red head-coverings. Kullu bazaars are as you imagine bazaars
should be – shops up a few steps with wooden-shutter doors; I

glimpsed a draper cross-legged on his wooden platform and, through another doorway, curvaceous, shining brass vessels stacked on each other.

By the time we arrived in Manali, at the head of the valley – it's at 7,000 feet – it was dark; hardly a street light. It seems an end-of-the-road place – a scruffy bazaar. We spent the night above the town, at a tourist log hut in a deodar forest. As I went to sleep I could hear the roar of the river below.

John and I planned to walk through the Western Himalayas to Kashmir; we thought it would take us five weeks. We had both been to India before but not to Kullu nor on any walking expedition – we were wide-eyed tourists. We had an introduction to a Dr Snell of the mission hospital who might help us.

The path through the Lady Willingdon Hospital compound was slippery mud. On the doorstep of what we assumed was the doctor's house there was a row of muddy shoes and sandals. A tall English woman in Punjabi dress said, 'Service is going on, do come in.' We had forgotten it was Sunday. The congregation sat on the sitting-room floor in silence, heads bowed, waiting to be 'moved' to speak. A red-headed woman whispered, 'Thank you God for the rushing river.' An emotional, dark-skinned Indian prayed for the people in Assam, who were worshipping ghosts and devils while missionaries were not allowed to help them. We cowered, hoping we wouldn't be expected to contribute our personal experience of the week.

After the coffee and Bournvita Dr Snell gave us a lift in his Land Rover to Gulab Das's guesthouse. It was up the hill at the very end of the road, then down a grassy path through an orchard. An outdoor staircase led on to an enclosed balcony. Gulab Das, a small, whining man wearing homespun tweed jodhpurs and swathed in a shawl, brought us apples and served a dinner of marrow and curds, rice and mint chutney. We ate by moonlight; the electricity had gone off. Tomorrow, Gulab Das told us, would be *sawan purnima*, the full moon of the month of *sawan* (roughly August). At Patseo, high above the villages, in the mountains in the north of Lahul, there would be a wool fair

2

that lasted throughout the night. *Pashmina* wool, from the fine undercoat of a special goat, brought down from Tibet and Ladakh by mule train, would be exchanged for sugar, rice and tea.

We woke to a perfect morning: the sun shone through an apple tree up against the window (Gulab Das claimed that he didn't sell its fruit but gave it to the Goddess Hadimba), and had *parathas* and apricot jam for breakfast.

Despite Dr Snell's practical trekking tips – like having cloth bags made to hold rice, *dal* and flour – and his introduction to Wangdi, a Nepali mountaineer who found us porters, it took ten testing days to organize our expedition. Finally we set off, with three guide-porters, heading straight up through the deodar forest above Manali.

For the first few days I didn't even think of writing in my diary. Once we had crossed the first pass, the 15,000-foot Kali Hind, I wrote:

> I don't have time to think, only to concentrate on the next step. The sphere of your concentration is so small; if you let your mind wander you've got off balance and out of breath. So there's no time and not enough energy to be frightened – you just put one foot in front of the other, even if it is vertical ice or a single log bridge.

This was my first experience of altitude; I had never even been to the Alps. I was struck by the eerie quietness of the pass and by the barren landscape, drained of colour like a monochrome print – dirty snow and stained ice.

We created a world of our own in a parenthesis of time. Strength and continuity grew out of the camaraderie that developed between us. Initially we were five. Sonam abandoned us half-way through (and from then on we had to find a local replacement, stage by stage), but Chamba and Taj became real companions. Chamba looked and behaved as though he were the younger of the two. He was the expedition's Puck, with a crop of vertical hair that stood up from his round, red face. He had a peculiar rolling gait and often fell over, haversack and all. Permanently dishevelled, he made no sartorial effort even when we arrived at the big bazaars like Kishtwar. His jokes tided us over moments of weariness or despair and he himself would roll on the ground with laughter at them. Rarely did he show any sign of stress or strain, but I remember him moaning softly on the long walk up to Bramour Forest rest-house. We had already walked twenty miles that day and weren't prepared for four more; and he was convinced that bears would get us. Below the Sinthan Pass, when we couldn't find water, he raged, 'Those Musulmans, no one is any good for travellers here. In Lahul one potato is enough *subji* for four, and if you go to any house they'll give you what you need without you asking for it.'

Taj danced across the mountainsides. Every morning, before we moved off, he spent a while in front of a two-inch mirror perched on a rock, combing and oiling his hair and twirling his moustaches to the required angle. Mercurial, sometimes moody, he was also a born organizer and often a brilliant bargainer. Chamba had little tact – he had a gruff, slightly insolent manner with locals – but Taj could wheedle a bottle of local liquor, a cauliflower or a leg of mutton out of an apparently barren hillside. Crucial to our enterprise, he could also persuade unwilling villagers to be our porters for the next stage. One evening, when we were still a week away from Kashmir, he was squatting dolefully in the cave that was our night's camp. 'Cheer up, we'll soon be there,' John said. 'There are plenty of lovely girls in Kashmir.'

'They're not that good, and they're dirty,' he mumbled. 'Anyway it's all right for you, you've got money. All I'll want will be a bottle of *sherab* [liquor].' Perhaps he was gloomy because we were approaching a Muslim country, where there was going to be little hope of finding alcohol.

Towards the end of the six weeks I wrote in my diary:

There are periods of ecstasy – sitting in the shade of a walnut tree cracking walnuts or lying stretched on a rock watching clouds, empty-headed. We don't talk much as we walk. I wonder, unconcerned, how far to the village or how long until the next cigarette stop (we smoke 'Scissors' or 'Panama'). I look at the trees and

4

flowers and the light and shade. I am exhilarated to be without everyday anxieties – or comforts.

It was that exhilaration, and the excitement of senses sharpened, that made me want more. An egg, wild pomegranates for *chutni*, or even (twice) a chicken; these were real treats. When we arrived in Kashmir, 'The terrestial paradise of the Indies' – so long looked forward to – I was disenchanted, and loath to accept the intrusion of the real world. John had to go to London, but I couldn't bear to abandon what we had created. So I went back to Manali.

Manali

'What a shame it's so spoilt, so squalid and dirty,' the tourists bemoan, assuming that Manali was once a picturesque village. But it never was. Manali village is up above, on the far side of the Manalsu *nala* which joins the Beas just upstream from the bazaar. The villages – with their substantial stone and timber houses – cluster on promontories among terraced fields and apple orchards. The white peaks rise thousands of feet above. On the precipitous slopes deodar forest gives way to spruce and fir; birches and rhododendrons grow below the alps and the permanent snow. From the bazaar, a couple of hundred feet above the river, you only catch glimpses of the snow peaks, for the valley is narrow here.

For centuries Manali was a trading post for goods coming to and from the plains and the North – Lahul, Ladakh and Tibet. Towards the end of the last century it grew from a traders' encampment to one or two shops and a post office. During the early years of this century a Forest rest-house and a Public Works Department rest-house were built for officers on tour or those on fishing and shooting holidays; the only other accommodation was at Captain Banon's guesthouse. The Captain was an Irishman who had retired from a Bengali regiment and settled here to grow apples.

A noticeboard beside the octroi post (a pole across the road, lifted by the toll-keeper when the vehicle had paid its dues) read 'Welcome to Manali', but during my early days there the bazaar didn't begin for half a mile. On the right a spectacular deodar forest hid the river; on the left was the potato ground and the shack of the civil hospital, then the petrol pump and the police station. Then you reached the bazaar – a mere two hundred yards long. Cobblers sat on the kerb, sheltered from sun or rain by umbrellas, with their tools and sample shoes laid out beside them. Next door, also sheltered by umbrellas, sat the umbrella-menders. The barbers' stands were more substantial: the customer's chair, and a mirror resting on a folding table, were protected by a thin cloth awning. Cigarette kiosks – with the colourful packets arranged to line three sides of the booth – and vegetable stalls jutted out on to the street. Substantial brick-and-mortar or timber buildings housed the cloth shops, the Bhutti Weavers' shawl shop, the State Bank and two or three grain merchants-cum-grocery stores like the Chandrabhaga, which also sold luxuries – tins of cheese, butter, sardines and, sometimes, bars of chocolate. Even these *pukka* shops didn't have glass windows; they were open on to the street by day, and closed at night with wooden shutters.

The bus stand was at the top of the bazaar, with Verma's tea-house just below it, the town's only restaurant to the left of it, and the tourist office – in a tin hut – to the right. The bus stand was also a crossroads. The road to Lahul went off to the right, to cross the Beas, while the road to the log huts and Gulab Das's went on up the hill. In the *Y* of the crossroads, with the forest as a backdrop, was a *maidan* used as a camping area (now a pretentious municipal park with a stone stage and a statue of Nehru), and overlooking it was the post office, in a room above the Rama bakery. In the early days I didn't know what to look for to distinguish a Tibetan from a Nepali or a shepherd from a buffalo man. Nor did I know what to make of what I was told. It wasn't that people tried to fool me; I just didn't know how to digest the information I was given – I had no context to fit it into. Everything was one-dimensional. Slowly I learnt who was who, and the significance of what I was told and the map of my surroundings began to emerge.

Manali is no model town. Open gutters run down the streets; the alleys are muddy and unpaved. There are dead rats, rabid and scabby dogs, and a rank smell of garbage, damp tweed, wood smoke, diesel and kerosene fumes. But only the purblind could find it boring. I could sit for hours in Verma's tea-house, pretending to read my newspaper but watching. Nowadays I can tell a Nepali coolie from a Kashmiri and a Spitiali from a Tibetan. I can see that a woman is from Saraj by her black-and-white checked *pattu*. I know a Gaddi flock of sheep from a local one, and a Gujar's large plastic jerry can for buffalo milk from a Lahuli's two-litre metal can for Jersey's milk. This hotchpotch is the fun of the bazaar. Manali is a lure – not just because of the shops, but also because of the lucrative opportunities of the market-place; there are hotels, guesthouses and taxis, trekking and climbing parties, the wool trade and shawl manufacture, seed-potato export, orchard-contracting, building construction, the drug trade (in the wake of the hippies), and timber operations. An adventurous boy in a remote, roadless village in Buddhist Zanskar hears about Manali and vows that when he grows up he will venture over the passes to find work there. Or a tea-shack owner in Kangra closes his shutters, spends his savings on the bus fare to Manali and finds himself a job as a uniformed waiter serving Chinese food to wealthy Bombay tourists.

The weather was autumnal during the two months I was in Manali after the trek to Kashmir. The light became less dense – it was pale and transparent – and the leaves began to fall. Porters strolled up and down in newly bought clothes. The season was almost over. Outside the grain store there were huddles of prosperous Lahuli women – their eyes flashing and observant – wearing velvet dressing gowns and discussing budgets and prices for their winter provisions. There were Zanskaris, down from even higher and more distant Buddhist villages, with greasy plaits under conical yellow hats and layers of unwashed wool; they were wild-looking, like Red Indians. Lamas from remote monasteries, who had also come for rations, were easily identified by their bristly shaven heads and thick maroon gym tunics, and had shaggy donkeys to carry the grain sacks back over the passes. Lines of tailors sat cross-legged in dimly lit booths birling their machines to make warm winter clothes; charcoal-filled irons on damp tweed gave out a distinctive smell in the cold air. There were less pleasant smells round the butcher's stall – warm blood and offal.

Mid-afternoon was peak strolling time. As I sat at Verma's tea-house reading the day before's *Statesman* and drinking a glass of tea or, if the electricity was working, a cup of weak, frothy coffee from the espresso machine, Chamba might shamble in and join me.

'I'll be leaving Manali soon. Can't stay here much longer, too cold and expensive. It's good down at Una, except there are so many of those noisy Punjabis. You get a kilo of cauliflower for a rupee, or free maybe, and we Manali people get plenty of work selling sweaters from the factories.'

It was Chamba who first told me the story of the Lahuli *thakur* who was a reincarnated lama. He pointed him out in Verma's, sitting with friends at a back table.

Some lamas, in disguise, once came to the house of a Lahuli who held a high rank in the air force, and were given work in the kitchen. They showed the young son of the house 'old things' which had belonged to the dead lama, mixed with other people's clothes and possessions. The boy picked out the dead lama's things and so, throwing off their disguise, the visitors announced that the boy was the reincarnation of a high lama. 'Nonsense. My son is to be a soldier, not a lama – please go from here and never come back,' said the air-force father, sending the lamas packing. But while his father was away, the boy was kidnapped. An uncle was sent to Ladakh to find him. 'All right, all right,' he appeased the lamas, 'he is your head lama, but you must bring him to Srinagar to have the papers signed.' The trick worked: at Srinagar the family succeeded in grabbing the boy and sent him quickly to Vietnam, where his father was stationed. Soon afterwards the father was killed in a helicopter crash; then the mother was sure that if they continued to thwart the lamas something would happen to her son, so she handed him over to the monastery. Now he lived six months as a high lama and six months with his family – just below Manali in a large house surrounded by an orchard.

This was the kind of story I didn't know what to make of; I found it so hard to believe.

Taj sometimes visited me. We would sit, on upright chairs, sipping a little Panipat No. 1, a bright pink 'English wine'. 'No, I don't know what I'll do in the winter.' Was he not going with Chamba?

'No. Okay, we're good enough friends for working together here but you don't go everywhere with someone. It's different for him; he has a family, but I'm all alone. I have one brother, in the army.'

At the time I wasn't sure what he was implying. I think he was hinting at the superficiality of friendship; stressing that it is family bonds which count. In his world, no one trusts another with his fears and anxieties; airing them would be more likely to arouse ridicule or scorn than to arouse sympathy. And there is pride: anyone in possession of detailed knowledge about you might use it and could acquire a hold over you. You protect yourself by assuming the world is uncharitable. Without a close family network you feel vulnerable. Taj's father, who had been a muleteer trading between their northern Lahuli village and Tibet, was dead; his mother, too. 'I was about eight when she died. I was sitting in her lap. I hate the smell of death, it gives me a headache.' He did have a married sister, living near Manali, but, Chamba told me, her husband frowned on Taj – on his drinking and on the fact that he hadn't married and settled.

I often walked up to the Hadimba temple, secluded among the tall, straight deodar trees of Dunghri forest. It is hard to describe the atmosphere there, yet it was so striking it was almost tangible – intense and pervasive. As you came in from the sunlight the forest was quiet, and dark-green. It wasn't just the age and the height of the trees that affected you, but also the immense primeval rocks. The three-tiered, sixteenth-century temple itself is built over a massive rock. It must have been a shrine long before the temple was built, for the Goddess Hadimba, originally a *raksha* (demon), has controlled the forest for more than twenty centuries. It was the rock that saved her from being washed away in the great flood that devastated the universe – her footstep is imprinted on it. Much later, at the time of the wars of the Mahabharat and the adventures of the Pandava brothers, she was deified and absorbed into the Hindu pantheon. During their exile the Pandavas had happened to camp nearby. The most powerful of the brothers, Bhim, took a fancy to Hadimba and there ensued a terrible battle between him and the *raksha's* brother Hadimb, who fought to protect his sister's honour. For forty-eight hours the forest shook and shuddered as they wrestled with each other and hurled trees about. Ultimately Bhim triumphed. As the grieving Hadimba attended to the bruised body of her dying brother, Bhim snatched and ravaged her. The seduction led to romance. But Hadimba would only agree to a continuance of their dalliance in the forest if she was allowed to bear a son; the enraptured Bhim had to agree. After Bhim and the Pandavas had continued on their travels, leaving the forest once again to Hadimba, she became a goddess, because she was the mother of a bona fide god, Ghatotkacha. So Hinduism expands – by adoption rather than conversion.

I visited the temple one afternoon with Raj Krishan (his family were the temple custodians) and Lady Betjeman, whose Catholicism didn't bar her from having an extensive knowledge of and enthusiasm for Hinduism. She wanted to know, 'Do you really worship the *Devi* or is it more the philosophy?' Inside the dingy temple, he had replaced his trousers with a scanty *dhoti* and at that moment, hands folded and head bowed, was reverentially at prayer. There is no icon or image in the windowless temple – only the footstep in the overhanging rock and, under it, on the damp earth, a conch shell, a bell, and offerings of coins and flowers. He must have heard her ringing tones but he chose not to answer her.

I was unaccustomed to being with people who had firm religious feelings. In Manali everyone around me assumed a natural familiarity with their gods, and their unselfconscious beliefs affected their daily lives. In the afternoons I sometimes walked with Sister Valerie – the tall woman in Punjabi dress who had let us into the doctor's house – in the arboretum by the river, to enjoy the autumn colours of the English oaks and limes and sweet chestnuts. She strode along with a bamboo pole, which I assumed was to protect either us or Kimble the spaniel. I described our walks to my mother, who was not an admirer of Jesus:

> Valerie told me how sometimes Jesus lets people go along different paths; they may be worshippers of Shiva or Buddha, but in the end, if they are really searching, He will show them *the* path, because it is the only truth. I did ask why God leads them such a dance; why not the main road, straight to Jesus? She explained why. 'When the man who carries our baggage when we go to visit the villages – he's a long-haired dervish – became a Christian, he asked us the same question. "How is it we haven't heard about this before?" I told him our army of good Christians spreading the word is just too small: there aren't enough of us.' I was tempted to ask, if His truth is so self-evident why aren't there more?

The bloom of the hippies' flower power was over; those that had lingered here were debilitated by drugs and an inadequate diet. Susceptible to disease and infection they often hung about the hospital looking for attention. Their rootlessness and claims to be searching for truth encouraged the missionaries in a way but also confused them; the Lord had sent the missionaries to India to help foreign heathens, not lost European youth. Dr Snell found himself irritated with the hippies' obsession with themselves and what they ate; he wished they would see the benefit of trusting themselves to Jesus and follow his example of service to others. Linda, a tall, elegant girl who had once been a beauty queen in Canada, told me that up in the village where she lived the children were apt to throw stones at her and boys had tried to climb into her room. 'It all happens because of the bad things in my head, because I think wrong thoughts. It's only because I haven't reached real peace within myself that I get upset about

11

it. I'm trying to get off eating tomatoes – when I succeed that will help me. Dairy products are bad for me too.'

One afternoon at Verma's, Chamba came to say he and his wife and little daughter were off to Una for the winter.'*Jhule*, go carefully. Don't eat too much in Scotland; not too much whisky either. We'll meet again. Come back to Manali soon – next year?' I certainly didn't want this to be the last time I saw his beaming, round face.

Before it became too cold and snow closed the road, Taj and I went up to the Rothang Pass. It took hours to climb the mule track from Kothi up to Murrhi, where we were to spend the night; it was steep and I was already out of practice. I had imagined Murrhi would be a stone and timber village built into the hillside, but there was nothing except three hotels, like a group of dry-stone fanks, with canvas roofs. Ours was the Nepali Dhaba, though it was owned by a tall and dignified man who came from Spiti; he was a little too reserved for a hotelier, but his wife exuded hospitality. A one-eyed Tibetan wearing plaits and a back-to-front army coat, one sleeve hanging loose, stood over the *chulha*. The dish-washer, stunted and deformed by curvature of the spine, spent most of the evening outside at the icy slops beside the water drum. From time to time he would shuffle in to entertain us to a show, like a Shakespearian fool. Customers sat drinking *chang*, the local beer, until the rising full moon lit the tips of the mountains. Taj had had my *charpoi* taken to the back of the hut and set beside the one belonging to the hotelier, who slept for only an hour or two at a time, then refreshed himself from his *chang* kettle. Three sheep's legs hung above my head, and rats ran along the meat line, squealing with excitement.

In the morning we climbed the last two thousand feet to the pass. At 13,200 feet it was cold, too bitter in the wind to linger and look over into Lahul, despite the spectacular view of the holy Mount Geyphang and glaciers that really looked like rivers of ice. Everyone was coming over from Lahul for the winter. Girls had their heads bound with head-squares or towels, pinned at the chin, to keep off the wind; Tibetan families whirled prayer wheels; mule trains rested on the summit – the lead pony wore a purple plume between his ears. We followed some Zanskaris, in big winged hats and felt boots, who scampered down, precariously balancing bent-willow packs high on their backs.

I stayed for a few days twenty miles down-valley at Katrain with Pandit Balak Ram and his son Raj Krishan, the custodian of the Hadimba temple, who was also a farmer, orchard-owner and politician. Here the valley was much wider than at Manali and, though not much more than a thousand feet lower, much warmer. We sat out in the garden, once formal now uncared-for – with jasmine in bloom and the last rosebuds – and looked across the valley to the old castle at Nagar. Old Panditji complained that you couldn't buy lawn grass seed any more, nor proper purple dahlias. He wore corduroys and a herring-bone tweed jacket and, as he couldn't get a deer-stalker, a brown trilby. He was a devotee of the old days.

One afternoon a small, old man, dressed in layers of homespun tweed, came deferentially to the steps and, squatting on his heels, began a long conversation in Kullui. The old man was the *chaukidar* (caretaker) at Duff Dunbar, a house my hosts owned up above the Dunghri forest. They were having trouble with the tenants, a band of British *hippinis*, who were using the old furniture as firewood. They had been told to leave by the end of last month, but Raj Krishan, embarrassed by the women's pleading, had allowed them an extra week. Now two weeks were up, and the *chaukidar* said the squalor was unbearable. These women didn't fit the picture of the British in his memory: 'It cannot be. Either I've never seen the British or they are just telling you they are British, because they are a different type of foreigner.' I saw the *chaukidar* glancing at me, sizing up my Britishness – or lack of it. Panditji said that the *chaukidar* couldn't understand why the British didn't stand for the elections these days; 'It's true that if they did no other party would stand a chance.' He decried the weakness and incompetence of the present administration and police, paralysed by powerful local politicians; in British times, he said, the administration was honest and strong.

In the evenings it was chilly and we huddled round a smoulder-
ing, British-style open fire; above the mantelpiece hung a blackened oil painting of a waterfall in the Lake District. The
window-sills were stacked with old copies of *Country Life* and the
Field, sent by a friend in Twickenham. We ate walnuts and maize
fried together, washed down with pegs of Black Knight whisky.
Raj Krishan drank in front of his father, whom he called 'Daddy',
but respectfully went out of the room when he wanted a cigarette.

The old man aired his disapproval of modern times and 'this
democratic form of government':'A gentleman cannot pull on.
In the old good days people had principles. There was a District
Forest Officer who shot a twenty-seven inch ibex – no less than
twenty-eight inches was the rule – up the Parbatti valley. When
he discovered what he had done he was so ashamed that he sent
a runner on a two-day journey to the Conservator. For those
two days, until the reply came back, he stood with a stone on
his head to demonstrate his shame to the locals and to his *shikari*
[hunter]. The Conservator fined him five rupees.'

I understood why the *chaukidar* had found the hippies a
'different type of foreigner'.

I went back to Manali for a wedding at the hospital. The New
Zealand lady doctor was marrying a padre from Kerela, and I
was to be the photographer. Sister Valerie gave me lunch –
cauliflower cheese followed by apples well scrubbed with carbolic
soap. The wedding was held under an awning in front of the
doctor's house. Taking the photographs wasn't easy; there was
little light under the awning and I didn't have a flash. Women
and children sat on the left, men on the right. Valerie struck up
'Here Comes the Bride', her long fingers thundering down on
the piano keys. Dr Snell, wearing an immaculate navy lounge
suit, gave the bride away. The Snell daughters were bridesmaids;
their blonde hair was decorated with yellow flowers and they
clutched yellow posies. Lahulis and Tibetans began to throng
over the wall and one woman calmly tied her sheep to an apple
tree while she watched the fun. The service was conducted

by the Bishop of North India in Urduized Hindi and English, punctuated by loud sucking noises from babies at the breast. Verma was the caterer and Gulab Das had made the cake.

Soon afterwards I reluctantly left Manali. At five in the morning, as I waited for the first bus to Delhi, it was dark and cold. Taj, looking forlorn, saw me off. The leisurely pace of the shaking bus lulled me into a state of suspended consciousness. Even after dawn there was little colour; the orchards were leafless and grey, the hillsides bleached and the fields, but for the green of winter wheat, a dull brown. My eye registered anomalous details — corrugated iron roofs, plastic flowers, concrete bungalows scattered along the roadside rather than clustered in villages, cliffs being dynamited to make a new road, the old rocks in the valley floor being blasted for building material.

I wondered what would happen to the next generation here. Would young men move away to the big cities, abandoning and debilitating their agricultural villages, as had happened to the hill communities in Europe? Or would the old rural order be revolutionized by a thriving cash economy? Politicians promise roads so that sacks of seed potatoes and boxes of apples can be trucked out from remote villages and rice brought in. As a cash economy replaces subsistence agriculture, spending power is generated for some; but for others, inevitably, raised aspirations will remain unfulfilled. Communism can't be a realistic alternative here, where people's tenacious belief in ownership and the importance of family is so strong. And how could you introduce concepts of equality to people who are taught respect for elder siblings from the cradle and for whom it is clear in every conversation who is giving and who receiving respect?

As the bus was about to leave Kullu valley and we drove into the bend after Bajaura, where the road follows an arm of the Beas, I decided I would come back and organize a trekking agency. I have passed along that bend in the road many times since, and often wondered what made me think of such an enterprise and what made me think I could do it.

The First Summer

I spent that winter in London. I whirled about, formed a limited company, found an accountant, calculated costs and budgets. With more literary flourish than tour operator's know-how I wrote a brochure:

> You can camp above the clouds where the peaks seem suspended in the sky, and where the only sign of man in the vast arena of mountains is the track made by a shepherd and his sheep . . . From your cosy camp, watching the sun rise across the peaks, all the cares that so burdened you in the lower world seem insignificant.

I knocked on the doors of Air India and travel agents with Indian connections. There were those who doubted the practicality of a lone foreign woman running a business in India; was it even legal? Others raised their eyebrows in a way that made me feel tight-rope walking or lion-taming would be more acceptable. Looking back, I am surprised anyone did take me seriously. My knowledge of the area was confined to the trek to Kashmir and a couple of months in Manali. I had no mountaineering skills nor expedition-leading experience, and I knew nothing about the travel trade or running a business.

By the early spring I had mailed five hundred brochures, made friends in Air India's tours department, and established an arrangement with Cox and King's, a long established (and faintly amused) travel agency with offices in London and India. They would handle my bookings (I had two) and forward the payments; rupee notes were to be sent from Bombay in a registered envelope.

In May I was back in Manali. My base for the first season was the top floor at Gulab Das's, with the use of a kitchen down below, but I spent most of the time out in the hills.

Initially there was no sign of Chamba, Taj or Sonam; I hadn't been able to write as I had no address for them. For my first recce I had to depend on Kullui men. They had no organizational flair – they were well-meaning, but had to be told when to make

16

a cup of tea let alone when we should be off in the morning or what constituted a suitable camp site. After a few drizzling days and unsuccessful attempts to find the way across a ridge that connected two valleys – I did at least see a pair of snow leopards and my first heartsease on the top of a pass – they said they wanted to go home. I was fed up and agreed. It was my twenty-ninth birthday.

For the next route-finding expedition I had the benefit of Taj's expertise, for he had arrived back from the spring ploughing in Lahul. He didn't seem surprised to find me in Manali, nor as pleased to see me as I had expected, but he readily agreed to join the trip. We bit off much more than we could chew. My map marked a useful-looking route leading from the head of Kullu valley over a pass to the headwaters of the Ravi river. Then there was a choice: either you followed the Ravi down to Barabangahal (the first village on our original trek) or you turned off to the left, high up the Ravi, traversed a stretch of snow field, and rejoined the path from Barabangahal – which crossed the Kali Hind Pass to Manali. I decided to try the latter.

We bought provisions for a week's expedition and spent two or three pleasant days walking up the Solang *nala* to Beas Kund, a saucer-shaped arena surrounded by snow-fields, rock faces and glaciers. In the early evening it reverberated with avalanches and rock falls, and the glaciers creaked. It was the end of June. Each day the long hours of hot sun melted tons of snow and ice off the mountains; everything was insubstantial. The night we spent there, a friend from England who had joined me for his first taste of the Himalayas had a good night's sleep; I did not. I may not have had much experience but I had had enough to know that what we could see of the way up the pass was no easy scramble. It looked like a vertical climb up a gully, and near the top there was an overhanging rock buttress to be negotiated. Taj was not one to show apprehension, but as we huddled round our nightcap cup of tea he had admitted it was a pity Chamba wasn't with us. I certainly missed Chamba's waddling gait and his jokes, and the reassurance of his loyalty. The two other men, Nepalis, inspired no confidence.

The gully which had frightened me from below proved to be so steep that Taj, the only one of us who could use an ice axe, had to cut steps most of the way. My English friend had never tackled a frozen, perpendicular slope before, and his long feet mutilated the horizontal toe-holds into vertical slashes. Out of a selfish sense of self-preservation I insisted on climbing in front of him. As we neared the overhanging rocks I could see pitted runs in the packed snow. It was all too clear: during the day the hot sun melted the ice gripping the rocks so that they rolled and bounced downhill, a mortal danger for anyone climbing up from below. Taj decided that we should negotiate our way round to a ledge and spend the night on it; in the early morning the precarious rocks would be held fast by the night's frost. It was an unpleasant prospect but relatively safe.

The last stretch was less steep, and at the top there was a spectacular view of Mount Hanuman Tibba, a shining elongated triangle against an azure sky.

Once you have overcome a hazard which for a time has absorbed all your mental and physical energy, you assume all will be well; you don't think any further ahead. We hadn't descended far before we were faced by a nasty fast-flowing stream. It was too fast to cross; we had to wait until the morning, when without snow-melt the water would be lower. Even then we had to fix a handrail rope, in case anyone lost their footing in the icy torrent. The snow field beyond turned out to be a gruelling ascent. My friend was finding his first encounter with the thin air at 16,000 feet testing, and the Nepalis were inadequately shod; we were slow. At last on the crest we could see no sign of the track marked on the map: we looked down on to a malevolent, dirty glacier. Rising mist veiled the dangers ahead, and it was impossible to assess which might be the least dangerous way down. But down we had to go; it was too late and too cold to wait for the mist to clear or to search for an alternative pass.

It was the sort of risk you shouldn't take. At that time I had no idea what was an acceptable Himalayan hazard and what was dangerous and foolhardy. My memory of the episode is vague. It was one of those occasions when ordinary observations and mental processes are suspended: you see and act only as you have to, from one fifteen-foot section to the next. I remember Taj cutting seemingly endless steps and resting on grey shale promontories. Now and then, for a few seconds at a time, the mist would lift a little, but we had hardly realized that our view had extended to fifty yards before the mist swirled and closed in again. I saw Taj slip, and he and his red haversack slid down the ice with a sickening scraping noise. Somehow he saved himself, his pride and temper the worse for the fall. I don't know how he found a way down and off the glacier; he must have smelt it.

Exhausted, we made our way off ice and rock on to grass. The mist was still down and by now it was twilight. It occurred to my numb brain that we needed sugar, for energy, and at the bottom of my bag I found some bars of chocolate. We pitched a tent, brewed a cup of tea (which smelt of kerosene, for the can had leaked into the sugar; kerosene, as I learnt then, must never be carried near food), devoured the chocolate and collapsed.

In the early morning, camped on an alp at about 12,000 feet, we were above the mist; it was clear that inadvertently we had crossed back into the Beas watershed rather than the Ravi basin. Our provisions were nearly finished: we had just a few hundred grams of the kerosene-stinking sugar and a kilo or two of flour. Without re-stocking we couldn't go on to explore the route leading to the Kali Hind Pass. It didn't look as though it would be far to Manali so Taj and one of the Nepalis volunteered to go down to buy rations and post a letter; we thought they would be back the following evening. I had recovered from the traumas of the day before and was looking forward to a couple of restful, if slightly hungry, days camped on the sunny alp. I scribbled what I thought was a reassuring note home, making light of our adventures:

We are out exploring a route and got a bit delayed because of hitches like steps having to be cut in the snow up to the pass, a river that was too fast to ford in the afternoon, and mistaking the way because of mist. As a result we have run short of supplies. But we've been all right because we've always had dry tents and

cosy sleeping bags, so no danger of suffering from exposure. I am
going to camp on this lovely alp – there's a primula and a transparent dwarf azalea all around – while two of the men go down
to Manali for rations. I'm so enjoying reading *Anna Karenina* again,
though I have to skip the descriptions of their meals. Don't worry
if you don't hear from me for ten days or so. I'll write as soon as
I'm back in Manali.

In the afternoon of the following day we lit a fire with rhododendron (*companulatum*) carried up from below; we were ready to
cook the expected meat and eggs. But the men didn't appear.
By the morning of the third day I had finished *Anna Karenina*
and I was hungry; we were reduced to a soup made from wild
garlic, thickened with what little remained of the flour. Before
the daily mid-morning mist engulfed us I had seen there were
two white tents and some ponies fifteen hundred feet below us,
and decided to visit them.

They turned out to be the tents of Khampas (traders whom I
later came to appreciate as some of the most interesting people
in the area), who were here for the summer to collect medicinal
herbs. As I approached the first tent I was welcomed by a man
with a peculiar squint or wall eye: 'Come in, come in. We were
wondering why you were staying up there. Why didn't you
come down before?' I didn't have to give any explanations. Taj
had passed here on his way to Manali, and the Khampas knew
all about us. 'Your men won't be back till tonight at the earliest,
maybe tomorrow. There's no direct way to Manali from here,
no way down the *nala*. Downstream from here it's cliffs. You
have to climb right up to cross the ridge and down the far
side.'

There were three men and two teenage boys. The tents were
professionally sewn, with the panels against the stretch of the
cloth, and reinforced with strategic ropes. Although they were
white I was reminded of pictures of black, yak-hair Mongolian
tents. These people were organized in the way of those accustomed to tent life. The men had thin, Chinese-style drooping
moustaches and eyes narrowed against sun, dust and cold. Their

possessions were methodically stacked around three sides of the tent – wooden chests, rolls of goat-hair mats and blankets, spoons, plates, kettles and churns for making butter tea, all arranged with kitchen-dresser precision and cleanliness. At the far end, a coloured photograph of the Dalai Lama hung above a shelf where polished copper cups stood filled with an offering of water. These were not humble rustic people. There was a pressure cooker and a large radio. The oldest man was wrapped in a fine homespun shawl, and all three of them wore Japanese watches. Without a moment's hesitation or a hint of awkwardness my boss-eyed host showed me to a blanketed corner where I could rest my back against sacks of grain, and made me a glass of thick, sweet tea. He welcomed me as though he had been expecting me to call, as though he was just round the corner from some shops. He didn't ask if I wanted anything to eat or drink, just placed the *tawa* on the stove to heat while he kneaded dough and began to cook. He told me they were here for two or three months. 'Our village is in Hampta *nala*' – he pointed over towards the peaks on the far side of the main valley – 'but in winter we go down below, towards the Punjab, and do business. Yes, selling these roots and other business too.'

I was given hot water to wash my hands and served spicy black potato curry and a well-brewed kettleful of *chang*. I ate eight large chapattis; never before or since have I eaten so many. My gratitude was effusive; I kept repeating that I would repay the rations as soon as ours arrived, though I could tell he considered my utilitarian attitude a little uncouth. He insisted that one of the boys should go up the hill to tell everyone at our camp to move down.

In the evening they gave what seemed to me a party – with vast quantities of food and *chang*. Taj and the Nepali (and the rations) arrived in the middle. Sitting down, I didn't feel much the worse for the *chang*, but when I got up and went out, the moon took arcs and dips through the sky and my knees and ankles wobbled.

The next morning it was raining. I decided that our exploration of the route to the Kali Hind would have to wait. We were adamant: our hosts must take our newly bought rations – it would be absurd for us to carry them back down.

The monsoon had begun. It didn't rain every day or all day; there would be three or four very wet days at a time and endless mist. Lady Betjeman was back in Manali, spending a few weeks across the hill from me at Duff Dunbar, the house owned by Pandit Balak Ram; at last they had succeeded in moving out the *hippinis*. One Saturday the Snells asked us both to dinner at the hospital; I wrote to my mother to describe it.

> We slithered down the hill through the forest – Penelope was carrying her 'party shoes' and her mending – a pinny and two pairs of beige bloomers. Sister Valerie was there too (she and Penelope cackled with laughter at each other's jokes – the British are noisy laughers). And there was a sullen *hippini* who wants Penelope to teach her how to be a lady.
>
> Afterwards Dr Snell offered us a lift home but the Land Rover stuck in the mud. So Penelope and I, clinging together, scrambled up through the pitch-dark forest. It was eerie round the temple – there was blood from a fresh sacrifice and swathed men lurched about under the trees – but Penelope shrieked so piercingly – to scare off the *joginis* (spirits), she said – that it would have frightened away a *raksha* let alone a drunken villager.
>
> I stayed the night with her as she wanted help having her ponies shod at the blacksmith's the next day – when she bawled at them in her rude Hindi to tell them how it should be done.
>
> This news is going to upset you: everyone in the village is busy shovelling apricots into pits, to rot the flesh and leave the stones clean; they crush the kernels for oil but consider the fruit worthless. Just think of the jam you would enjoy . . .

I assumed that monsoon conditions only entailed braving the discomfort of sodden sleeping bags, dripping tents and the irritation of slippery mud, and that I could continue to explore routes. Chamba had turned up, wreathed in smiles, and once again I had warned my mother, 'Don't worry if you don't hear from me for some weeks because I'm off into the hills.' Despite

22

my considerate efforts her anxiety got the better of her some time during that summer. She sent a telegram to Dr Snell asking for news and he wrote back to comfort her, clearly amused by his British women visitors: 'She is incredibly tough and is looking fantastically well. She is trekking with Penelope Betjeman, who is also incredibly tough and determined. They should make a good pair.'

When I arrived back from the hills I found a note in my typewriter and the copy of an article. Stanley Johnston, a *Sunday Times* reporter, had come for the weekend from London to visit me. Much of his article was devoted to quotes from my trekking brochure; he had found it so funny that he had determined to come and look for me. Reaching Manali at last, he had discovered where I lived from some hippie friends of Penelope's.

I reach the Himalayan Guest House, just a few rooms set on the hill overlooking the valley.

'Hello, Mr Gulab Das. Is Miss Christina here? Miss Christina of the Kulu Trekking Agency?'

'Miss Christina,' he repeated, nodding. Then he shook his head. 'No, Miss Christina not here, she gone on trek. She come back in ten, maybe eleven days.'

Since it was still only Saturday evening, I decided to spend the night at the Himalayan Guest House. Mr Das cooked my dinner and brought me the Guest Book to sign. I looked through the entries. There was a heavy sprinkling of missionaries and church workers . . . As I read on Mr Das put his finger on the page.

'Miss Christina come first time here.'

I read what it said. Entry serial number 37 indicated that the first visit of C. Noble, British, took place in August 1970. Occupation was shown as Tourist, aged 28, coming from Scotland. Purpose of visit shown as 'holiday', sex F. According to the book, Miss Noble returned in October 1970. This time purpose of visit is listed as 'pleasure' and occupation is shown as 'nil'.

With entry serial number 67 of July 1971, C. Noble arrives for the third time. Age has risen to 29. More significantly, her occupation is shown as 'Tour Operator'.

23

I sit there on the balcony and look out over the valley. The monsoon clouds still shroud the mountains and the rain begins to spatter on the roof. Somewhere up there C. Noble is trekking away. I remember with foreboding what the brochure said: 'You will not be playing at being isolated.'

Then, as the clouds clear briefly on the mountains, I understand the vision which, between entry number 37 and entry number 67, has converted Miss Christina from a Tourist into a Tour Operator. It may take her a while to put the Kulu Trekking Agency on the map, but I have no doubt she will succeed in the end. It is too good an idea to go wrong.

I took out my duty-free scotch and raised a glass of Black Label to the mountains and the improbable girl who had apparently made them her life. The storm broke all around, washing away the road in a hundred places and ensuring, beyond a shadow of a doubt, that I would be late back to work on Monday.

When we arrived back in Manali, Chamba squeezed off the bus near the petrol station; he was in a hurry to see if his wife had had a baby. He hadn't even mentioned the expected birth while we were in the hills. It turned out that the baby had been born but it was a girl. He was disappointed: he already had a daughter of three, and he wanted a boy.

I called the next day at the house Chamba rented from a lay lama for fifteen rupees a month. The room was eight feet by six, made of two-inch planks and scraps of offcuts, papered inside with newspaper. It was immaculate; every spoon and cup hung in its proper place. The silver bowls containing holy water under the shrine to Buddha were burnished with years of loving polish. On the shelves I noticed some things which were familiar from our trek to Kashmir and which I didn't remember having given away: a torch, a French water-bottle and a boy-scout frying pan with a folding handle. It felt as if we were inside a tropical house at Kew: the thick timber walls let in the damp air, the windows were shut against the rain, and the newly delivered mother had a good fire going in the sawdust-fuelled stove. On the shelf-bed lay a bundle swaddled in layers of shawls. Poking into it I found

24

a blotchy red head. The lines of its eyelids were marked with heavy black kohl and a black smudge had been made off-centre on its forehead – to make the child ugly lest the gods, coveting her beauty, went off with her.

I was given two 'half-fried' eggs, a little tangy as they had been fried in a generous quantity of *ghi*, sent from Zanskar. Both Chamba and his wife had family and village homes in Zanskar. Chamba had found his way to Manali ten years ago, after being turned down by the recruiting officer as too short to enlist in one of the Dogra regiments. His wife and a group of relations had been on their way back to Zanskar from a pilgrimage to Dharamsala, where they had received the Dalai Lama's blessing, when Chamba and his friends had abducted her. My eggs were served with slices of white bread, bought specially for me from the bakery, and thick tea flavoured with cardamom.

The three-year-old, Tsering Dolma, clung to my knee. She had large doleful eyes and seemed to have an even more bloated stomach than most of the under-fives in the bazaar and villages. Her little teeth were blackened, and I asked why.

'It is since she has the medicine from the mission hospital – she has to take it for two years. It used to be injections, every day; she screamed so much. Now the two years are over she can have the pills.'

They showed me the hospital card so that I would appreciate that they had regularly kept up the treatment and see how expensive it was. She had TB.

The new baby had been born in this room, delivered by the grocery-shop manager's wife; she wasn't a local woman, but came from Darjeeling. 'She is very good at it. She always comes when you go for her. She charges me twenty rupees. If you go to the mission hospital it costs a lot of money. They won't let you leave the hospital for three days and someone has to take your food there. It isn't worth it.'

I didn't know the Manali or Zanskari custom for greeting a newborn baby so I fell back on the Scots. I crossed the child's palm with a rupee coin, hoping it would have enough silver in it to bring her good luck, and left it slipping from her tiny clutching palm among the shawls.

Living alone during that monsoon I learned to be unruffled by the unexpected. Day after day would pass with no event to interrupt the monotony. Then there would be a day when everything happened. One morning I was interrupted by a boy I had met on a bus coming from Simla. He wanted advice about the way to Beas Kund (wisely he was not planning to go beyond). I lent him some *dekchis*, a *tawa* and a tent and told him to go over to Wangdi's to find a porter.

Not long after he had gone Chamba waddled on to the veranda, beaming. 'The Raja of Mandi is downstairs. He was asking for the trekking memsahib in the bazaar. I brought him up. He wants to see you. He has a *sadhu* [a wandering holy man] with him, he found him on the way.'

I had met Raja Sahib of Mandi the previous year. John and I had had an introduction to him and visited him at his palace on our way up to Kullu. He had entertained us with the greatest civility, feasting us with a five-course dinner and lively conversation late into the night. Now I found him downstairs, standing with a half-naked *sadhu* on the big rock; they were having their photograph taken by a small boy. They made an odd couple. The *sadhu* wore only a loincloth and had bleached tousled hair hanging to below his waist. Raja Sahib was wearing a Western-style summer suit made of green *khadi*, a hand-spun cloth. His Nehru cap was green, too, with the Mandi crest on it. He kissed my hand and explained that he had been searching Manali for me since his arrival the evening before.

To my relief the *sadhu* disappeared. Raja Sahib and I were absorbed in conversation (about his hopes and fears on the eve of Independence in '47) when Wangdi and his wife came up the steps. Conversation became difficult. Wangdi spoke a little hesitant English, his wife none. Raja Sahib spoke fluently and very fast. He didn't want to change to Hindi, politely not wishing to imply that the others were poorly educated. At last they explained why they had come – to ask me to type a formal letter to the District Commissioner regarding the purchase of their house. I did my best, with everyone watching my slow fingers on my old typewriter.

Raja Sahib persuaded us all to accompany him down to the bazaar, stopping at the fancily designed new Tourist Cafe for a Fanta. He complained to the uninterested bearer, 'Why don't you sell cakes like they do in the mountain cafes in Austria?' And then to me, 'I have an idea you and I should start up a restaurant together, or maybe two, one in Mandi and another in Manali. We could have snacks, both Indian and European, and good music, and we could commission artists to paint colourful murals.'

At the bazaar he insisted I join him on his search for two nuns said to be at the Buddhist monastery, over the river and up the hill on the way to Vashist. But first we must find two foreign *sadhus* who were to meet him in the evening.('You see, I want to find out about the modern religion, what all these young people think.') He knew one of the *sadhus* was American, and the other Italian; they were both tall and reputed to be staying at a disreputable hotel behind the school. But they weren't there and no one wanted to help.

At the monastery the head lama entertained us in his guest room, seated on piles of carpets. He was engulfed by maroon robes and rolls of fat, and was almost as keen to be photographed as Raja Sahib was to have a photograph of him. I was asked to be the photographer. It was a pity I only had a black-and-white film, for the shafts of sunlight coming through the window brought out the rich colours on the maroon and yellow lama and the green Raja, the old *thankas* on the walls, and the fine Tibetan carpets. We were given butter tea, sweet tea, dried apricots and toffees. The lama's son (he belonged to a non-celibate order) was brought in, a sickly pale child who clung to the rags of the ruffian Tibetan servants. We were told his health was still very weak despite the expertise of the best Tibetan doctors and the mission hospital; I think the lama thought we might be able to help.

Finally one of the two nuns was found. Her shaven head and

maroon robes and her obvious fondness for the head lama didn't disguise her natural jauntiness, and her vivid blue eyes expressed a great zest for life. She said she was Mary Campbell, from Glasgow. The other nun, from Croydon, was still sealed up in a cave in Lahul, meditating; she wasn't to come out for six months. Her food was passed in and her dirt taken away through a trap in the door. It was a very hard meditation. Mary Campbell had been in a solitary cave too but had had to come out to go to the police in Kullu about her visa. She hadn't divorced herself from thoughts of Scotland; on the contrary she was delighted to find that she and I both knew the hills of Argyll. 'Oh yes, I know the head of Loch Fyne well – that's near where the Duke of Argyll lives, and he's the head of my clan.'

I was exhausted by my unusually sociable day. Raja Sahib and I walked back to the bazaar, discussing the significance of coincidences, the result of the manoeuvring power of the gods. 'If you are attuned you can understand the significance. But to people like you many things are pointless. You must search, search. I have been searching all my life.' We said a prolonged goodbye in front of the Tourist Office, and I promised to go and visit him soon down at Mandi.

On one of our monsoon trips we had tried again to explore the route over the pass to Barabangahal, but after three or four days we were defeated by rain and mist. Nevertheless, I was confident that what we had seen of the route, combined with information we had gathered from some helpful shepherds, would allow us to find the way in sunny September weather without trouble.

This was my first party of real clients: there were eight of them. Their leader had run for Eton and was a professional walker, experienced in the Alps and the Andes. We sauntered up the Phojal *nala*. I knew that leather was anathema to the *Deota* of the twin villages at the top, and had warned the clients that they should bring alternative footwear. Two thousand feet beyond the villages, after fording the stream which was the boundary of the *Deota*'s territory, they had changed out of their canvas shoes back into heavy leather boots, when some villagers coming down-valley accosted us, almost barring our path. We were to sacrifice a goat for having offended the deity with the leather – no, two goats; there were a lot of us. Things looked bad. We couldn't afford a thousand rupees, for we wouldn't have enough to buy essential rations in Barabangahal. I sat on a rock by the river and smoked a *biri* with the old men. I explained how deferential we had been; they could ask their relations back in the village who had seen us all walking through in our canvas shoes. For some reason it worked: the old men were smiling. And the clients were impressed by the ease with which I had extricated us from what had looked like a tricky predicament.

Two days later we were lost: the route didn't seem to follow the description given us by the shepherds. We came to an impossible crest at about 15,000 feet and had to retreat to a chilly improvised camp site. Early in the morning Taj, Chamba and I went ahead to explore another ridge – my anxiety drove me to a turn of speed I never knew I had. We stood at 16,000 feet looking down on to a spectacular red and brown view and a precipitous drop which obviously led back into the Beas watershed, not over to the Ravi and Barabangahal. Tears of shame at our incompetence began to roll down my cheeks in the biting wind. Taj encouraged me: 'What's the good of that? Come on, we've got to get on with it before the sahibs arrive.' There was no choice: we had to get them down this precipice. We set up a fixed rope and prepared the slings and karabiners, with an air of being in command of the situation.

We never reached Barabangahal. But the first trek wasn't a disaster, for several members of that party returned to trek with us in later years.

II
FOOTLOOSE

Sial

No one could have construed my first season as a commercial success, but I had proved, at least to myself, that I was able to live in Manali and organize trekking expeditions. The next April I was back.

I had long ago made friends with the telegraph signaller, a helpful and efficient man whom I had met while sending and waiting for endless telegrams, and before I left in the autumn I had arranged through him to rent Postman Luder Chand's house in Sial village, above the bazaar. It was to be a two-year contract, conditional on the installation of running water and a 'flush'.

I arrived in the evening. I had so much luggage that I treated myself to a taxi up from Chandigarh, cutting the thirteen- or fourteen-hour journey to ten. The bazaar was in darkness, the electricity off. Familiar figures emerged out of the dark – the tourist officer, Raj Krishan from Katrain and the signaller himself; they had gathered for a political meeting on the *maidan* opposite the post office. Without electricity there was no microphone, and the meeting was lit by hissing petromex lamps. Verma's café was open but his espresso machine was boarded up; he had failed to pay tax on the extra revenue it had earned him last season. I had an omelette and tea.

Sial village is at the opposite end of Manali from Gulab Das's. As you come up from the octroi post past the petrol pump and the police station there is a lane off to the left, which leads into the Buddhist area where Tibetans, Ladakhis, Lahulis and Zanskaris live. On past the Lahuli *gompa* (a Buddhist monastery or temple) the path zigzags steeply up the hill behind the Zanskari

31

gompa through an evergreen oak wood. Those who live below, round the *gompas,* and the Sial villagers above, use the semi-secluded oak woods as a latrine: the path stank. But the less steep path which runs from the back of the *gompa* along the stream up to Sial was filthier still.

The house I had rented was at the far end of the village; at that time it was the last house, with only orchards and fields beyond. Taj and Chamba appeared as soon as I was up; somehow they had heard I had arrived. Chamba busied himself brewing a cup of welcome tea on the open *chulha*. The kitchen was on the ground floor, on the side of the house facing the village. My living quarters were the two rooms upstairs. They opened on to a veranda, which looked out across the valley and ran the length of the house. On the back corners of the veranda, against the bank of the terrace – now vivid green with winter wheat and dotted with striped tulips – there were to have been a bathroom at one end and a store for the trekking equipment at the other. There was no sign of either, nor even of the promised water supply. In the meantime, Luder Chand explained, they had dug an earth closet in the orchard, so that I wouldn't be inconvenienced, and today he was going to erect a sackcloth screen round it.

The house had been built during the last few years; the veranda balustrade still had only a single handrail. I had decided to use the room at the far end of the veranda for myself, because it had the best view, but I couldn't move into it straight away because Jabbu, Luder Chand's younger brother, had to move his belongings out. Luder Chand and the rest of his family, including his parents, lived in their original house in the other part of the village, across the stream.

Inside my room it was dark; Jabbu had papered the windows with newspaper to keep out the winter cold. I could just make out a gallery of garish calendar posters of gods and goddesses set against imaginative mountains, waterfalls and gardens. Outside, the light made me blink. The brilliant April sun was reflected off the unsullied snow on the opposite side of the valley; the snow line hadn't yet receded even above conifer level. In the orchard just below, the apple blossom had faded from its earlier pink to almost white. Scarlet and orange minivets, blue stonehatches, green and rose finches, and sometimes a pair of Himalayan magpies – drawing attention to themselves by their distinctive undulating flight – cavorted in the branches.

In the late afternoon the telegraph signaller called. Perhaps he felt some responsibility for the unfulfilled terms of the lease, or perhaps Luder Chand had asked him to be an arbiter. The three of us sat on the one *charpoi* on the veranda. Luder's old father was there too, a spare man of few words but underlying determination; he squatted against the handrail and called for his hookah. I was annoyed because I had considered that both a lavatory and a room with drainage (where, with a bucket of water, I could have an adequate and private bath) were essential. 'You said that when I arrived there would be a bathroom and "flush". How can I take a bath? Out here on the veranda? And there isn't even any water. I can't carry buckets from the tap [a hundred yards away in the middle of the village]; I'm not strong enough and I'll spill the water.'

'Memsahib, we have built the water tank,' the old man said. 'It had to be a long way up the stream. We have been working on it all the winter. It was very difficult, too cold for the cement to set; and anyway we couldn't get any. In a few days we will lay the pipe – I am going to Kullu for it tomorrow – and then there will be a tap by the kitchen. Until then Jabbu will bring you water in the morning.'

The everyday pace was easy going. Chamba arrived early. I would hear him approaching with my bed tea, his footsteps on the wooden boards of the veranda, then the doors of my room would burst open letting in a flood of light. '*Jhule, jhule,*' he would beam as he thrust the enamel mug of tea at me. By the time the sun rose above the opposite hill he would have two half-fried eggs and chapattis ready for me; I breakfasted outside on the *charpoi*. During the day the place became busy. Taj hung tents and sleeping bags out in the sun. Luder Chand's old mother plastered the rooms, spreading the mixture of cow dung, straw and mud over the walls with her hands, preparing it for the whitewashing that I had insisted on. Two carpenters arrived from Senogi village up the hill beyond the Hadimba temple, and intermittently measured, planed and sawed. Much of their time, though, was spent drinking glasses of tea, smoking *biris* and exchanging jokes with Jabbu – who had shifted his belongings and his calendars into one of the downstairs rooms. Poor Jabbu. When he wasn't chatting to the carpenters (or carrying my pails of water) he passed his time sitting on a metal chair in the sun. Since he was a graduate of Kullu college it would have been undignified for him to till the family fields. He was looking for appropriate employment – but during the years I was there he never found it. Around midday Chamba went home to his timbered room in the orchard behind the petrol station. In the evenings I would cook my own potato and pea curry with rice on the round tin stove I had had installed; it was easier to master than the open clay *chulha*.

To Sial village and Manali bazaar I must have seemed like any other hippie. Children would chant 'Ya, ya, *hippini*.' Linda, the Canadian ex-beauty queen, admired my long frilled skirts, but I did wear trousers and a *kurta* to go to the bazaar. I didn't think of myself as a hippie. I kept aloof from people who were, lest a hint of friendliness might lead to squatters on my veranda. I considered myself a businesswoman. This year I had several parties booked, but I felt ill at ease. I was Managing Director of a 'trekking agency'; what did that mean? It was just me sitting here, my feet on the veranda rail, while Chamba and Taj mended the zip·on one of our five tents. Now that I had time to think about what I was doing, it seemed tenuous and pointless. And why was I making such a fuss about running water and lavatories? What if I left? I had assured Luder's old father that the improvements, made for my convenience, were a good investment; in the future they would be able to charge a higher rent for the rooms. But would they? Sometimes, rarely, I was aware of an undercurrent of satisfaction. Now I was engulfed by a more familiar feeling – a tight pain of emptiness in the ribcage, a sense of the futility of effort. Part of the attraction of living here was that I found the scale of the landscape reassuring; it put man and his puny efforts into perspective.

> 'Tis all a chequer board of nights and days
> Where destiny with men for pieces plays
> Hither and thither moves, and mates and slays
> And one by one back in the closet lays.

But now I felt I had been fooling myself.

The first clients of the season annoyed me. A holiday in the Himalayas was a considerable commitment for them, in both time and money, but they seemed to ruin it for themselves. They complained that they couldn't be really comfortable without an armchair, that the jam pot was dirty and that the natives didn't smile. Chamba tried to cheer me up by imitating the portly sahib stumping downhill.

Out in Saraj, in the hills between Simla and Kullu, we needed flour. Lama Le (a recent recruit to the team) volunteered to go down 1,500 feet to the nearest shop. In the meantime, Chamba or Taj had the bright idea of enlivening the evening meal with a dish of the wild spinach they had noticed in a nearby wood.

I ate after the sahibs – some of their left-over rice, one or two chapattis (made with the newly bought flour) and lavish helpings of spinach – and said good night. I had just nestled into my sleeping bag when I realized I was about to be sick. The rest-house was several hundred yards from the spring; there was just one bucket of water, intended for the morning bed tea, in the kitchen. I was sick, repeatedly, discreetly, behind the forest guard's shed, then I grabbed a large mug of water from the kitchen. I had been the first to succumb. For hours the camp site reverberated with the sounds of vomiting, and there was no more water. We left as quickly as possible in the morning, with profuse apologies to our clients.

The argument over what had made everyone sick continued for years. Some, including me, believed it was the wild spinach – not spinach at all but a virulently poisonous weed. Others, including Lama Le, who was responsible for it, thought it was the flour; he was convinced it had rat poison mixed with it. No one ever listened to me when I pointed out that the sahibs hadn't eaten any chapattis.

That rest-house was later the setting for another misadventure. I had carried a large live cock 2,000 feet up the hill in my haversack with his squawking head sticking out of the top. At the rest-house we butchered him and with hungry expectation put him in the pressure cooker. We were drinking tea on the kitchen steps when there was an explosion: his remains were on the rafters, where they clung for many years.

Such incidents became part of a store guaranteed to enliven a chilly evening round the kitchen fire and have Chamba grasping his stomach with laughter. Jokes, good times, hungry times, memories of cold and fear, began to bind us together. A similar bond of companionship is familiar to anyone who has participated in a long expedition; ours was all the stronger for being continuous – we were together year after year, behaving well and badly, enjoying and suffering the ups and downs.

Not long after the spinach (or flour) saga I made my promised visit to the Raja of Mandi. The bus took seven hours to cover the hundred kilometres; the driver stopped at every tea-house, every shrine, to make an offering, and often along the way to talk to a passing friend. At Mandi bus station, one of Himachal's most congested and squalid, I was met by a palace retainer; I was to wait there, sitting on some boxes, while he went for the Mandi car.

The Raja had moved since my last visit, from the spacious modern palace built in the twenties or thirties on the outskirts of the town, to the old palace overlooking the central square. *Mandi* means a market, here built at the crossroads of three main routes. It is a medieval town. Crowded buildings hang over narrow cobbled lanes, where silversmiths sit in alcoves well above street level and sleek bulls lie outside secluded temples. It used to be the capital of a princely state – Mandi was never under the British Raj; then, after Independence in 1947, several of the hill princes combined their territory to form the embryonic Himachal Pradesh.

On the first night Raja Sahib gave a dinner party. The Rani was absent; she was at their house down in Poona. 'She prefers it there or in Bombay; she has her bridge friends, and racing, of course.' The District Commissioner was the principal guest. His profile, with languorous eyes, prominent nose and down-curled moustache, belonged to a Pahari miniature. But below the profile he was disappointing, short and squat, and he had little to say. His wife wanted me to appreciate how trying it was to be stationed in Mandi; she was accustomed to sophisticated Simla society and to her friends from Miranda College, Delhi. Clearly she didn't consider either the local doctor or his wife to be out of the top drawer. Then there was a gaudy Punjabi lady who sang. Both the latter and the doctor's wife were fasting; it was Lord Krishna's birthday. The doctor himself was not, and he had obviously fortified himself with a few pegs before he arrived. He didn't need much persuasion from Raja Sahib to enliven the party by reading the ladies' palms. He explained that he also had the gift of telepathy. Any night he couldn't sleep he knew there must have been an accident somewhere; the next morning he would expect to hear there had been a suicide or a drowning, or he would read in the newspaper about a train disaster. He must have had a lot of bad nights.

Two tables, each with a silver vase of flowers, were laid for dinner. The smaller table was set for only two, for the 'fasting' ladies were to eat separately to avoid the danger of pollution. Their meal consisted of salad and yoghurt followed by a bowlful of mangoes, bananas and grapes. Raja Sahib apologized for the lack of meat at our table; it was because he was respecting the god by abstaining from eating meat before performing the midnight *puja*. We were served clear soup followed by cauliflower cheese, then a main dish – vegetable cutlet 'Maryland' with sauté potatoes. After that we began on a full Indian dinner – *pilau*, *sag panir*, *puri* and *raitha* and many chutneys and pickles. Raja Sahib talked of his plans of starting a dining club (as well as our two restaurants?). The final course was fruit sponge in custard.

Afterwards we sat round the piano in the drawing room, sipping coffee out of angular 1930s cups from Heal's and thimblefuls of brandy, while the Punjabi lady played and sang. At a late hour we were suddenly joined by Raja Sahib of Kullu and his son; they were staying the night, on their way back from a visit to Bombay, but had spent the evening at the Mandi cinema house rather than attend the dinner party. I had the feeling Raja Sahib of Kullu had little time for the formal conversation the District Commissioner's wife hankered after; he enjoyed more robust and jocular company. Shortly after his arrival his mother came waddling into the room. She was about four and a half feet tall, and wrapped in a white sari – widow's weeds. She hadn't been to the cinema – and no explanation was offered as to why she hadn't attended our dinner. She wasn't introduced to anyone and almost disappeared into one of the chintz chairs. She enjoyed a laugh and considered she had reached an age when she could make remarks as outrageous as she liked, in Hindi – not for her Miranda College English.

'Ha, don't say you've been giving that doctor a chance to hold your hands and breathe liquor all over you. What did he tell you – by this time next year you'd have twin sons?' She cackled behind her white headcloth. The District Commissioner's wife was not amused.

The doctor wasn't disconcerted by the new arrivals. He continued to entertain us with stories proving the accuracy of telepathy until Raja Sahib burst into the room just before midnight. 'We're late. Come on, dear guests, we should go.' He had changed from his *khadi* lounge suit into holy clothes – a yellow Gandhi-style cap, a silk *kurta* printed all over with 'Hari Ram, Hari Krishna', and a yellow silk *dhoti* with a red border.

We were led by torchlight through long passages – smelling of rats or bats – under the palace and up into a room where two *pandits* were attending to the image, barely visible under marigold garlands and vestments of silver and gold. Raja Sahib sat on a spotted deerskin beside the old *pandit*. Together they chanted the Sanskrit mantras, the *pandit* nudging Raja Sahib to tell him when to throw rice, *ghi* and rose petals into the fire. The younger *pandit* waved yaks' tails and peacock's feathers over his head. At the appointed moment, attendants – I recognized the bearers

38

who had served us at dinner – clashed cymbals to announce the birth of Lord Krishna. Fireworks and gunfire were already resounding in the town. Raja Sahib of Kullu didn't participate in the ceremony or even enter the sanctuary; he stood looking in from the doorway, and when his mother offered him the *prasad* he had to toss away his cigarette quickly and throw off his shoes.

My room in the *zenana* (the women's quarters, although there were no other women staying there) had a velvet bedspread, lamps with shades made of gathered silk, a desk with cubbyholes, and stationery embossed with the Mandi crest. In the blue-and-white tiled bathroom, linen face towels hung on a sword which served as a towel horse. Breakfast was brought to my room on a silver tray; Raja Sahib and I ate other meals together in the darkened dining room.

We spent one long afternoon in the cool of the drawing room – hung with sepia photographs of the Princes of India at Delhi *durbars* – discussing religion. There was no aspect of any faith which didn't interest the Raja. He had never allowed Christian missionaries into his state, not because he disapproved of Christianity but because he thought their proselytizing might upset his people. We compared Buddhism, Confucianism, Hinduism and Christianity. He had always felt attracted to the idea of an invisible power. I was cynical, and ignorant.

On the death of his uncle, the British Raj had chosen him from the various contenders to the throne. They wanted a young malleable boy whom they could educate to their way of thinking. 'At that time I wasn't interested in religion. I performed the necessary religious rituals because my British tutors told me my people expected it.' Later he became intellectually curious; he began fervently to study the philosophy of the Gita and the teachings of the great Hindu thinkers. More recently, the doctors attending him during an illness had been amazed by his mastery of yogic techniques. 'Images and Divinities are very useful. If you can do without them you have made great progress, but few can.' For hours he told me dramatic stories of the lives, deaths and rebirths of the heroes and heroines of the Hindu pantheon.

Now something new had happened to him: in a confiding tone he explained that over the last few years he had become attached to a famous *mataji* (guru) from Madras.

'She has taught me much I didn't know. I have made progress but not enough. Last year, I had gone to Bombay station to see her off. She said, "Come, come with me to the Ashram." I said, "No, you have to make me *really* want to, there is still something in me too much of this world, something that makes me hesitate." One of my companions was shocked. He said, "What could be more wonderful for you than the *Mataji* asking you to come to her?" In this life I don't think I am going to get any closer to understanding the infinite. I have done enough, I have had a full life; maybe I'll understand more in the next one. So I said to the *Mataji*, "Forgive me. The light is going out for me, let me go home, with your permission and with your blessings."'

After dinner, when the two of us sat out on the *zenana* veranda, I saw something of his worldly attachment. He had told me how much he loved London and Paris – 'I used to be known as Prince of the Night Clubs' – and now he had a bearer bring out a heavy, antique gramophone. Smiling as he fondly turned the handle he said, 'I used to be so fond of dancing I would spend night after night in night clubs for months on end.' We sat side by side on the cane sofa and listened to 'Why am I lonely, Why am I blue?' and 'Tea for Two'. He fondled my feet, 'the most erotic part of a woman'. I tried not to be embarrassed, to accept it as a *zenana* custom, in the starlight.

I admired his lively mind, his refusal to take anything for granted, and his subtle perceptiveness. I was intrigued by his obsession with the machinations of unseen powers. Although he was physically frail, the old man's intellect was so vital and enthusiastic it seemed he might explode.

On my return from the Mandi Palace, Taj and Chamba were welcoming and I was pleased to come home to my familiar room – to the red tablecloth, yellow cotton carpet and *khadi* bedspread with its rustic orange tiger. In Mandi I had gone out to buy an electric kettle and Raja Sahib had come with me; he said he wanted to give me a present. I wondered what: an antique Tibetan bowl, or an enamelled silver pendant? It turned out to be a blue-striped cotton carpet. It was useful beside my bed but not quite of the style I imagined befitted a prince's gift.

The monsoon had set in. The sackcloth screen round the earth closet in the garden was black with mildew: the EC had turned into a WC that never drained away. We perched an old umbrella as a roof over the pit, but it was still an unpleasant experience to squelch out there through the mud. The umbrella dripped on to you as you squatted over the slippery planks, and fat white caterpillars lived in the murky water.

The gorge road into Kullu was blocked by landslides for five days; no mail came through. When the road was cleared it took the post office two days to sort the backlog – I always suspected they cleared some by hurling mail-bags into the river. I was sure one of the sorters couldn't read. He turned the envelopes this way and that; I think he sorted by instinct. In those early years, going down to the post office for the mail in the afternoon was an anticipated excitement round which the rest of the day took shape.

Then it was the apple season – with the smell of apples and of the pinewood packing boxes everywhere. Women and little boys came down the hills staggering under the weight of *kiltas* full of apples. Packers squatted under tarpaulins beside mounds of Royal Delicious, and trucks loading the boxes blocked the roads. For the hippies it was the beginning of the 'dope' harvest. It was *charas*, the resin, rather than *bhang*, the dried leaves and seed, that was popular, and this is at its best in August, when the plant reaches maturity. While it is still growing the whole plant is rubbed between the hands. The dark, sticky gum accumulates on the palms and is then rubbed off into a black lump. Local people smoke it sometimes in the winter, and a few use it regularly; it was always an export from this area down to the plains. But it was the hippies who created local dealers and caused the export market to escalate. For many foreigners *charas* is the reason they choose to be in Manali, and funded by it they set off to Goa for the winter. Over at Jugatsukh there was a 'factory' where, with the connivance of the police, balls of the drug were individually wrapped in toffee papers for export.

At the tail end of the monsoon we set off into the hills to explore a route on the opposite side of the valley, but it rained and rained. Taj, Chamba and I were stuck in a tent for two days. We could see nothing and had little idea where we were. We played cards, slept and told stories. I told them about Highland cattle, the rain and midges in Argyll, and they told me about Zanskar and Lahul.

'I used to go to school some of the time,' Taj said. He spoke good Hindi and could write a bit. 'But often I'd be away helping my father with the mules. I liked that; you met people. It's boring in the village. Except in the marriage season, then it's good.

'At night when everyone was asleep I used to take the white pony out of the stable, tie some hay in a blanket and gallop miles through the moonlight to the marriage, to drink and to dance, for days and nights.

'Then I heard about the good money you could make in Manali as a trekking guide, so I came here. Once a year I go back home. My brother's wife is there alone; he is in the army. I go back to plough the fields – that isn't woman's work.'

Chamba didn't mention boredom, and his description of life in Zanskar made one wonder why he had ever left. 'In my village there are fifty or sixty big houses and two hundred and fifty lamas in the *gompa*. On the winter evenings everyone gathers together in one house and tells stories and sings and the *chang* never runs out; there are caskfuls of it. You mustn't sit too close to the fire or when you go out you will freeze. It is easy to travel because you can walk, or ride on the rivers. So you go visiting in other villages and the parties last days at a time. Then when the spring comes, perhaps it's May, there's the ploughing. It's not like here with fields the length of your arm and little bullocks like donkeys. There the fields are wide, and huge yaks pull the great metal plough. Everything grows so well. Potatoes are ready in a month and wheat in a month and a half.'

I wasn't bored stuck in the tent but the mist was claustrophobic; we couldn't see further than the flowers at the entrance. One afternoon Taj, with meticulous care, made some *halwa* (a fried-semolina sweetmeat). Chanting an evocation to the gods, he placed it on a nearby rock. I laughed, I thought he was joking: then I realized he was unselfconsciously making an offering to propitiate the mountain deities, and I was ashamed of my cynicism.

Two hours later the mist had lifted. We looked out at a breathtaking view. Suddenly we could see for miles and miles. There were mountain spires that cut into the sky, and away up the valley the glaciers were more impressive than any I had seen. Even Taj and Chamba were amazed. We had been camping there for days, and had it not been for Taj's offering we might never have seen what lay in front of us.

Incomers

It was to be my third season in Kullu. The pattern of my migrations was established. I spent winters in London and Scotland, and from early April until the middle of November in Manali. I wasn't ever frightened, either in Manali or on expeditions into the hills (except when there were river crossings or shale slips); I didn't feel alone or vulnerable. By now my mother had accepted my living there and was encouraged that I was among people I so evidently trusted. As the years passed she became interested in them, particularly Chamba and his family, Taj and the hospital sisters. My letters described the changing flowers and scenery of my new landscape, while hers described the weather and colours in Scotland. To feel attuned to the passing of time I needed to know whether the azaleas were out or the raspberries or brambles ripe in Argyll.

Leaving home was always painful. Then at some moment during the cramped journey in the pitiless plane the magnetic force that held me to the familiar I had left behind began to tug me in the direction of the familiar I was going towards.

I came by the night train to Chandigarh, then caught the bus. On the plains of the Punjab it was harvest time. Bullock carts took up two-thirds of the road, looking like prehistoric monsters mounted on small stands – they bulged with chaff wrapped in sackcloth. Over the first pass, around Bilaspur and in the fertile wide valley of Suket, the roses were out and the wheat just beginning to ripen; it might have been the end of June at home. Suket is well-tended; the houses are trim and white, and in front of each there is a mud cone storing dung cakes for fuel. The cattle tethered to the front porch wear quilted coats – each one has a pouch like an egg cosy for the hump. Below Mandi there were white Khampa tents down by the river: the traders and their mules waiting for the snow to melt before moving further up. And just beyond Mandi there were Gaddis, grazing their sheep and goats on the threadbare scrub jungle before their spring migration towards high summer pastures.

The gorge, usually so dismal, was pink and white with bauhinia tree in flower – it looks like magnolia blossom from the distance. By the time the bus rattled up Kullu valley and into Manali it was dark; I spent the night with the Sisters at the hospital.

Now I'm sitting out on my veranda – the apple trees are still bare; only the apricot blossom is out, such a vivid pink. It's hard to believe this time last week we were Easter egg-hunting by the loch at home. Our *deota* is being carried round the village. Ahead goes the band, two drummers and trumpeters – several curly brass trumpets and two long copper ones which need two men each to hold them. The burnished metal glints in the sun. The *deota* itself is a *rath* – a wooden sedan chair carried by poles which rest on the shoulders of one man ahead and another behind. Masks displayed in rows face ahead – silver and bronze ornamented with earrings and pendants – and red and orange silk brocades stream from the top, brilliant in the sunlight. Little boys carrying a trumpet gave a blast when they passed my veranda. Old men spin as they vaguely follow the entourage. Women carry *kiltas* on their backs into which villagers toss their offerings – money or balls of *ghi*. Nearby the sound is less cohesive, but from a distance the call of the drums and trumpets is irresistible. The valley is filled with the echoing beat, for yesterday was Jugatsukh *mela* and tomorrow is Vashist; everywhere the gods are on the move.

Now there was a functioning standpipe outside the kitchen, but the bathroom was a skeleton timber frame yet to be enclosed and there was still no 'flush'. This was the second year of my two-year tenancy. I threatened Luder's father. 'My old mother and my aunt want to come to visit me' – untrue: my mother wouldn't have thought of undertaking a plane journey – 'and they cannot stay here without a working flush.' At last we had been issued with a permit for the cement, but by the time Luder's father went to Kullu it was out of date.

Chamba, his wife and the little girls had moved into one of the two downstairs rooms (Jabbu was still in the other). On chilly spring mornings Mrs Chamba would bring me a large bowl of steaming *thuppa* – broth. My early-morning version was made with barley flour and dried yoghurt, strongly laced with *chang*. 'In Zanskar we make it like this for the old people; it's good for them in the mornings.' It would knock me back under the bedclothes for another half-hour.

Mrs Chamba was a handsome, high-cheekboned woman. She wasn't loquacious, her Hindi was limited, and she had only left her Zanskar village five or six years before, but even when she was among Bhoti speakers she seldom told a story or gave more than an incidental comment on the day's events. She was unusually efficient: everything was always in order and the daily chores executed according to a disciplined regime. Chamba, on the other hand, would have been a shambles left to his own devices.

The dried yoghurt for my *thuppa* came from Zanskar. From time to time a food parcel arrived from Mrs Chamba's mother (Chamba never received one from his home), brought by one of her burly, taciturn brothers. Groups of Zanskaris would come to Manali to buy winter rations or on pilgrimage to visit the Dalai Lama at Dharamsala or even to distant Gaya in Bihar, Lord Buddha's birthplace. They would stroll four or five abreast up the bazaar, conical hats at an angle over black pigtails, maroon cloaks swinging. Some had needles and plaited twists of barley tucked into their yellow tweed hats, or primulas, picked as offerings to the gods of the pass and worn as talismans. They didn't appear daunted by the worldly hurly-burly of Manali; an enthusiastic curiosity shone in their eyes. Later I might find the group crowded into our kitchen (which began to reek of rancid oiliness from unwashed bodies and heavy tweeds in the unaccustomed warmth), recounting months of news to eagerly listening emigrants. There was one gentle old man who kept picking up and admiring one of my china egg cups. Finally he couldn't resist asking for it – to serve *arak* in, for visiting lamas, he said.

The food parcel was always wrapped in carefully stitched cloth. In excited anticipation Mrs Chamba unpicked it to find three greasy bags of dried yoghurt, a bag of tiny black peas, half a dozen dusty dried apricots and perhaps a well wrapped packet of dried yak meat. 'Don't tell anyone. They think it's cow's meat. They'd chase us out of Manali if they knew. Here the people eat fish – in Zanskar we don't, because fish belong to the gods.'

Everyone in India busily differentiates his own group from others, establishing its exclusiveness. 'Oh no, we never kill an animal in Zanskar; it is against Buddhist religion. The *lohars* do the killing. They come to the house, and we give them food and drink, but they don't come upstairs.'

It was lucky that Chamba's inherent jollity and good nature endeared him to everyone, for it wouldn't have occurred to him that it is prudent for incomers to be tactful. 'The Kullu people are all right, but they are greedy; they want everything for no work. I don't talk to Sikhs because they drink, and eat meat. If they were proper Sikhs they wouldn't. As for Kangra people, we see them when we are down there in the winters; they think only of eating money.'

The younger of Chamba's daughters, the one I had visited as a day-old baby, was now a lively two-year-old and Chamba's joy. In the evening, in our cramped kitchen (half taken up with the gravel stored for the day the cement might arrive), he would hold her hands and sing for her while she danced between his knees. I never knew her name; she was always called Nomo, which means 'little girl'. The older child, Tsering Dolma, was less favoured. When anything was lost or broken it was always her fault. Perhaps as a result she was often upstairs on the veranda outside my room, playing jacks with chips of stone and two or three marbles or pieces of kitchen debris, her little sister tied on her back with a shawl.

Taj rented a room in a house just above ours. In the mornings he was very much part of our household, often sharing our tea, teasing and entertaining Chamba's daughters. Then he would disappear to the bazaar. A roving bachelor, he lived life on a dangerous brink, often despondent and often drunk. Chamba hinted that he was unlikely ever to be considered as a desirable bridegroom. He did go home to his village in northern Lahul each spring, but he was more established as a Manali man, less romantically attached to his childhood home than many of the recent incomers.

I appreciated Chamba's steadfast friendship and found his spontaneous affection and his jokes irresistible. But I felt sympathetic to Taj's deep-rooted pessimism: 'I will do the *charas* business, take plenty from here to sell to the hippies in Goa. If the police catch me they can put me in the gaol. I don't care.'

Gentle Lama Le, the animal-lover, came from Ladakh proper, north of Zanskar. He lived in a room down by the *gompa* and was less a part of our everyday life. I only got to know him when we were out in the mountains, where he was a natural – steady and slow, never off balance. In the evenings he would sit alone by the fire, thumbing his way along his rosary and murmuring prayers. Occasionally he would interrupt his murmurings and talk about his earlier life in the *gompa*, very quietly, almost in a whisper. His parents had given him to the *gompa* when he was seven or eight. When he was twenty he ran away because he was fed up with working in the kitchens. Now he didn't dare go back home; if he was caught the punishment would be five years of washing dishes. Judging by his physique, *gompa* rations had not been body-building; he was pale and lightly built, with long-fingered hands. He remained a lay monk, with shaven head, maintained his vows of celibacy and never drank. He spent his winters in a monastery down in Gaya. Though he was younger than Taj or Chamba he had an air of venerable sagacity. No one used his name; he was always called 'Lama Le', the 'Le' being a mark of respect. He was esteemed for his steadfast character and his reliability. Just occasionally he would betray his youth by a demonstration of supple gymnastics, or by dissolving into an uncontrollable fit of high-pitched giggles.

During my third Kullu season Dorze joined us. He was younger than Lama Le, twenty-five perhaps, and wore a tremendous moustache. Understandably it was a great source of pride to him, for most Mongoloid people have little facial hair. He too was originally from Zanskar but as a young boy he had been sent to be a servant in Lahul – his father had died and his mother had run off with someone else; he wasn't wanted at home. He had worked, almost enslaved, as a house servant and then as a shepherd. During his time in Lahul he claimed he had seen a cockerel lay an egg. He had arrived in Manali recently and, with Chamba's help, kidnapped a Zanskari girl on her way back from a pilgrimage to Gaya. Arranged marriages are the proper tradition but kidnap marriages are an accepted alternative, absolving the family from marriage expenses. I was told that no girl is ever kept against her will. 'Of course she cries and cries and says, "Let me go to Zanskar to my family." It wouldn't be proper for her not to,' Dorze said, though I didn't see how anyone could tell whether the sobs were feigned or real. 'These days she is always crying, she stays inside the house saying she wants to go home. I tell her it is nothing, not to worry.' They lived in half of a small tin shack on the far side of the lower *gompa*, at the entrance to the Buddhist area.

My earliest memory of Dorze dates from the time we were out with a group which included several keen birdwatchers. Late one afternoon I noticed them standing round a small bushy tree from which a peculiar high-pitched call was emanating. The women were excited, and their binoculars had been trained on the tree for some time when down jumped Dorze. They were not amused.

From early times Mongol Buddhists were to be seen in Manali; at various stages in their history the upper valleys were actually ruled by the Ladakhis and the Spitialis. Later, Buddhist traders and their mule trains set up encampments at Manali while they bartered the wool and borax they had brought from the north for salt and cotton cloth which came up from the plains – but they were temporary visitors. In the 1950s Lahulis began to buy property here. A combination of the closure of the border between China (Tibet) and India, after the 1961 war, and the advent of transport by truck, curtailed the activities of the Lahuli and Khampa muleteers and encouraged them to establish themselves round Manali. During the sixties the Buddhist population was further swelled by the arrival of Tibetan refugees.

Through Chamba, Taj, Lama Le and Dorze, silent, smiling Chawang, old Wangyal and Sonam (who had abandoned us on our trip to Kashmir), I came to know many faces among the community of Lahulis, Zanskaris and Ladakhis. Most of their dwellings, intermingled with the Tibetans', congregated round the *gompas* and formed a substantial Buddhist enclave.

To Buddhists, whether they are Tibetan or Zanskari, Ladakhi or Lahuli, the Dalai Lama is God. For some time it had been rumoured that he was to visit his people in Manali and the new Ge-lugs-pa *gompa*, and at last the day arrived. Chamba's children were immaculately prepared and bathed. Their hair was oiled and beribboned, and they were dressed in the Mothercare suits I had brought them from London. Mrs Chamba was spruce in a brown velvet Lahuli gown, tightly waisted. About two hundred of us gathered down by the octroi post, beside the Ladakhi *thanka* painter's house. Decorative arches lined the road, and stone hearths had been built and whitewashed for the fragrant juniper to be burnt in. Everyone had brought white muslin scarves to present to His Holiness. The children lit *agarbatti* sticks, and our local lama showed us how we were to bow. Dorze kept nipping into the wood to have a smoke (it wouldn't be proper to be seen smoking along His Holiness's path). Chamba stoked the cairns with juniper, and mothers settled down on the roadside to suckle their babies. A jeepload of fat lamas arrived to organize us. We were to stand not in a bunch but in a line, women on one side of the road, men on the other. Nothing happened, so we began to huddle together again and chatter. Our *agarbatti* sticks went out. Then ahead there was a flutter of excitement and, with a swish, two jeeps and a Mercedes swept by. We hardly had time to bow down, and not a moment to glimpse the great man.

We ran through the civil hospital ground, behind the petrol pump and through the orchard past Chamba's old house, dragging or carrying the children, to the new *gompa*. It was surrounded by security guards and soldiers with guns, and they wouldn't let us by.

Few of the bazaar wallahs were Kullui, although there were exceptions – the sewing-machine agent was a charming, ineffectual man from Manali village and our butcher was a Kullui woman. Chandrabhaga, the grocery store, was Lahuli-owned and the manager was from Darjeeling. Most of the grain shops and the 'fancy goods' shops belonged to Punjabis. Many of the tailors came from Kangra, while the cloth-shop owners were Punjabi or Lahuli. Some of the Tibetan refugees were fast forming a successful business community. Fate dealt them a curious helping hand: quantities of old clothes intended for the flood victims in East Pakistan found their way to Manali. (The aid agencies may have decided, rightly, that overcoats and sweaters were more appropriate here than in Dacca.) The Tibetans set up open-air stalls at the edge of the forest below the bazaar – opposite which there is now a thriving Tibetan market dealing in imported knick-knacks. Wangdi, the climbing outfitter who had helped us on our first trip, was a Nepali. Except for Postman Luder Chand and one other local, the post office was run by Punjabis.

One day the acting postmaster, a Sikh, wanted me to check the English in a letter he had just written to the area manager.
It read:

I appealed for a transfer from this place last year. You said you would look into it when you came on tour, but your honour was not able to come to Manali after all. My wife is chronic hysteric, she is in the civil hospital Hoshiapur under constant care. I myself am an APS veteran with severe burns on legs and cannot stand hill stations. I must suffer the burden of keeping two homes, on top of all this, this year my daughter is to be married. You will appreciate honoured Sir that owing to the utter dearness of my situation please grant the transfer.

I said I thought it was a very persuasive letter.

The next request for help from the post office was more testing. Kranti, a Bihari friend who was teaching at the University of Simla, used to come and stay. During one of his visits the signaller called, and we drank tea and exchanged some bazaar gossip. Then the signaller beckoned Kranti aside. He said he had noticed on a letter that Kranti was Dr K. Singh (he has a Ph.D. in English literature). 'Excuse me asking you a favour. Will you do a sperm count for me while you are here? For seven years we have been waiting for children. People are saying I should take another wife. But my wife says it is the fault of my sperm. I have had sperm counts done in Simla and Kullu but I know that being foreign-trained your testing would be better.'

Kranti explained that he wasn't a medical doctor. The signaller was unabashed: 'Well, then, when you go home to Bihar will you take some of my sperm with you? They must have good testers there.'

I liked to think that I had begun to understand how the people I lived among thought and reacted, but even now I often found myself at a loss.

Between Taj and Chamba there was, from time to time, a ripple of jealousy. I knew I must be careful never to criticize one to the other: a hint of criticism would be interpreted as an invitation to tell tales. Chamba implied that Taj took a commission from what I paid the mule man (his contact). He also insinuated that Taj had had the idea of hiring out some of the tents and equipment to an Italian climbing party while I was away in the summer. In answer to my casual enquiries Taj implied that it was Chamba who knew the Italians and had organized it. Neither of them mentioned it directly; I had found it out for myself. Nor had they passed on the rent.

I braved the issue one morning, fortified by a bowlful of Mrs Chamba's *thuppa*. I sat behind my desk, still in my dressing gown. It was Taj who had had the key so I addressed my remarks to him. He didn't deny what had happened; he just said, 'It was about a thousand rupees. The Mountaineering Institute charges twenty-two rupees a day per tent. There were three tents for fifteen days. Deduct it from my pay. Is that all right?' I tried to murmur some sort of reprimand. 'What's done is done,' he said. Chamba said nothing and didn't look up. I don't know if they ever sorted out the damage between them.

But most of the time they were good friends. Round the camp fire in the hills or at home in the kitchen they told jokes at each other's expense. Taj loved the story of how Chamba had been turned down by a Dogra regiment for being half a foot too short. And Chamba mercilessly teased Taj for having lost his smart foreign watch on his drunken way home from the bazaar. 'See how much better my old one is,' Chamba would say, holding up a wrist tattooed with the hands of a watch-face which read three o'clock.

I was always intrigued by incidents in their lives, and sometimes found myself involuntarily involved. The evening before a party was to set off into the hills was always an anxious time for me. Had the porridge and dried meat been packed? Had anyone remembered to collect the butter from the grocery shop? On this occasion I had waited until 9.30 p.m. for the party to arrive at the guesthouse and then given up, assuming they had missed a connection.

In the morning I discovered what had happened. The clients – just one couple – had taken a taxi all the way from Delhi, as Chandigarh airport had been flooded. They had comforted themselves with the thought that 'It'll be all right when we get to Manali and meet Miss Noble,' but when they arrived at the bazaar at midnight they had found no one to ask, and the Delhi taxi didn't know which guesthouse to go to. They had slept in the taxi until five. 'You see, my wife is not a good traveller; she

Ploughing a recently terraced field above a village

Terraced cultivation surrounding a village with its temple to Shamsher Mahadev

Above: A house in Jugatsukh village; the photograph was taken while the carpenter and I were looking for local veranda styles.

Below: On the way to Rahul's hair-cutting ceremony at Hadimba's temple, Dunghri forest

Above: Duff Dunbar. Lengths of deodar timber bond the walls in the local style.

Below: The veranda of Prini Ropa, looking up Kullu valley

Above: Boura Singh and Tara

Above right: The carpenters – Sunk Ram and his brother – with the house they have just made for the children

Right: Sunita patterns Tara's hands in the traditional way for brides, with a lichen and mud dye.

Below: Rahul and Tara taking a morning bath at Gulab Das's

Gungru, the *chaukidar,* and his wife

Karma (*photograph by Tom Miller*)

Taj and Chamba

Kranti, Dorze and Rahul on a picnic above Kothi

doesn't like it.' She was perkily sitting up in bed at the guest-house, dressed only in her bra. I wasn't sure whether or not to shake hands with her. They wanted to set off on the trek after breakfast.

Back home I found that Chamba had been taken off to the police station because of an argument in the *chang* bar. Mrs Chamba said she would tell him to catch us up as soon as he reappeared, and so an hour or two later, more or less complete, we waited for the clients at the bus stand. As they arrived – he in a heavyweight fishing anorak, she in a strapless top made of old fashioned bubbly swimsuit material – Luder Chand's father came up and urgently whispered, 'You must come to the police station, otherwise Chamba isn't going to get out.' Our bus was about to leave and the Sahib was fussing about posting his postcards. I said I was sorry, I had to go to the police station (I didn't mention that it was to extricate one of our chief guides), and that I would catch them up later in the day. They looked panic-stricken. Having finally arrived under 'starter's orders' as the Sahib put it, they were now being abandoned.

At the police station there was turmoil. It wasn't easy to understand either what had happened or what was to happen. Chamba and a nasty-looking man with angry round eyes, who said Chamba had insulted him, were both in the lock-up. An ancient Zanskari ruffian had been summoned as the Solomon who would settle the dispute. Everyone was ready to bow to his judgement; the question was, when would it be? He would have to hear the ins and outs of the case and the police wouldn't release the culprits until he had. I wanted Chamba out now. The Solomon was going away for a month. Luder Chand and his father looked uncomfortable and said at intervals what a good man Chamba was. Mrs Chamba arrived sobbing and enraged. A Tibetan girl who was attached to the Solomon shouted and shrieked. The constable kept beating the table with his stick. Suddenly it was fixed. The hearing would be in two weeks (that would seem to be while the Solomon was away, but we didn't question the decision). In the meantime Chamba could leave the police station.

The Sisters

Dr Snell and his family had left Manali after my first year there, but I often used to call on the nursing sisters, Joan and Valerie, at their bungalow overlooking the untidy garden, between the hospital and the doctor's house. The living room – where there hung a prayer: 'Lord give us strength to go and possess the land, the harvest is plentiful but the labourers are few' – and the bedrooms had bow windows on to the connecting veranda, where we would sit in the sun for eleven-o'clock coffee and biscuits. They provided homely snacks like toast and jam, and occasionally toast with dripping from a Sunday roast of goat. Valerie was dark, tall and strong; Joan was fair and almost frail, and grateful for her friend's strength and ebullience, although, as Valerie would be the first to acknowledge, it was Joan who had the greater medical expertise.

They had worked at the hospital here for many years, going home for a few months' furlough every four or five years. They spoke adequate Hindi and I never saw either of them wearing European dress; they always wore a *salwar* and *chemise* (Valerie often took it upon herself to adjust Joan's *dupatta* if it slipped immodestly low). But whatever reason the Lord had for choosing them as missionaries it can hardly have been that they showed signs of being natural travellers. They had heard His voice loud and clear, directing them to leave home and carry His torch to the heathens in the hills of India. Their trust in Him was unflinching, but they felt isolated in an alien world. In their simple rooms and with each other they sought to create a homely haven. They called each other 'dearie' and 'love' and would discuss at length the problem of whether to indulge themselves and buy a tin of ham roll or make do with rice and *dal* again. They craved plain English food.

My relationship with them was equivocal. I think that to their surprise they became fond of me, though they continued to consider me a bit outlandish. Their attitude towards me was reminiscent of my school teachers', though much more affectionate. There was a moment when Valerie thought there was hope for me. I had asked for the full words of 'Onward, Christian Soldiers' – but I hadn't mentioned that it was because I wanted to quote a verse in an article about the Moravian mission in Ladakh. She told someone that she was praying for me because I was beginning to see the Light. In a way they belonged to a world I knew – cauliflower cheese and Sunday walks. But they also thought and behaved in ways that often seemed uncharitable to me. Out-patients didn't open, no matter how urgent an emergency, until after morning prayers were over; on the grounds that the soul was more important than the body. Their work was heroic, and without the glowing light in their souls and their selfless devotion to a cause they couldn't have endured the long hours and frustratingly primitive facilities. They dealt with sixty to eighty out-patients a day, attended to four wards, and struggled – often by torchlight – in the operating theatre. One or other of them was on call every night.

Linda believed that all 'bad things' – like stone-throwing boys – emanated from within herself. Valerie believed they were the work of Satan. When one very sick toddler was admitted to the ward, Valerie told the parents to remove the amulet round its neck. They explained that it contained a talisman from a powerful *guru*. She ripped it off and made a show of throwing 'the filthy, Satanic magic' to the far end of the compound. The child was seriously dehydrated from dysentery and had to be kept on a saline drip. A few hours later, when Sister's attention was diverted, the family took it away from the hospital. By the next morning it was dead. On another occasion Wangdi, the Nepali mountaineer, was very ill with TB and spent months in and out of the hospital; ultimately he died there. His widow and her brother came to take the body home for the pre-cremation rituals, but to their consternation Valerie forbade them; the body was to be given a Christian burial because, she claimed, Wangdi had given himself to Christ on his deathbed. From her meagre missionary's salary, Joan paid for a deaf and dumb girl to be sent to a special school in Delhi. But when one day the child was found playing with *deotas*, making little *raths* out of sticks and leaves in a corner of the hospital compound, Joan assumed that the devil must be getting at her at the school and threatened to cancel payment of the fees.

I did witness one rare triumph of their proselytizing zeal. A Nepali who suffered from TB of the hip had been sent to Delhi by the mission hospital for treatment – expenses paid. On his return to Manali, cured but semi-paralysed, he found his older child had died and his wife had run off with another man, taking the younger child with her. Soon afterwards he made it known that he wanted to become a Christian. A baptism by total immersion was planned, and a padre, attached to the army, was to conduct it. We gathered on the bank of the Manalsu *nala*, which was swollen with monsoon rain. Women grazing their donkeys came to watch. Kullui children abandoned their cattle and sat on the mill roofs, their eyes bulging with excitement at the spectacle. We stood in a circle round a knoll while the gentle old padre led us in the prayers and hymns. He stripped down to green nylon shorts and the convert was helped off with his trousers; then the padre and two sturdy Nepalis hauled him out into the current. The three of them bowed their heads in prayer, then, waist-high in the icy, racing river and struggling to keep themselves upright, they held the victim's nose and whooshed him backwards into the cloudy water. Shivering but elated, they heaved him safely to the bank.

A New Zealand doctor ran the hospital for a while, but then no replacement could be found. Joan shouldered the burden. Unassertive and tentative, she didn't view it as an opportunity to exercise her considerable skill and knowledge, and she was only too aware of the risk involved in tackling the simplest operations without a doctor's qualifications. She felt she had no choice: she believed it was God's will that she should be needed. Sometimes she looked so frail and so close to tears that I thought He was expecting too much of her. For a time she had no company, for the stalwart Valerie was away on leave.

I offered to help, although not in a nursing or medical capacity. I would arrive after morning prayers, having breakfasted at Verma's on the way. I read the day before's *Statesman* as I ate *chena* and sizzling hot *puri*, with a splash of yoghurt and a lump of mango pickle. My role at the hospital was to organize the queue of out-patients. I gave out numbered tickets, took temperatures and wrote up a summary of each patient's complaint. I tried to establish how long they had been ill and whether there was a record of any previous treatment. This was crucial if they were TB patients. TB is the scourge of the hills. The initial treatment consists of twice-weekly injections for a year or six months; it is expensive and inconvenient for the patients, many of whom have to travel a long distance. Often the patient stops the medication when he feels better. Then he has a relapse. The disease inures itself to the drugs and the resilient form can infect others.

When an English chest specialist on holiday in Manali suggested that he might, in return for free board and lodging, work at the hospital for a few weeks, Joan was delighted. It didn't take us long to realize he was not a godsend. He spoke no Hindi, so my role extended to acting as his interpreter. I was soon making very free translations of his advice to the patients. The local women are ill at ease when being examined by a man, and nudity in any circumstances appals them. He would bawl in English, 'Clothes off, *off*, OFF', on the basis that if you shout loudly enough anyone ought to understand. He would shout at a frightened anaemic woman, stretched naked on the bed, that she should eat more meat. Of course she would if she had a chance, but here meat is beyond most people's daily budget. Another of his favourites was 'Eat plenty of roughage'. Roughage was the one ingredient not lacking in anyone's diet. We were relieved when he went back to London.

Eventually Valerie came back from leave and a new missionary doctor arrived from Britain. He was six and a half feet tall and very thin. Joan was relieved because the responsibility was off her shoulders, but she wasn't happy. He worked very, very slowly, so they were never finished until late at night. And he had odd ideas. As local people couldn't afford a torch he felt it would be wrong for him to use one; one night he fell over some rocks in his own compound and broke his nose. Oxfam suggested that they might buy the hospital an X-ray machine, but the new doctor said they wouldn't be able to accept it; a gift from Oxfam might have been bought with donations from non-Christians, so he couldn't use it at the mission hospital.

On my thirty-first birthday Joan and Valerie gave a party for me. I described the evening to my mother.

> The sisters invited me for seven o'clock. I found Valerie, still in her white uniform, pumping the primus stove. She greeted me with 'The best laid plans o' mice and men gang aft agley.' They had had to perform a Caesarian operation. A Tibetan girl had been brought in who had been in labour for four days. 'Idiotic people,' said Valerie. 'They only live over the wall, and by the time they brought her the baby's head was half out but there was no way the rest of it was going to get out that way.'
>
> So they hadn't started cooking the birthday supper. There were to be eight of us and everything was a treat – two packets of Knorr chicken noodle soup someone had sent from Canada, a tin of frankfurters and one of real English ham, some bars of Bournville chocolate and a Dundee cake made by Valerie's aunt and brought out by two visitors from the mission at home. I was touched by their generosity in providing these treasured delicacies for my birthday; the trouble was that there wasn't enough. I could have gobbled all the cocktail frankfurters myself, it was a small tin of ham, and there was just one small cucumber with four tomatoes and a loaf of stale bread. We began with a sung grace. Valerie conducted, using an aluminium ladle as a baton – I promise . . .
>
> 'The girls' insisted on walking me home. We climbed the hill in a crocodile (Valerie brandishing the *lathi*) like schoolgirls, with loud jokes and screeching laughter. I knew that Luder Chand, Chamba and Jabbu were having a party to celebrate dynamiting the cesspit. To avoid the two parties meeting I managed to dissuade 'the girls' from escorting me beyond the village tap.

My diary received such a different account of my birthday that it is unrecognizable as the same day. It doesn't mention the sisters' party, but tells of how I woke paralysed by indecision.

Kranti and I were struggling to decide whether or not we should settle down together. It wasn't easy for him. I was a foreigner, his family in Bihar disapproved, and would he abandon his university teaching career? I was apprehensive too. Could I trust myself to be steadfast, to be a wife and perhaps a mother? Could I abandon my hankering for adventures with unforeseeable ends? Should I leave my newly found Manali world? I spent the hot day tossing on the *charpoi* on the veranda. I was in limbo. I had been brought up to accept that I should be in command of my own individuality and that it ought to be possible to find a rational path out of emotional turmoil. Now I was absorbing ideas that gave little weight to the concept of individuality, and the idea of gods who cast an arbitrary glance at our short span of days in this world.

The Map

During my early days in Manali a map of the area was just a flat sheet of paper with dark blue rivers, pale-blue hatched patches of glacier, closely packed contour lines and incomprehensible names. Now when I looked at a map I could envisage the passes and gorges, and familiar stretches began to fit together. I knew that the dotted line marking a path was wrong, because there was a new bridge (and a tea hotel just above it); the path no longer ran along the left bank of the river. The bluff above the turn in the river I remembered as a good camp site shaded by birch trees. I knew that generations ago the friendly people living at the head of that high valley had come over from Zanskar – before receding glaciers opened up crevasses and made the path too dangerous. The villagers in that wild narrow valley to the west of Kullu were isolationists, treating all outsiders as untouchables, and spoke a language whose origin was unknown. By keeping my eyes and ears open I now understood the meaning of some of the place names – a *tach* and a *got* were both grazing grounds for shepherds, Kullui and Gaddi respectively. A *galu* and a *jot* were both passes, but of very different kinds; a *galu* is a neck cut through the mountains, while a *jot* is a pass like a saddle.

I learnt to be circumspect when it came to information about the way ahead. You have to work out what question might elicit the information you need and phrase it carefully, to discourage your informant from giving you the easy answer. If you ask a passing ploughman, 'How far is it to Chikka Tach?' he is apt to reply, 'It's near, just up the hill.' But if you ask him, 'If you had to carry a sack of corn to Chikka Tach would you eat before you set off? And would you get back home before dark?', you are more likely to discover how far and how gruelling a climb it really is. I began to acquire an eye and an ear for a potential route and, crucial for the trekking organizer, for the daily stages into which it could be divided. You must reach reasonably flat ground to pitch tents and there must be fuel and water; an idyllic camp site with a snow-fed spring in April can be waterless when you arrive in the autumn.

I learnt how the valleys and ranges fitted into each other. I could assess altitude from trees and flowers, taking into account whether I was on a north- or a south-facing slope. I became aware of distinctions between people of neighbouring valleys, of which deities must be revered where, and of their relationships with each other. The god of Malana (the unfriendly village with the unusual language) is Jamlu, brother of Geyphang, the presiding deity of Lahul. But the people of Lahul and of Malana village have nothing in common. It isn't just that the Malanese have a reputation for being unwelcoming but that they have always maintained a policy of keeping themselves apart; even the British considered it prudent not to try to interfere in their administration. It is only recently that a schoolteacher has been accepted within the village.

On one of our early recces we set out to explore a pass beyond Malana, not intending to visit the village; if its inhabitants objected to outsiders I saw no reason why we should impose ourselves on them. But it turned out that we had to stop there – there was nowhere else flat enough to camp. We had to remove every leather item that we wore before we could enter the village

60

– boots, watch straps, belts and camera cases. I had to hide my haversack with its leather straps. The Malanese had an inbred look; I had never been aware of it anywhere else but there was no mistaking it. And when I peeked over a bank to look at a house under construction I was alarmed by the vehemence with which I was warned off. I felt ill at ease. The next morning, when we were already some way beyond the village, we met two or three men on a narrow path; their glower told us to move our polluting presence out of their way.

Although stretches of mountain may appear to the unaccustomed eye not to be inhabited, it is often a false impression. Dense, steep-sided forest may hide contractors' labourers – poor Nepalis or Kashmiris – or professional woodcutters from Kangra. And in forest glades at 9,000 or 10,000 feet there are encampments of Gujars. For four or five months of the year they and their herds of buffalo occupy well-built summer houses with mud walls and flat roofs. Gujars belong to a semi-nomadic tribe which grazes animals through the lower mountains from Afghanistan to Nepal. They are taller and better built than most of the hill people and boast aquiline noses and a handsome bearing. They are the only Muslims in the area; many of the older men sport henna-dyed red hair and beards, showing that with the best of Mohammed's faithful they have made the pilgrimage to Mecca. Higher up, from the edge of the treeline up to 13,000 or 14,000 feet, the Gaddi shepherds graze their flocks of cream-coloured sheep and goats. The Gujars, with wives and children, travel a comparatively short distance from their winter quarters to their substantial summer encampments; the Gaddi shepherds cover much greater distances and camp in the open, in caves or dry-stone igloos. They wear white homespun tweed cloaks kilted at the waist with coils of black rope, and are staunch Hindus and worshippers of Lord Shiva, to whom they believe they owe their shepherding *dharma*, or calling. On the alps just above the treeline there may be a Buddhist encampment – perhaps one or two white tents belonging to Khampa herb-gatherers, like those who looked after us so generously when we ran out of food.

I met those generous hosts again several years later, when I was exploring a route for a party from Thomas Cook's, planned for the following year, with an ex-Everest mountaineer.

The mountaineer wanted to travel 'light and fast'; against my advice he insisted that we should leave Manali in the afternoon rather than early the following morning. We had no tents and minimal provisions. As dusk turned into night we were still struggling up a perpendicular path through deodar forest, and it was raining. At last a dim glimmer led us to a hut where a disagreeable Kashmiri apple-picker was asleep in some hay. We slept on the veranda.

Next morning at about ten we were walking through a hamlet of houses when there was a shout – 'Come on up here!' My boss-eyed friend had recognized me and was leaning over his veranda. We went up. 'You can't just walk through our village without visiting us, and you've come on a good day – there's a party.

Have a glass of tea – our house isn't grand but we don't lack anything – and then we'll join in.' Out on the green at the back was a large circle of people who were sitting drinking; they were honouring the memory of a woman who had died on that day the previous year. The widower, a spruce, trim man showing no signs of emotional upheaval, welcomed us. He had had two wives. It seemed odd that the surviving one should be presiding over a memorial feast for her deceased rival; but maybe they had been friends. Two boys, skinny twelve- or fourteen-year-olds in new white tweed jackets, served the *chang* and the bottles of *arak*. They had a sad, drawn look: were they grieving for their mother and suffering at the hands of an unkind step-mother?

Superficially the Khampas of this village – with their tweed clothes and Kullu caps – weren't very different from the Malana people, no more than twenty-five miles away as the chough flies. But when you looked more carefully it was clear that they had little in common with those inbred recluses. Hampta village wasn't as remote as Malana, though it was still some distance from a road, but the people here, of Tibetan or Mongolian origin, were worldly traders. They had acquired their land a generation ago and turned the nearby hillside into a profitable seed-potato farm. The people of Malana spent their lives holed up in the village. For the Khampas the village was a base; in the summer some of the men camped in the mountains, herb-gathering, while in the winter they all went down with their mule trains to the foothills to trade.

My mountaineering companion, who had been in such a hurry, drank copious quantities of *chang* and silver cups full of *arak*.

It was the afternoon before we moved on; Lama Le, our only companion, had been murmuring his impatience. We climbed for less than an hour, and were resting above a Gujar encampment when he dozed off. When he woke he didn't look too good, and a steep half-hour defeated him; we would camp here, beside a pool of stagnant water, and sleep on a ledge under a rock. Lama Le, taciturn, began to make kedgeree. The mountaineer rolled himself into his Everest sleeping bag and slept soundly, but I was cold and uncomfortable on the narrow ledge. The next morning I decided that he and the disapproving Lama Le could make the recce on their own, and I left for home.

Confronting Death

I had always wanted to go beyond the Inner Line – to cross the Rothang Pass into Lahul; John and I had intended to walk that way on our trek to Kashmir but permission had been refused. Now I decided to try again.

I went to the office of the chief of police in Kullu. When I had submitted the necessary forms in triplicate the clerk asked me, 'Are you a virgin?' I quaked; did he require a yes or a no to give me the permit? I decided to assume he meant, 'Are you married?' and answered no. He didn't comment, but told me to come back in the afternoon. At four o'clock, trembling with excitement, I clutched the chits for the police checkposts along the route; they permitted me to travel all the way through Lahul to the Darcha bridge at its northernmost point.

Over the Rothang Pass everything was so different that I felt I should be carrying a foreign currency. I knew that this region was beyond the reaches of the monsoon, but I wasn't prepared for the contrast. In the clear dry air the white peaks seemed even shinier than on the Kullu side. There were glaciers, textured with patterns in greens and greys, in wild architectural tiers, with flying buttresses and pinnacles of velvet-smooth ice. Man would build like this if he knew how. The mountainsides were arid desert, except for the tiny circular patches of green where generations of Gaddi camps had nurtured rank docks and nettles. In the beige and grey rock, as though they had been painted with a giant's brush in thick oil paint, were strata of ochre, red and acid yellow. Down below were the fields, not sprawling haphazardly along the valley sides, but arranged in solid blocks of pattern. In this arid climate, crops won't grow without irrigation. The blocks – fields of potatoes, barley, buckwheat and, lower down, wheat – are fed by irrigation channels taken miles across the hillsides. The villages here bore no resemblance to those of Kullu: the houses were square, flat-roofed and mud-plastered. The only trees were a few poplars and groves of willows; the supple, thin branches of the pollarded trees tossed in the wind like a choppy sea.

The willows are pollarded because sheep and goats feed on the bark of the twigs during the winter. Winter is so long, from October to May, that the women spend all summer cutting and carrying grass. Without it the cattle would starve. Everything that grows is used; I even saw potato shaws drying on the roofs. I also came across my first yak. If I had ever tried to imagine a Highland cow crossed with a Shetland pony it would have been a yak.

Despite the disadvantages of the arid climate and the high altitude of the villages, on average 9,000 to 10,000 feet, Lahulis are not poor. They are industrious and efficient cultivators. Their cash crop used to be *kuth* (*Saussurea costus*), a plant like a thistly rhubarb; it is cultivated for its root, which is used as medicine and valued by the Chinese as an aphrodisiac, and recently its oil has been exported as a base for perfumes. But today it is the seed potato that makes money for the farmers. The neat, even drills and meticulous irrigation channels would make the finest Ayrshire potato farmer blink. The Lahulis are wise enough not to put all their eggs in one basket: they have also begun to grow hops for the rapidly expanding brewing business, and chicory for export to the coffee-drinking states in south India.

Traditionally, cultivation isn't the only source of livelihood for the Lahulis. At least one son or daughter would become a lama or *chomo* (nun), and be supported by the *gompa*, while other brothers would often be traders and muleteers, spending many months away from home.

Taj hadn't come with me, for he was out with a party of climbers, but I spent a night at his village. I had imagined the picturesque village with its wide green *maidan* where he galloped white ponies, and imagined too that I would be welcomed and feasted by his family. But I was disappointed. There was little cultivable land and it was very high – at 11,500 feet the crops were poor. The village had depended on its mule trains' trading with Tibet, and since the Indo-Chinese war and the closure of the Tibetan border it had felt a severe loss of income.

I had sensed some reluctance in the people I spoke to when I asked directions to Taj's house. It was evening, and the house seemed deserted, unlit. No one answered my shouts and knocks. I went in, and in the murky shadows found a lone woman and an ill child, lying swathed in blankets, by the stove. I unwrapped the grimy blankets and found a pale boy of about six; he looked as though he had chickenpox and was soaked with sweat. I suggested he should be covered with something lighter and looser. Yes, yes, the woman said, tugging at a corner of blanket, but I could see she wasn't going to pay any heed to my advice. She wanted to tell me her troubles.

'My elder husband is away all the time, he is in the military. He sends money sometimes, but very little. My younger husband, the one that works with you, he never sends money. This year he didn't even come at the ploughing time. It is very hard – I cannot manage everything by myself. I have to depend on neighbours to help cultivate the fields. That isn't right, it brings shame.'

What did she mean? That she was Taj's wife? I knew he did have a brother in the army. Then I remembered that in Lahul and Zanskar brothers often shared their wives; one woman married all the brothers of the family. 'He hasn't been home for so long his son here hardly remembers him, and he never sends anything for him.' She clutched my arm. 'You should tell him to come home more often to bring his son good clothes; he goes to school now.'

The unplastered room was dark and dishevelled and chilly. I didn't want to be involved. I pressed some money into the boy's hand and left.

Sometimes my interest in what I saw was given shape and focus by the thought of describing it to my mother. I knew she would appreciate my surprising afternoon in Keylong, the capital of Lahul. I had been staying, grandly, in the suite used by Mrs Gandhi at the Circuit House. It had been refurbished for her visit the previous year – when, so the story goes, she was given a kilo of *ghi* made from the milk of yaks specially fed on rose petals. It had a pink-tiled bathroom with pink toilet paper, and there was even a working bedside light in the bedroom. My stay had been arranged by the district Public Relations Officer, to whom I had an introduction from an antiquarian bookseller in Simla. He turned out to be knowledgeable on a wide range of subjects from potatoes to Buddhist iconography – like most Lahulis he was a Buddhist – and his company enhanced my visit to Lahul.

This afternoon I was on my way to visit the Moravian missionaries' graveyard – there were Moravian missionaries here for a hundred years, although they had few converts and there are no Christians here now. They invented the iron stove (like the one I use in Manali) and the idea of a chimney, taught everyone to knit patterned socks and, most importantly, introduced the potato. On my way I met my friend the Public Relations Officer. He knew I was interested in agriculture because we had discussed hill sheep and Jersey cattle, and I had promised that next year I would bring some Golden Wonder potato seed for him – please don't let me forget. He asked me if I would go and judge the cattle show – the judge hadn't turned up. He refused to take any notice of my protests that I didn't know enough, insisting that because I came from abroad people would accept my decision, assuming I knew best.

The cattle and many owners and spectators were assembled in a gritty yard, and the dust blew into my eyes. My task wasn't as hard as I had imagined. There was only one class of about a dozen beasts, and it wasn't so much a case of choosing a champion for its fine points as of choosing the least disabled; they were a motley bunch. One had a withered hindquarter; another was in poor health with a large swelling on her rib cage. They were both casualties from grazing on the steep mountainsides. Some were all horn and hairy-pony tail – showing their yak parentage – and others showed the influence of the Indo-New Zealand Jersey breeding project.

Finally I picked a Jersey who was nicely built, if not in the first flush of youth. Then, as I was about to present the owner with the prize envelope, I saw to my horror that one quarter of her udder was 'blind'; it had presumably never recovered from acute mastitis. The only thing to do was to pretend I hadn't noticed.

I continued the letter the next day, after attending the cremation of a Buddhist nun. I wanted to describe the event to my mother because it was so far removed from her own idea of funerals – which she rarely attended because they so upset her.

A nun of eighty had died, and the Public Relations Officer took me to the funeral. We climbed two thousand feet up the mountain until we reached the Buddhist monastery in a pencil-cedar grove. It was a large, flat-roofed building with smaller flat-roofed buildings beside it, washed with translucent beige mud, where the monks and nuns lived. We were welcomed at the door by the dead nun's sister, who was wailing noisily. My friend bent down to her (he is very tall), held her fondly by the shoulders and murmured comforting words. Inside we sat among the mourners on carpets round the room. Both monks and nuns wear maroon robes and have shaved heads, so it's hard to tell the difference. The village women wore a lot of jewellery; several necklaces of large corals and turquoise and seed pearls, and heavy gold rings pulling down their earlobes. Many of the older women were bald above their foreheads because of the silver pieces they wear tied into their hair. I sat with them drinking cardamom-flavoured tea and *chang* and ate patterned fried chapattis. Each time a new guest arrived all the women rushed towards her, wailing, pressing their noses, rubbing their eyes with the edges of their gowns, and clinging to one another's arms and shoulders. Then they would sit down and chat quite jovially until someone else arrived, when they began to wail all over again. I didn't know how to compose myself and from time to time had difficulty not laughing. It seemed wrong for me to sit there with a blank face while tears gushed down everyone else's.

The wails rose to a crescendo when they went out to bid farewell to the corpse. Some pulled forward, others tried to hold them back, as though the actual moment of its departure would be too painful to witness. The body sat upright on a bier. It was tied on with lengths of new tweed. A shawl covered its shoulders, a headcloth and a silk hat covered its head, and a red silk umbrella was carried above it. The lamas on the roof of the neighbouring building wore scarlet brocade hats and had flowing beards; they were picturesque against the snowy peaks. They beat drums, blew trumpets and conch shells, and clashed the cymbals. As the body and the procession of mourners moved downhill, wails mingled with the sounds of the instruments.

The bier was placed on the ground in the cedar grove. Now the body was partially unwrapped for the ritual of purification: you could see the face and shoulders. Little piles of grain were laid out on a blanket – provisions for her journey. Lamas sat in a row, chanting prayers and sometimes chatting and exchanging jokes.

I found the scene very moving: the ritual and ceremony helped to make death acceptable. There was no pomp, no awe. Women sat in the shade knitting while the children, sheep and goats scampered about. The body, sitting on its colourful bier, didn't seem horrifying. My friend explained that people are taught not to be frightened of death, to accept it. For lamas and nuns there are special exercises, which they use to prepare themselves and to help others. They keep guard over the dead and use thigh bones as flutes, skulls as drinking vessels. The more advanced perform meditation and mental exercises which enable them to enter a state of trance or *samadhi* – sitting upright in the lotus position – after death; the body doesn't then decompose. There were traces of blood from the dead nun's nose, apparently an indication that she had achieved *samadhi*. She had been in it for two days, but some great lamas achieve it for ten days, even for weeks. The corpse was given advice as to how to proceed on its journey. My friend said the instructions were very well done.

I feel I have learnt a lot today, seen things I have never been faced with, been made aware of how narrow-minded I am.

My newfound reactions to death were tested all too soon. One morning in the autumn, soon after my visit to Lahul, I was coming up the hill from an early trip to the bazaar when I met Chamba's first wife in the wood on the steep slope above the *gompa*. 'Come quickly,' she said. 'Nomo is ill.'

The child had had diarrhoea and hadn't looked well for some time. Up at the house I found Mrs Chamba looking really anxious, her face swollen with tears. Nomo was wrapped in a cocoon of blankets. She had had a very high fever in the night and was delirious; to me she looked close to death. Tsering Dolma had been sent to call Chamba's first wife (Chamba was out in the hills), who had gone to fetch the *vaidya*. He had given Nomo powders for weakness.

'We must get her to the hospital.'

'Memsahib, it's not good to take her out.'

I knew they were loath to take her to the hospital, but I paid no attention and tied the cocoon on to Mrs Chamba's back.

I wished she would walk faster down the hill; I just wanted us to get to the hospital before the child died. Tsering Dolma scuttled along, clutching my hand. I jumped over the back wall, so that I could search for the sisters or the doctor more quickly, and found Joan. Then there was no sign of Mrs Chamba and the child. She had said she was going round by the gate, but had she decided against coming in? At last I found her sitting patiently on the out-patient benches. Had Nomo been my child I would have been making a hue and cry, running here and there and demanding attention.

Joan went quite pale when she examined Nomo and told Valerie to prepare steroid injections. They took the child to the ward, unwrapped her and put her on a drip. Mrs Chamba was quietly crying. I wanted to leave, I didn't want to see her die, but I knew I must stay. Nomo was in a semi-coma. From time to time she came out of it for a little while and called '*Amma, amma*, I am very ill, water.' Then she would slip back into unconsciousness.

In the bazaar I found Jabbu Ram, Luder's younger brother, and explained what had happened. He looked unenthusiastic when I asked him to set off towards the ridge above the Jugatsukh *nala* where Chamba and the party of trekkers were meant to be camping that night. I knew he and Chamba had fallen out recently but hoped that he would be generous-spirited. He said he would go.

Nomo's breathing got worse; otherwise there was little change. Time passed slowly. I slept at the sisters' house. They too were anxious. No one understood what it was that had come on so suddenly and dramatically, although later the hospital decided that it must have been TB of the stomach.

Chamba arrived the next day, frightened and bewildered. I was so relieved to see him: I could hug Chamba. I had wanted to hug Mrs Chamba, but felt I couldn't.

That night he came knocking on my window to tell me Nomo's breathing was shaky, irregular and sometimes stopping altogether. We fetched Joan. Chamba hovered over the child as though he could breathe life into her. He murmured to her, and then just sat there reciting *mantras*. She survived that night and the next. I thought her breathing was gaining strength and that she seemed more as though she was asleep than in a coma. The mission prayed for her at morning prayers; and at grace, before our mashed potatoes and vegetable pie, Valerie prayed that God should keep her safe from the devil's work.

It was beautiful early-autumn weather. The leaves of the acacias in the compound were just turning and the mountains above were sharply defined; even at night, by the light of a full moon. Valerie said I looked too *deshi* wandering around with a blanket as a shawl and with ill-kempt hair.

On the third morning I went to the bazaar to buy eggs and bread for everyone's breakfast, and was on my way back to the hospital when I met Chamba's first wife once again. She said, 'Where are you going? There's no one there. She's dead and they've taken her home.' Only an hour before I'd met Chamba on his way up to the house to fetch milk for the patient.

They were sitting in the first wife's house. Mrs Chamba was wailing, and now I did hug her. I didn't know what else to do. Chamba sat looking very upright and dignified. I noticed a bundle on the bench beside me: it was the body, already wrapped in white. Soon Tsangpo brought white scarves and Chawang brought incense sticks. Mrs Chamba howled, 'Oh *Bhagwan*, why have you taken my girl away?' The lama came with his prayer books and settled down to chant the required prayers. Everyone was doing a task, without fuss – churning salt tea, cutting vegetables, buying spices. More mourners gathered. Mrs Chamba wailed and sobbed; no words of comfort could quieten her. Just as they were preparing to take the little corpse away, Taj and Dorze arrived – they had been up in the hills with the trekking party. They dumped their haversacks outside, came in without taking off their boots and knelt down to the bereaved mother, holding her in their arms, holding her head between their hands.

The procession left; the women stayed behind. The oil lamp burnt dimly, and Mrs Chamba and I lay down and slept, exhausted. Later I was told that as the pyre was lit, down at the *ghat* by the river, Chamba himself finally broke down and sobbed.

It seemed impossible to accept the loss. What arbitrary will had decided to end Nomo's life? There was no comfort to be offered and I could find none for myself.

The Last Footloose Trip

By the autumn a decision had been made: from next year Kranti would live with me in Manali. The plan was that we would run the trekking organization together. It would be not so much my fanciful creation as a proper business; we would buy additional equipment and a jeep and be able to take more clients.

Taj, Chamba and I made our last expedition together. We were to go from Manali over to Barabangahal, and then explore a new route over the Thamsar Pass to the south, down to Kangra valley. It was October. We started off straight up our *nala*; in fact we passed Luder's father and the *mistri* working on the water tank. During the three days' climb up from Manali I had never felt fitter. I was intoxicated with well-being and the feeling that I could go on for ever, taking anything in my stride. The moon was waning, and the dark nights were lit by the white glow of the Milky Way. Just below the Kali Hind at 13,000 feet, where we camped, it was cold. I cut vegetables and watched the *dal* as it cooked on a hearth in the shelter of a Gaddi stone igloo, while Taj and Chamba scavenged for wood, searching for any the Gaddis might have hidden before they left for the winter.

On the day we crossed the pass I was painfully slow. Breathing hurt, and I thought I would never make the trudge up the last snow slope. I arrived at the top bad-tempered, miserable and blind behind my misted-up goggles. On the far side the snow was thicker and softer, more tiring, and more snow began to fall, quite heavily. Somehow I stumbled on down until almost at dusk we reached shelter – another Gaddi igloo, damp this time and full of goat dung. I knew I had a high temperature.

The next day the pain in my chest was worse. I struggled down to rhododendron level where we camped; here we could have a proper fire. I dosed myself with Disprin and antibiotics and fell into a fitful sleep, interrupted by nightmares about two beautiful Lahuli girls with ping-pong balls for eyes. I couldn't eat and I was frightened. The weather was far from set fair and we couldn't afford the time to rest; a substantial snowfall would mean spending the winter locked into Barabangahal. And winter lasted until the end of April or beginning of May.

Taj decided that he could make out a track down the left bank of the river. It had to be a quicker and easier route than the one we had followed before, which involved a climb of 3,000 feet, and, because the river was now low, it should be possible to cross it somewhere to reach Barabangahal.

Hours later we found ourselves in virgin forest, among a tangle of fallen timber on a precipitous slope. It was primeval: there was no sign of man's ever having been there – not a vestige of an axe stroke or a fire. I had always searched for landscape unscarred by man, but this was too eerie and quiet. If we died no one would find our remains for hundreds of years. Walking through tangled timber was tiring. The pine needles were slippery, and the forest was so dense that we couldn't see out far enough to maintain any sense of direction. None of us spoke. We all knew we had to make our way down; there was no choice. We didn't ask each other what we would do if there was a cliff face down to the river.

There were no cliffs, but Taj's calculations were wrong: the river was not low. He searched up and down and scanned the banks for tracks showing where others might have crossed by a hidden bridge. There was none: we would have to try to wade through. I didn't bother to feel the temperature of the water. I knew that it was freshly melted snow and ice, and far deeper, wider and faster than anything I had ever had to face before. People often died crossing rivers; if you stumbled and were submerged it only took moments. We were all carrying haversacks which we would hardly have time to throw off if we fell. Arms crossed over our chests as if we were about to begin a chorus of Auld Lang Syne, we grasped one another's hands and plunged in. Half-way across I knew that I could only bear a second or two more: the cold hurt so much that it took my breath away. 'Hurry! hurry!' I gasped. 'No,' shouted Chamba. 'You must do it slowly, slowly – don't fall.' I fixed my sight on a boulder on the far bank and reached it half conscious. Chamba took off my boots and socks and trousers and Taj blew life into a driftwood fire. Slowly our circulation returned.

At Barabangahal we were feasted on potatoes and fresh maize cobs, and we slept. Many of the houses were abandoned. The schoolmaster had left; so had the shepherds and flocks and most of the families. A few had to stay – some who were too infirm to cross the pass and some to look after the cattle through the rigours of the winter. I visited the Shakti temple, an unimpressive shrine above the village, to give thanks for our safe arrival. The old temple and the village itself used to be on the other side of the river; it was swept away by a flood when a glacial lake burst the moraine high in the Ravi valley, across the watershed above Beas Kund.

I wanted to stay and rest for a day but Taj was insistent that we should set off at once towards the Thamsar. The villagers too urged us to leave, pointing to the shredded cotton-wool wisps in the blue sky which presaged bad weather: 'If you go quickly you'll make it down to Chota Bangahal in two days; it's not far.'

As we climbed up out of the valley the clouds did begin to build up. By two o'clock I couldn't go on. We had only just pitched the tent when spits of snow began to fall. Now Taj showed his anxiety. 'See, if you hadn't gone so slowly we would have got over the pass today. Now we may never make it.'

'Nonsense, I'm getting much better. Tomorrow I'll be able to walk all day, through snow or whatever, and we're comfortable enough here,' I said, trying to reassure myself as well as him. Within an hour the spits of snow had become a blizzard. Taj lay in his sleeping bag listening to Radio Ceylon while Chamba mumbled his prayers and I read *The Idiot* by torchlight. We were all trying not to listen to the soft *pud, pud* of snow falling on the tent. Taj and Chamba got up several times during the night to batter it off the sagging flysheet.

In the morning it was still snowing. We set off one behind the other, close together. Two dark figures emerged from the whiteness: exhausted Barabangahalis, wrapped in blankets, who had spent the night out. They gave us the briefest of directions, for they were loath to loiter. We should have known better than to attempt a recce of so high a pass so late in the year, and it was turning out to be a pointless exercise anyway. In these conditions we could hardly make out the lie of the land, nor could we assess stages and camp sites. The going was very slow. The soft new snow carpeted the loose boulders. One step held; the next would sink through to above the knee, and it was painful as well as a waste of precious energy to extricate your foot.

At about three o'clock, between the squalls and mists, we could make out cairns on the horizon which must mark the pass. We realized that we couldn't reach it until after five and it would be foolhardy to go on and risk having to spend the night at 15,000 feet in this weather. (This was the night, according to the villagers, when we should have been down in the valley at Chota Bangahal.) There was a relatively flat stretch of snow below us. We trod it firm and drove the pegs into the beaten snow. We cooked kedgeree inside the tent. I retched at the smell of kerosene fumes mixed with onions and couldn't eat. Taj didn't turn on the radio; this time he murmured prayers with Chamba. He wouldn't have been able to hear it anyway, for all night the wind battered the tent like a dog shaking a rat. Would the pegs hold? Taj and Chamba slept, but I didn't. Should I struggle out of my sleeping bag, out of the double layers of the tent, into the dark and bitter wind to check the pegs?

In the morning the tent stank of kerosene and damp clothes.

We would have to crawl up through the snow to get out. Taj and Chamba put on all the clothes they had. Normally so resilient and ready with a joke in the face of adversity, they were now taciturn and looked submissive, as though resigned to their fate.

It wasn't snowing any more, but the new snow was so deep that it was too tiring to lead for more than twenty yards at a time. The leader's legs sank to thigh level at each step, while those following had the benefit of his path. I took my turn with the others, for I was feeling much better and inexplicably cheerful. It was Chamba who began to lose heart. 'You two go on, it doesn't matter about me. Don't you worry, just move on. I don't think I can make it to the pass.'

It took us four hours to reach the cairns – it was just as well we hadn't tried to get there the night before. The pass was clear; we could see down the other side. But we were in no mood for admiring the view. Far below we could see rhododendrons. There was less snow on this side, but it would still take us several hours to reach the wood.

With legs like feeble jelly we staggered down, and came upon a lone dog standing on a rock, looking expectantly up at us. His track showed that he had come up from below. Was he searching for a master and flock that had perished in the blizzard? The sight of him brought home to us how lucky we were to be alive and safe. In the colourless, bleak valley there wasn't a sign of another living thing. But Chamba and Taj began to lose their mask-like expressions of resignation, and to scamper downhill with their accustomed turn of speed, too fast for me. We weren't going to reach the rhododendron wood before dark, but it didn't matter: we were off snow. We pitched the tent among some sheltering rocks and pulled sleeping bags over our wet clothes. We didn't even bother to try to cook. We were safe – it could snow and blow as much as it liked but we knew we weren't going to perish, nor have to spend six months in Barabangahal. We didn't talk about it, but we shared enormous relief.

The following day, in the middle of the morning, we reached a 'hotel' run by a Khampa woman. She made us tea with slightly sour milk and *gur*; it might have been ambrosia. She cooked us a stack of chapattis and hot potato curry. In the afternoon we played cards with a group of Gaddis who were impressed by our hardiness, and assured us that we were the last to cross the pass that year. Our sleeping bags and clothes were spread on the rocks to dry in the warm sun, and our stomachs were full. The day before was already a memory; already it was impossible to relive the discomfort and exhaustion and the effort required to overcome the apathy of resignation. In the evening the three of us shared two bottles of fine *arak* provided by the hotelier.

III
Expansion

Home-making

The 'flush' was not materializing. (You find yourself using the continuous tense in India not just because it is a direct translation from Hindi but because so often it is apt.) I had tried both the carrot and the stick. I had given Luder Chand's father advances for the tank, cement, pipes and cisterns. Then I had reduced the rent to an appropriate rate for accommodation without plumbing, explaining that I would repay the balance as soon as I had a working bathroom. It was two years now that I had been living there flushless. Kranti pointed out that since the landlord hadn't managed the promised sanitation in all this time it was unrealistic to hope he ever would.

In the third spring we arrived to find he had refused to give the Chamba family their room; instead they were camping in the kitchen. There were five of them now, for during the winter twin girls had been born, replacing Nomo twofold (though I don't think she was ever replaced in Chamba's heart). The old man said he needed the ground-floor room, which I had rented for them the previous year, for when visitors came to attend marriages and *melas*; it was an unconvincing explanation, but nothing would change his mind.

We went to my old friend Pandit Balak Ram down at Katrain, hoping that we might rent Duff Dunbar, the house above Dunghri forest. We sat out on the lawn amid the roses and magnolias. He was pleased to see us. He liked conversational company, and as he and Kranti both belonged to Brahminical landowning families they met on common ground. They discussed caste ideals, Gandhian principles and today's dirty politics.

77

Panditji began to reminisce about 'the old, good days', when a bottle of Mr Mohan Meakin's Scotch whisky cost 2 rupees and 8 annas, and a packet of Senior Service cigarettes a mere 3 annas. Every day he used to go down to tea and then stay for a peg with Mr and Mrs Tyacke at their guesthouse. 'They left to go home in 'forty-eight. I still miss their company, though they write regularly and send me *Country Life*. They live in Twickenham now, but they say there too it's not like the old days.'

Trying tactfully to turn the conversation towards the reason for our visit, I asked about Garden Duff Dunbar, the Scots forest officer who had built Duff Dunbar in the early 1870s.

'All the deodar forests round Manali – no, not just there, all of them up and down the valley, all that you can see – were planted by Mr Duff Dunbar.' This must have been an apocryphal story to aggrandize Duff Dunbar, as most of the forest was the result of natural regeneration. 'You see, he was a hard-working man, an old-fashioned type of man.' Manali was often referred to on maps as Duff Dunbar and now I discovered why. 'He was the most important person in the area. At that time Manali bazaar hardly existed. There was Manali village up on the hill across the river and there were two or three traders' shops where the mule tracks met; that was all.'

It seemed there was a dichotomy between the Garden Duff as he had been in Kullu, squire and upright forest officer, and the Garden Duff Dunbar who was Laird of Hempriggs in Sutherland. On the death of his uncle some time in late 1875 or early 1876, Garden Duff, aged about forty-three and unmarried, had to leave his newly built house above Dunghri and shoulder his Scottish inheritance.

It wasn't until after his return to Scotland that he acquired the 'Dunbar' part of his name, so it was puzzling that Manali post office and the house should have been given the double-barrel version. The Scottish version of his character is very different from the Indian.

A month after inheriting the estates he married his cousin Jane Louisa Duff . . . he left the estates after only eight short years.

78

Having begun to waste money and to sell the family heirlooms, his marriage soon failed, and eventually he ran off with his wife's sister. Not only was this considered incestuous in those days, but she is said to have been under-aged. He went into 'exile' in Ireland and in 1884, the estates were handed over to a succession of trustees.[1]

Panditji chose to ignore my slanderous Scottish account of his hero. He went on to explain how the house had come into his family. A year or two after his departure from the valley Duff Dunbar had sold it to a Mr MacKay, who was childless, and became so fond of Panditji's aunt that he gave it to her as a wedding present.

After the stale biscuits and tea, which took so long to arrive that we had begun to think they must have had to go to the forest for fuel, he said yes, we could rent Duff Dunbar. We could have it in a month's time, once it had been whitewashed.

I wasn't sure what to feel. I was excited at the prospect of such a lovely house – a mansion house, set in its own grounds – and its Scots connection, but it would be a move into another kind of life. I was loath to leave my old life in the village. First we had a trek to organize; we would leave the final decision until afterwards.

When we got back we found there was still no sign of any effort being made to provide a functioning lavatory so we told Luder's father we were leaving. He addressed his rage to Kranti: 'You people from the plains think you know everything. I tell you I could read and write before you were born. Memsahib was our guest, and with her it was all right. Now you come and it's "This hasn't been done, do this, get this done." You think because we are just farmers, villagers, we don't know anything.'

I felt sorry. He suffered from a common Kullui inability to grasp the laws of cause and effect. I had never been inside the old house where the family lived. Whenever I was passing by and they invited me for tea, I was given it out in the courtyard. I had been asked inside very few Kullui houses. This reluctance to offer hospitality to strangers may stem from fears of caste pollution but I think it also comes from a lack of curiosity. Kulluis are unworldly in the sense that they lack interest in what they don't know about. Luder's father had never managed to instal the 'flush' because he lacked the enthusiasm and confidence to tackle anything unfamiliar. Then he felt resentful about losing his rent. This same lack of interest and sense of purpose was the underlying cause of the Kulluis' more general resentment against the successful incomers to the area – Lahulis, Khampas and Punjabis.

Mrs Chamba had said she didn't want to move with us, because Duff Dunbar was too far from the bazaar. Hoping she might change her mind if she had company, we suggested Dorze and his wife might come too. He was willing, and happy not to pay rent for his hut near the *gompa*, but she was reluctant – it would be too cold up there and too far from work.

The evening before the day of the move the landlord called. 'Now I understand,' he said. 'It's not because of the "flush" – it's all because of that servant. You make such a fuss about one man, giving him such importance. I don't want to give the room to Chamba. You know what he did when they were out on trek? Jabbu knows how to cook good food. When Chamba hadn't put enough fat in the *thurka* for the *dal*, Jabbu put some more in and got abused. Chamba shouted that Jabbu didn't know how to work and what did he think? That he was in his father's house and that he could use up all the fat? Then do you know what Chamba did? He put the meat ladle in the *subji* and the *dal* so that Jabbu couldn't eat anything, because he is a vegetarian. That's the type of uncivil man you chose to make such a fuss about.'

Mrs Chamba had been listening to this tirade. I think she had hoped to stay on in the house, living in the kitchen. But by the next day she was coming with us and had persuaded Dorze's wife to come too.

The next morning I was sent to guard the luggage at the bottom of the hill. I sat on the wall by the *gompa*, shaded by an umbrella. Taj, Chamba, Lama Le and three hired Nepalis brought down load after load, and Mrs Dorze brought a large kettleful of *chang* to refresh them. I drained the dregs left in the cups and soon felt quite merry, chatting with passers-by who stopped to admire our belongings. The Lahuli girls particularly liked the long mirrors and old lamas too took surreptitious glances at themselves as they shuffled by. Anything larger than a small hand-mirror is a rare luxury; people excitedly admire themselves if they catch a full-length reflection in a shop window or in the back-wall mirror of a tea shop.

Rumours came down the hill that an argument was in play between Kranti and the old landlord. Luder Chand's father was claiming the 750 rupees of rent I had deducted because of the lack of 'flush'. Kranti was claiming half of the furniture I had had made; I had paid the carpenter to make the bed, bookcases and cupboards, while the landlord had provided the timber. Lama Le came down with a steel trunk on his back, saying the old man had locked the big yellow *duri* inside the room and that a lot of shouting was going on. Chamba added that Kranti was threatening to break down the door. At last one of the Nepalis staggered downhill with the *duri*. By now so much household bric-à-brac was assembled that it took a passer-by a good ten minutes to admire it all. Chamba's first wife was particularly nosy, picking everything up, lifting up lids, peering inside and making admiring hissing sounds.

At last Kranti appeared and everything was stowed either in the truck or on the jeep trailer. Our half-wild cat mewed hysterically under a basket. The Chamba family's stock of fire-wood had to be thrown on board; outraged by the old man's attack, they were determined not to leave him a stick.

At half-past three we lunched on the lawn in front of Duff Dunbar. It was a hundred years since Garden Duff was said to have taken his first – and as it turned out his last – cup of tea there. It was while he was drinking it that the telegram arrived summoning him back to his Scottish inheritance. Now we ate hard-boiled eggs, *dal* and chapattis, sitting amongst the last of the apple blossom. The magnolias and clematis were not yet out.

Duff Dunbar

Chamba and I washed generations of sparrow droppings off the veranda. Lama Le and Kranti cleaned window panes with newspaper and spit and pieces of cuttlefish. I found a tin of well-matured furniture polish in the bazaar and painstakingly rubbed it into the sitting-room mantelpiece. This was made of fine walnut, velvet-smooth, and in its simple elegance reminded me of one in an eighteenth-century Scottish manse.

Downstairs there were two rooms; the sitting room, where I worked at a desk in the window, was separated from the dining room by an entrance hall. Here there was a handsome hall table where vases of gladioli or delphiniums should have stood; instead it was always piled high with oddments to be taken upstairs or down to the bazaar. The dining room was dark and the least attractive room in the house; we used it as the trekking store. We ate in the kitchen, which was a separate building at the back of the house, or on the lawn at the front, or on the upstairs veranda, depending on the time of the year and the time of day.

Garden Duff had had the sense – apparently unique among the British in Kullu – to appreciate local architecture and local craftsmanship; his house was a fine example. The only concession to British design was an indoor staircase; at the head of the stair was a nicely turned banister which bordered the landing. From there you looked out through a double door on to the veranda. Nine crenellated arches, supported by curved brackets of foliage, framed the view. An intricately fretted balustrade ran the length of the veranda, and under the roof hung wooden tassels that gently knocked against each other in the breeze.

The two upstairs rooms, the visitors' room to the right and our bedroom to the left, had dormer windows looking on to the veranda. The visitors' room was panelled from waist-level down, to protect the skirts of Garden's guests from the flaky whitewash. In our room the bed was under the dormer window, and I opened my eyes each morning to the view framed by two of the veranda arches. I could see the large pear trees at the top corner of the drive, and the old apples in the orchard; then at the far end the edge of Dunghri deodar forest and, up above, the snow peaks on the opposite side of the valley. The Scotsman must have searched for some time before he found such a site. In these hills the land falls away precipitously but here, in front of the house, were 150 yards of flat ground for the lawn, the garden beds, what was once a tennis court (where Pandit Balak Ram's aunt had fluttered as a charming ball girl at Mr MacKay's tennis parties?), and the orchard. Grey tits perched on the veranda balustrade, and one nested above the front door.

Our bedroom was carpeted with the yellow *duri*. A geometrical patterned patchwork hung on one wall and an appliqué hanging of two symmetrical elephants with monkey riders standing under a mango tree hung opposite the window. Below it stood an old travelling chest with drawers – a fine example of tongue-in-groove joints and brass fittings – which must once have stored neat piles of Garden's (or Mr MacKay's) shirts and collars.

I was taken by surprise; I hadn't anticipated the satisfaction a house might give. I was thirty-three, and had never been tempted by the idea of home-making. Now, looking out on to the veranda as I drank my bed tea and listened to the whistling thrush and the cuckoo, or as I wandered from room to room, I purred with appreciation. I sowed lettuces and cucumbers and pansies and sunflowers; Kranti planted coriander and radishes. Sunk Ram and his brother, carpenters from Kangra, set up their bench on the downstairs veranda and worked (for £1 a day) from seven in the morning until seven at night. This time, wiser from experience, we bought the timber ourselves – well-matured deodar in ten-foot sleepers. First they had to plane the raw wood, shaving off fragrant coils, a laborious and time consuming job. They made cupboards and bookcases, a desk with drawers for me and a low stool with a back for my precious Tibetan carpet.

The plumbing issue had to be faced again: there was neither running water nor any sort of sanitation. In the meantime we had an earth closet dug in the orchard: it filled with water.

The newly arrived Indian doctor at the hospital, who prided himself on his village-health expertise, came and spent some time locating the ideal site and digging it out according to the latest theory. His EC too filled with water. The theory now was that water would be piped from the stream that ran past the kitchen to the bathrooms, which were to be constructed on the corners of the back veranda, behind the bedrooms. But where would we build the tank so that there would be pressure enough to fill it, and so that it would be higher than the bathrooms? Up on the hill, which would mean a very long stretch of pipe? In the branches of the oak tree above the kitchen? Panditji had agreed to pay for the sanitary fittings, but we were to pay for the pipe and the plumber and supervise the work. We decided that the tank would be an old petrol drum, and that it would rest on a platform in the oak tree. The *chaukidar* pointed out that in the summer months the stream would run low, even dry out. So, according to a revised plan, water would be piped up from the Public Works Department pipe that ran across the orchard. The pressure in it was said to be tremendous, more than strong enough to take the water up to the tank in the oak tree.

Then there was the question of whether we should have a cement cesspit or a dry masonry 'soak' pit. As it was to be built in the orchard below the house where both the ECs had already filled with water, it seemed to me likely that the 'soak' would be into rather than out of the pit. But after my failure at Sial no one wanted to listen to my views about lavatories.

During our early months at Duff Dunbar we seemed to receive very few letters. Could it be that Luder Chand was venting his father's rage by interfering with our mail? Mr Prakash the telegram signaller, temporarily promoted to acting postmaster, and his barren, squint-eyed wife leant over their balustrade above the post office every day, asking us to come and call. We had avoided visiting in case we should be asked any more embarrassing favours, but now *we* wanted to ask one. The day we called was Mrs Prakash's fast day; she fasted every Thursday to propitiate the gods so that she would conceive. She was confident of success, both because of the fasting and also because she and her husband had been to Triloknath in Lahul, where women hoping to conceive go to carry a rock three times round the shrine. (A year later my own pregnancy would confirm the power of the Triloknath rock in popular opinion; I knew I was pregnant before I went but hadn't told anyone.)

'By this time next year I know I will have a child,' she said. 'It is such a shame for a woman not to have a son. You must be feeling it too, *behinji*?' She ate nothing herself but gave us cardamom-flavoured tea, *pakoras* from Verma's and coconut macaroon biscuits from the Rama bakery below the post office. We discussed the Signaller's career predicament: he was acting postmaster only while the old Sikh was on leave. We promised to write to the authorities recommending that he should be officially promoted. Then we mentioned that we were worried about our mail. We didn't mention, of course, that we suspected Luder, but we wondered if it was possible that some of our letters were being mixed up with those sent to the hippies in the poste restante pile? I had found one or two for us among the tattered postcards from lonesome lovers – 'Pam where are you? When my path is not yours I cannot live' – and distraught parents – 'You don't have to come home Darling, just tell us you are alive, we'll send the money.' We left with Mr Prakash's assurance that we were to have our own mailbox in the post office.

Luder didn't show any sign of being upset by the new arrangement and was friendly enough when I met him on his way home, refreshed by an afternoon in the *chang bhatti*. But we had a new worry: Chamba's twins had begun to cry all night. Mrs Chamba was beside herself; she was convinced that Luder's mother had put a curse on them. Lamas were asked to the house to exorcize the spirits troubling the babies. For two days they read mantras, sitting on the kitchen veranda, with the long strips of prayer sheets piled on plastic jerry cans. Mrs Chamba kept them supplied with both salt and sweet tea. Chamba wandered about with his transistor blaring Radio Ceylon. It wasn't that he was sceptical about the benefit of the lamas' chants; it was just that he considered it was his role to pay and feed them, theirs to pray. It worked: to everyone's relief the twins slept soundly again. But they were not the only ones to be troubled at Duff

Dunbar. Boura Singh, who was to come to live with us the following year, refused to stay a night there by himself. Ghostly noises made his skin go taut and all night his ears vibrated with someone's cries. So maybe the ghosts were nothing to do with Luder's family at all. Maybe they were the ghosts of Garden Duff and Panditji's aunt.

Every morning Gungru, the old *chaukidar*, made his way up through the orchard with his flock of two sheep and a lamb and an old black cow. He lived in Dunghri, a village of Harijans (untouchables) below our orchard. Whatever the season he wore a tweed jacket over a tweed waistcoat and tweed jodhpurs. He and his wife, younger than him but so bent she was almost a cripple, owned only a tiny patch of land – a garden rather than a field. They had no children. Decades of being the *chaukidar* at Duff Dunbar may have given Gungru status but his real source of self-esteem was his role as the Goddess Hadimba's oracle's cap-catcher.

Like Gungru, the oracle himself was a Harijan; I assume that when the converting Hindus arrived from the plains they thought it expedient to leave some power in the hands of the indigenous population. Even though he was the oracle, he was prohibited as a Harijan from entering the temple, and sat out on the entrance platform. When he was about to enter a trance so that the goddess could speak through him, he would shake off his cap and let his uncut hair hang loose. This was the *chaukidar*'s moment: he had to be ready to catch the cap.

Soon after we arrived at Duff Dunbar it was Devi Hadimba's birthday *mela*. We invited people to a house-warming lunch party on the *mela* day, not realizing that it was a two- or three-day fair; some came one day, some the next. For weeks before the *mela* it hadn't rained. In Kullu it is the *nag* or snake gods who control the rain. Though Kulluis regard their gods with respect and awe they also treat them with rough familiarity. If one of their gods fails them the villagers may punish him (or her) by locking him up, or simply by not taking him on his customary outing to visit a brother or sister deity or to a fair. On this occasion the people had appealed to Senogi *nag* (in the village along the

86

hill below us) for rain. His oracle had retorted, 'You want rain? You want it to spoil the fun of your *mela*? All right, just wait and see.'

The *mela* ground was a few hundred yards to the right of the temple, along a path through the deodars. It was an almost flat glade of turf. The slope above had been terraced; stone walls supported three long lines of banks so that it looked like a stadium. Devi Hadimba, the hostess, was the first to arrive. You could just hear her band, its beat like a pulse gathering strength as it climbed up through the forest on the far side of the temple, followed by the troop of dancers. At the temple, where the *rath* of the *Devi* had spent the night, it was brought out to welcome them. Several of the small masks displayed in the middle of Hadimba's *rath* are three or four hundred years old. The more showy ones have been melted down and recast. The masks' silver earrings, enamelled head ornaments and pendants glowed against the rich colours of silks and brocades draped under the *chattri*, the umbrella. The sound of trumpets echoed out through the forest as musicians and dancers paid their respects. And as they processed along the path towards the *mela* ground, sun and shade played on the silver and copper trumpets and on the purple, orange and scarlet cloths. The dancers waved red handkerchiefs, while their hats swung to the laconic beat of the dance.

We sat up on the terraces among Kullui women in their *mela* finery – elaborate patterned *pattus*, red headscarves and gold rings in ears and noses. A crowd of young boys ran past behind the terraces, following something or someone. In seconds they had gathered momentum and numbers and dashed across the path of an arriving *deota* and its procession. I noticed the crowd pushing and bunching round someone among the trees below, and glimpsed a crazed-looking hippie behaving like a medieval jester – pulling faces and performing acts. The crowd giggled and jeered, but no one accosted him though he teased and jostled groups of women.

The *chaukidar*, proudly beaming on this important day, and sporting a white tweed jodhpur suit and his best hat with a flower tucked into its brim, stayed near Hadimba's platform. We gave him our five-rupee offering for the *Devi* and were given a red rose from the *rath* by the *pujari*.

It wasn't until the early evening that the oracles began to perform. In the semi-darkness, fitfully lit by torches of flaming resinous wood, the trees and dancers threw weird shadows. It began to rain. A full circle of dancers now enthusiastically bent their bodies to the rhythm, arms and legs swirling. The drummers thundered out the beat, while the *shehnai* player tried to keep control of the tune and the pace. Hadimba's *gaur* and another older oracle were dancing, twisting arms with each other. Their hair flowing, their torsos naked, they moved jerkily on thin, stick-like legs. Then, in turn, each of them pretended to slash himself across the armpits and over the back with a sickle, and lashed himself with a heavy chain. I spotted Jabbu among the crowd. 'Why are they doing this to themselves?' I asked. 'What's the significance?' But he wasn't helpful. 'They're just playing,' was his explanation. There was a smell of *chang* and damp, warm tweed. I was loath to leave but it was raining hard. The trumpet players used their trumpets as umbrellas.

As I set off up the hill out of the torchlight it was very dark. The capricious gods and their oracles were at one with the natural powers. Lightning seared the sky, thunder shook the ground, drums and trumpets echoed in the forest. Westerners like to think of Indians as fatalists who lack personal aspirations and who view their lot without anxiety or desire, but it isn't true. Men and women appeal to the gods with prayers, fasting, good deeds, offerings and sacrifices. They hope that in gratitude the gods will intervene against fate on their behalf and allow them good crops, propitious marriages, sons and prosperity. But if the gods' intervention fails, Indians are better than we are at accepting fate's injustice; maybe because they accept it as the result of their misdeeds in a previous life, or because they are aware that this one is transitory.

The next morning a man came running up from the village. 'Come, please, quickly, someone is dying. They say he is dead.' It turned out to be the hippie who had been performing at the *mela*. During the night he had broken into a friend's room and gone to sleep. He had been heard snoring but in the morning was found to be dead. Soon the whole village was standing about outside, and the police arrived. The head constable claimed that death was due to *chang* and *arak*, but in a leather pouch in the corpse's pocket they also found *charas*, opium and 'speed'. The friend whose room the dead man was in had identified the body and then disappeared. Neither his passport nor anyone else who knew him could be found, and no one knew how to inform his family.

Living alone in a couple of rooms in Sial village I had been a barely noticeable *hippini*. Now, the fact that we owned a jeep, lived in a house with a name set in its own grounds and were seen to be busy with regular groups of tourists began to change both our way of life and people's view of us. Kranti's presence made a difference too. His respectability – not just in his distinguished grey hair and handsome moustache but also in his manner of being used to authority and his 'abroad-educated' English accent – was immediately apparent. From the driver's seat of the jeep he would pass the time of day with the local dignitaries – the Director of the Mountaineering Institute, the Forest Officer and the Secretary of the Municipal Committee – and he would call on the District Commissioner when he visited Manali. Customers didn't send us registered envelopes full of rupee notes any more; we had a bank account. We were Manali's largest foreign-exchange earners and were given generous credit terms at the ration shops. Sometimes I found it reassuring to be so established, but at other times I hankered after the little world of my incognito life.

On my own I had been unconstrained. I reacted to events and made decisions as I saw fit; if they turned out to have been mistakes it was only I who suffered. But now when Kranti went away I was hesitant lest my decisions should turn out to be wrong.

Kranti is out with a party and today everything has gone wrong.
I took a couple of elderly entomologists down to stay at Nagar.
Dorze was squashed in the back of the jeep with their butterfly
nets and butterfly boxes. The jeep has been spluttering, and I had
to drive up the steep climb from the valley floor to Nagar in first
gear. To my relief we did reach the castle and parked in the
courtyard. Nagar has the grandest view in Kullu – it was the Raja's
seat and then the British administrator's – but our reservation was
only for an inner room, with a window and door opening on to
the courtyard. I demanded one with the view up-valley to the
peaks of Mount Geyphang. Back at the jeep, 'Fine,' I said, smiling
reassuringly. At that moment I saw smoke billowing from the
bonnet. I opened it far enough to see a dull flame coming from
the dynamo and to be engulfed by a terrible smell. I feigned calm
– 'Oh, it'll be all right, it does that sometimes, it'll cool off. Come
and see the view from the veranda.' The old couple's reaction was,
'It's not much like Chobham. I hope your man will help us with
the net on those steep slopes?' Dorze didn't look enthusiastic about
four days' butterfly hunting.

I freewheeled downhill, not daring to try the engine, and crawled
up the valley to Manali, thankful that our mechanic's workshop
was nearer than the bazaar. But it was locked up. Someone said
there was a mechanic at the bus station, but I know you shouldn't
trust any old mechanic; they'll pinch good parts or sell you dud
ones. The bus-station mechanic didn't inspire confidence. He hit
some things and kicked others, and then admitted he knew nothing
about electrics.

Walking down to Verma's for a restorative glass of tea I met
Amar Singh of the Chandrabhaga store. 'Your pipes and sanitary
fittings have arrived from Chandigarh. They are lying up at the
bus stop – you'd better get them collected.' The man in charge of
transport demanded 109 rupees for the carriage. Kranti had told
me it should be 40 or 50. Amar Singh advised that without a note
of the agreed sum I would have to pay, though it was double the
proper charge.

I hired the Chandrabhaga's truck, which couldn't make the last and muddiest steep stretch. The precious pipes and plumbing fittings couldn't be left in the forest all night, so I paid the *dudhwalli*'s children to carry them up to the house.

I forgot to give you the garden news. Fat maggots have eaten the bean and pea seeds underground and caterpillars have devoured everything above ground – like the lettuces and spinach. Every early morning Kranti goes to the garden to inspect his chillies and coriander. For a long time he refused to believe his coriander wasn't germinating. One evening Chamba stole some from a plot in the village below and at night, by torchlight, he and I pressed the feathery green sprigs into the earth. Next day Kranti came to the kitchen before breakfast, triumphantly announcing that the coriander was four inches tall. Chamba laughed so much that he spilt hot tea all over his lap.

Zanskar

As though the experience of home-making wasn't novel enough, I became pregnant during our first season at Duff Dunbar. That June, after twenty years, it was decreed that foreigners were to be allowed into Zanskar, and I was determined to go. Trekking over passes of 17,000 and 18,000 feet must be easier, I thought, when you were four months pregnant than it would be with a baby or toddler. Nevertheless I didn't tell my mother of the plan until I was safely home.

At last I was to see the country I had heard so much about; the place where, according to emigrants in Manali, there were broad rolling fields, chests full of produce, vats of *chang*, yaks the size and strength of elephants, ponies that could run up frozen rivers and ibex with metre-long horns on every crag.

After a five-year absence Chamba was going to visit his in-laws' home and his own. Mrs Chamba wanted to come too, to visit her home after her mother's recent death, but Chamba considered travelling with the twins would be too much trouble. His preparations were extensive. Not content just to give the tailor the cloth and the measurements for shirts and trousers of many different sizes, he spent days sitting in the shop to supervise the work. He bought a dozen packets of tea, lumps of sugar crystal, pounds of tobacco, matches, and lengths of the coiled bark used in brewing salt tea.

Our party was to consist of Kranti, my brother Johnny, Taj, Chamba, Lama Le, and Dorze and his wife, who was to spend the rest of the summer at home helping with the grass-cutting. A pony man, Gyal Chand, would join us at Darcha, the last village in Lahul. Our plan was to trek through Zanskar to Kargil on the Leh road, or to wherever we could find transport which would take us to Srinagar in Kashmir. We had to reach Srinagar within a month; we knew we were cutting it fine.

The expedition got off to a bad start. Our bus broke down a few miles out of Manali and there wasn't another that day. Kranti went back to fetch the jeep (and the mechanic who would drive it home). So we arrived at Darcha late in the evening and spent a dismal night in damp sleeping bags. The next morning it was discovered that Lama Le's haversack had been left behind with the medicine box in it. Rather than waste two days waiting while someone went back, we decided to make do with what the local dispenser could sell us: some aspirin, some grubby gauze bandages, a leaky bottle of gentian violet and a shelf-worn course of a sulphur drug.

I had a romantic idea of the Bara Lacha La – the first big pass on the trade route north to Leh and Yarkand, and the pass over which Kim's Tibetan Lama crossed on his way to India. It was a dull, relentless climb. The three of us took turns on the two riding ponies. The skinny white mare with a black mule foal was more popular than the fat black pony because the former had a European saddle, the latter a wooden frame inadequately padded with blankets. Our tedious climb was not rewarded with a grand view; the summit was bleak and eerie – half a mile of brackish flats and a shallow lake. I waited for Johnny by the lake; Kranti and I had been riding ahead of him. I didn't want to stare at his slow approach, but out of the corner of my eye I noticed his wandering gait. Even when he had sat and rested, his face had a purple tinge. His lips were bluish and he said he felt giddy; I was frightened. We went on down. It was too rough to ride, and the shale slipped underfoot. I hurried on, dragging both ponies, to tell Kranti and Taj, whom I found waiting at the foot of the descent, that we should camp immediately.

Taj had told the others to camp on a green knoll which we could see in the distance, but they had gone on miles ahead. Along the meanderings of the river we could see moving black dots only recognizable as people and pack ponies through binoculars. We fired shots into the air (we had a gun for pigeons and snow-cocks), but the noise dissolved into the vastness. Our men and ponies didn't even hesitate: on they went on the upper path. I knew Johnny's symptoms indicated a serious case of altitude sickness. We had none of the drugs we normally carried for such an eventuality, nor could we take him down to a lower altitude. To go back up to the pass and try to descend at this time of night, without tents or sleeping bags, would be crazy. We had lost a couple of thousand feet immediately after crossing the summit, but now the descent had flattened out.

Round a corner we found Dorze sitting on a rock. He seemed to expect us to be pleased that he had thought of waiting to help us across the river ahead. 'Why the hell didn't you camp where you were told?' I bellowed, but it seemed a waste of energy.

Now Kranti led the pony while Taj and Dorze supported Johnny in the saddle, one on each side to keep him semi-upright; he was barely conscious. I went on ahead, riding the white pony. It was nearly dark, and soon the track became too rough and rocky to ride on. At last I saw the outline of the pony man's tent, and then out of the darkness Chamba appeared on the path. My rage and anxiety burst out of me: 'Why didn't you camp back there where you were told to? Why didn't you wait? Is this the first time you've been out in the hills with a party, idiot – don't you know you wait for those behind? When my brother is dead it'll be your fault. Get back there and help them.' He said nothing, but shuffled off into the night.

We helped Johnny off the pony and carried him into his tent.

He murmured, his speech very slurred, that he was sorry to cause so much trouble, but that he did want to go back for his tam-o'-shanter hat which he had left on the summit.

I lay rigid all night: I was my brother's murderer. I knew enough to know that he was dangerously ill. Altitude sickness causes fluid retention, frequently on the lungs – pulmonary oedema – and sometimes on the brain; it was clear to me that Johnny was suffering from the latter. The risk from altitude sickness is immediate; you can die within hours or, if you survive a severe bout of cerebral oedema, you can be left brain-damaged. We had taken him up too high too fast. I should have known better and should never have set off without the drugs; if we had waited at Darcha while they were fetched he would have had time to acclimatize. In circumstances like this, even while administering the necessary diuretic drugs and even if it involves travelling at night, you are advised to take the patient down as far and as fast as possible. But from here there was no way down: it was back up to the pass we had just crossed or on up towards other passes. Several times during the night I crept round his tent to see if I could hear him breathe.

In the morning I heard him say 'thanks' for his bed tea. He was alive and conscious, he had lasted the night, there was hope.

There was nothing we could do but stay put and rest. There was no point in sending for stretcher-carriers or medicine, for by the time they arrived he would either be dead or acclimatized. We stayed for three days, and slowly he did get better. He was cheered by the arrival of his tam-o'-shanter; a Gaddi shepherd had spotted it lying by the lake and brought it all the way down to our camp. 'I know when you're in the hills you can lose something a thousand rupees wouldn't replace. It happened to me. I lost my dog last year – the whole year I didn't see him – then I found him just this month, at Darcha when I was on my way up from Kangra.'

We had our first contact with Zanskaris when we camped by the river below the Phitse La. On the far side of the river there was an encampment of yak graziers which turned out to include Mrs Chamba's brother. He must have heard of our approach, for as soon as our yellow tents began to go up he forded the river on a spirited piebald pony. Chamba and I rode back with him in the late afternoon. At our arrival men, women and children stared and pointed and stuck out their tongues in amazement. The women wore black fur head-dresses with ear-flaps, the backs and crests of which were encrusted with turquoise. Their maroon tweed gowns were girdled at the waist, and over the gowns some wore cloaks made of inside-out goatskins, while others wore colourful tweed cloaks decorated with tie-dye designs. The help-lessly giggling children also wore tweed gowns, and conical yellow felt hats with triangular brims. Both men and women wore amulets, as well as amber and coral necklaces. Few of the men had any beard and their moustaches were sparse, though their hair was luxuriant and worn long.

The shieling was substantial: two 'streets' with half a dozen tents down each side. The base of each dwelling was permanent, made of dry-stone walls up to about waist level. Over this was stretched a felted yak-hair tent, so dark a brown that from the distance it looked black. As we walked up the street towards Chamba's brother-in-law's tent, yaks were being herded down it; they had to be corralled at night because of marauding packs of wolves. Later we would see a stone-lined wolf pit. A kid is tied as bait in the middle so that wolves jump in and cannot get out; then they are stoned to death, or left to die.

We were given salt tea with yak butter – at this altitude you begin to appreciate that the salt and fat are good for you – and also bowlfuls of curd and *tsampa*. The cooking pot rested on a three-legged iron stand over the open fire at the far end of the tent. The entrance was the only source of light, and it was almost obliterated by the crowd of onlookers. They nudged each other into peals of laughter.

The climb to the Phitse La (18,000 feet), initially relieved by swathes of a deep-purple delphinium, was bleak and breathtak-ingly steep. Johnny had acclimatized and suffered no more than the rest of us, including the ponies, who gasped their way up. Gyal Chand, the pony man, on the other hand, strode uphill as though striding into the camera in a Western. With high cheekbones and a swarthy complexion, his belted cloak worn off one shoulder, he had the presence of a Red Indian bandit-hero.

This time the summit, decorated with prayer flags battered by the icy wind, rewarded us with a view which, had we had the breath to speak, would have silenced us. I looked out over hundreds of miles. The far-distant ranges were dark blue and deep purple; in the foreground rocks and hillsides were brown and red against white peaks that cut angles out of the azure sky. I could see so far that the horizon tipped away from where I stood.

The next day Mrs Dorze was up early. Dressed in her finery – a brocade Lahuli dress trimmed with gold, so new that the tailor's pressed pleats were still in place – she was away before we had breakfasted, tripping off down the sheer shale in pink plastic slippers. We didn't see her again until we arrived at Testha village.

I won't forget my first view of Zanskar. I was riding along a narrow path, absent-mindedly aware that the others had stopped and were sitting on a rocky rise. Suddenly I saw why: there, stretched below, was Zanskar. The river, thousands of feet beneath us, crashed through a red and ochre gorge; ahead the valley widened and the river took a more leisurely course. Sometimes beside it, sometimes curving round and over great humps of moraine, was the track, marked by a line of white *chortens*. In the distance, where the valley opened out, there were two villages of white houses with flat roofs. The vivid-green fan shape on the moraines – cultivated barley, pea and hay fields – contrasted with the yellows and browns of the unirrigated desert. Irrigation channels ran for miles, cutting across the cliffs and the mountainside. I felt like an explorer. This was how you should come upon a new country – reaching it by your own physical effort and viewing it spread below you like a map.

The light had a peculiar quality: it was harsh and dazzling, reflected off rocks and dry earth where there was no greenery to soften it. The glare ought to have washed out the detail, as it can in photographs, yet there was meticulous definition, even far away. It upset our sense of distance; we were unable to estimate how long it would take to reach a landmark ahead. And it was hard too on our eyes – they ached and longed for shade. It was with relief that, having descended by a rocky side-valley to join the main valley, we found a small willow grove and lunched in the soothing shade by its irrigation channel.

Chamba was to leave us for a day or two. His brother-in-law reappeared at the willow grove, this time with a pony who jingled a high-pitched, resonant bell. We didn't understand how he had reached us from the yak camp; we hadn't seen him on the way. 'See you the day after tomorrow,' Chamba called out as he waved goodbye and headed up the valley, riding pillion on the little chestnut stallion.

Testha village was our first goal: we planned a day's rest for ourselves and the ponies at Mrs Dorze's home there. As we entered the village we were greeted by Mrs Dorze, now a welcoming hostess, and her father – who was not in the same league of sartorial elegance. His gown was frayed and patched, and he wore a fur hat that had done duty for many seasons. Out there by the stream they quenched our thirst with a kettleful of *chang*, its spout anointed with a lavish blob of orange *ghi*. Then we were given bowls of curd with *tsampa* and salt.

In the evening we were invited to their home. Mrs Dorze was apologetic, and I could understand why: the house didn't live up to the picture of plenty that had been described to me. We sat on rugs and sacks rather than fine carpets, in a low-ceilinged, unplastered room darkened by an aeon of smoke. Unless you bent down almost to floor level, you couldn't open your eyes because of the smoke from the chimneyless, flameless yak-dung fire. Mrs Dorze's mother's arms and scalp were badly scarred by a branding iron. 'She had very bad fever with headaches three or four years ago. We thought she would die. But the lama is clever with the hot iron and he gave her good medicine. She was very weak, and even now in the summer when she has been out gathering grass all day, she feels giddy at night.'

This was Zanskar for real, not through the rose-tinted spectacles of an emigrant's memory. Here in one smoke-filled room the members of the family huddle through the long winters, passing on to each other virulent TB and epidemics of devastating measles for which the lamas' branding irons are a poor remedy. On our way into the house I had noticed a garden patch, hardly bigger than a window box, where potatoes grew. The growing season is so short that even potatoes barely reach fruition – and they survive only in the shelter of a house, not as a crop in the fields. No fruit is grown, and the little pea, munched as a raw snack by children when green, black when dried, is the only vegetable. The diet isn't adequate. It consists of parched barley, dried peas, a little wheat, even less rice and *dal*, which have to be imported, dried *lassi*, *ghi*, and some milk – very little during the seven or eight months of winter when the cattle are on meagre rations.

The next evening we were invited to Mrs Dorze's sister's house. It is an unfair world where one sister is married to the *Thakur* of Testha while the other has to settle for a kidnap marriage to the landless Dorze. The *Thakur*'s mansion was set apart from the village in its own willow grove. At our approach there was a deep and angry barking. By the weak light of our torch we could make out with relief that the beast was tethered by a chain. We stood where we were, not entering the courtyard, and shouted to announce our arrival. A girl came out and held the mastiff by its iron collar to let us pass. We stepped down into the house and made our way through semi-basement cellars – store rooms full of goat and yak hair, sacks of grain and massive iron vessels; the *Thakur* obviously entertained on a large scale. Then we passed through an antechamber with a dipped drain in the middle of its mud-plastered floor: the goat-butchering area. The *Thakur*'s family wouldn't butcher any animal themselves; they hire *lohars*[2] to do it for them.

Upstairs we were shown into the reception room, which was set out with fine carpets and *chogtses* (carved stools) for cups and glasses. There were two glass-paned windows, wooden shelves, and alcoves set into the plastered whitewashed walls.

Our salt tea was served in porcelain cups with lids and there was pea *tsampa* to be moistened into a lump with the tea and then dipped into a bowlful of hot *ghi*. It was all washed down with beaker after beaker of rum, bought from the military in Kargil.

As we left I asked to see the prayer room. Oil lamps burned and the juniper incense had been lit, but it was unkempt; the rolled-up *thankas* were covered in cobwebs and the images were dusty.

The next morning we all suffered from too much rum, though we didn't feel as bad as Chamba looked when he rode in behind his brother as we were dismantling camp. The chestnut stallion's bell was muted to a dull tinkle; any faster pace would have unseated the wobbly pillion-rider. In his red-and-white shirt, his hands clutched behind his back, Chamba looked like a despairing prisoner. He topped himself up with a few cupfuls of *chang* before we moved off down-valley through fields of geraniums, delphiniums and beautiful yellow columbines.

Our next halt was unexpected. We came upon an old woman crouched on the path in the middle of nowhere, clutching a once-grand, well-used kettle. She was Dorze's mother. We dismounted and sat in a circle in the sun on the gritty path while she ceremoniously poured the *chang*. Dorze unpacked from his haversack an uncured goatskin which he had brought from Manali as a cloak for her, and gave her packets of tea and lumps of crystal sugar. It was seven years since they had met. She looked woebegone and poor. A tall, thin and equally unkempt man stood some distance off; he didn't join our circle. Was he the man she had run off with, abandoning Dorze to servanthood in Lahul? As we left, son and mother embraced; she was crying.

By the time we reached Padam, Zanskar's capital, we were short of time. To my disappointment it looked as though we would have to forgo the visit to Chamba's village if we were to reach Srinagar as planned. From Padam we could see the Karsha *gompa* standing up against the cliffs across the great plain; but it was further than it looked, for the only bridge across the Zanskar river was some way downstream.

All night I tossed and turned. By dawn I had a proposal: if we moved off immediately and reached the bridge across the Zanskar river before midday, could we ride (using one of the pack ponies as the third riding pony) to Karsha and return to the bridge by nightfall? If that were possible, then the next morning we could carry on west towards the final pass without having lost a day. The answer seemed to be yes: it was agreed.

Chamba had assured us that he would be able to borrow a pony at the village just beyond the bridge so that he could keep up with Johnny, Kranti and me on our ponies. The others were to stay at camp by the bridge. But he returned from the village on foot – 'Useless pony; its leg was all fat.' We passed some fine examples of the famed Zanskari ponies, small and sturdy, trained to 'pace' and to cover a long distance in good time with the least discomfort to the rider. I was impressed too by their saddles, which had high brass pommels ('That's nothing, you should see the solid silver ones,' commented Chamba) and were covered with fine carpets. I hankered after their ornate stirrups and high-pitched brass bells whose ring could be heard a mile away. We made slow progress, not so much because Chamba was walking as because he greeted everyone along the way. It wasn't just a casual '*Jhule, jhule*'; the passers-by would dismount and settle down beside him for a chat and a *biri*.

On one narrow rocky stretch of the path, Chamba had a confrontation with an Indian Memsahib – not a Zanskari grandee but a pukka Memsahib from the plains, as foreign to the area as we were. Accompanied by two mounted men, she herself was well mounted and nicely turned out, her travelling costume topped by a red-and-white polka-dot hat. Chamba barred her way. For the past hour or so he had been wearing a wreath made of pea plants complete with pods; it acted both as protection from the sun and as a source of juicy snacks. The Memsahib was not amused by the faun-like creature standing across her path. 'You go this side,' she said haughtily, shooing him out of her pony's way. 'No, no,' Chamba retorted from under the trailing peas, '*you* go that way.'

The valley widened. A curving line of trim, whitewashed *chortens* marked the path from one village to the next; the *mane* walls were half a mile long and the prayer stones were carved by craftsmen.[3] I had to admit that the barley and pea fields, if not quite on the scale described by Chamba, were by far the broadest we had seen since Kullu.

At last we approached Karsha. It was built against the craggy hillside like a massive white fortress, with deep-set, black-edged windows. From a distance, village, *gompa* and mountainside were fused together.

Word had travelled ahead: Chamba's old mother had struggled some way from the village down the path between the high dry-stone walls to greet him. He bent down to touch her feet, she put her arthritic hands on his back and they embraced, briefly. She was too overcome with emotion to show pleasure: her cataract-clouded eyes filled with tears. At the house itself, more than a dozen members of the family had gathered out in the courtyard. As we dismounted we were offered the ceremonial welcome of *chang* from a kettle-jug lipped with *ghi*, and we drank from silver cups. It was most welcome, for we were hot and thirsty.

A lop-sided youth was ordered to take our ponies away to graze and we were led up steep stairs; coming in out of the dazzling sun we found the inside of the house as dark as night. We passed through a large kitchen and up a narrow ladder into a small, plastered room, decorated with calendars and laid out with carpets and *chogtses*. The deep-set, unglazed windows framed a view out across fields to the Zanskar river and over the plains of Padam.

There were three brothers present. It seemed they shared a wife, as is the custom in Zanskar.[4] One of the brothers had been in the army and spoke some Hindi. With some panache Chamba played host to us and simultaneously to his family; though he offered nothing he had provided himself. There was *chang*, salt tea and hot yak milk from the household, and tinned meat and biscuits which came unmistakably from our stores.

The worse for wear from copious *chang*, we staggered up to the *gompa*. It was on a grand scale, tier upon tier, like an imaginative illustration in a children's book. It was a medieval world. Lamas of all ages gossiped and giggled, lounging on the steps in front of heavy wooden doors with iron studs. In the evening sun the angles of the roof and squared lintels cast black-and-white shadows in geometrical patterns. Mastiffs still sheltering from the day's heat stretched out in shady corners squalid with *gompa* debris – old bones, pieces of cloth, and the odd tattered boot. Despite the midsummer warmth the old lamas' maroon cloaks were of heavy tweed. The cheeky, shaven-headed boys wore their cotton cloaks slipped off one shoulder and their yellow hats at a rakish angle. A bearskin hung above the door into the main shrine; its massive head loured from above as though it might at any minute bare its fangs.

Lamas wearing red and yellow robes and brocade hats sat in lines to chant the evening prayers. Serving lamas, two to each heavy copper kettle, moved up and down pouring salt tea. Ibex heads looked down from the ceiling, and there was a banner depicting running deer, yaks and a leopard, partially hidden by dust and cobwebs. Murals illustrating scenes from the life of the Buddha glowed with rich pigments, and multicoloured *tsampa* and *ghi* offerings were displayed like exotic wedding cakes. The last rays of the sun glinted off the gold brocade in the altar cloth and off the rows of *thankas*. Images of the Buddha, three times the size of man, stood above the altar, dominating the theatrical scene. Trumpets blasted, cymbals clashed and conch shells were blown through cupped hands; the sound escaped through the closed windows and curtained doorways into the courtyards and out across the valley. It isn't hard to appreciate the impact of the *gompa* on villagers accustomed to colourless mud and stone dwellings which are dwarfed by the silent landscape.

At the bottom of the *gompa* hill the rosy nephew Nawang stood waiting for us with a pint-sized tumbler of neat rum rimmed with *ghi*. This was 'one for the road': they insisted that we drain the tumbler through its *ghi* rim and wanted us to go back to the house for more, but sadly we had to go. We summoned the deformed pony boy, Nawang's brother (I thought it unlikely he would be sharing Nawang's blushing new wife).

Chamba seemed to be coming back with us, and had acquired a brown pony. Nawang would come too so that he could bring it home (he longed to come all the way to Manali but Chamba wouldn't hear of it). After five years' absence it had been a brief visit, but Chamba didn't seem to want to linger. The emigrants in Manali certainly consider themselves Zanskaris and identify themselves with their home villages; and the women go home in the summer months to help with the grass-cutting. But the men spend no more than a day or two at a time in Zanskar, stopping off to deliver gifts when they are escorting a wife or sister or passing nearby. Perhaps it is that once they have left home and established themselves in Manali they are economically independent: if they stayed in the parental home for any length of time it would upset the status quo and they would be expected to contribute to the household.

As we rode off, the sun was sliding behind the snow peaks on the other side of the plain, beyond Padam. They became black silhouettes against a green and pale-purple sky. Soon it was so dark that I couldn't see the pony in front, only hear its hoofs on the stony path. It would be some time before the waning moon rose and lit our track; we had to trust the ponies' instincts. We knew that somewhere near the last village we were to turn off the path. It seemed a long way. There were no lights in the villages, but we could feel the proximity of buildings and hear the dogs. Oil-wick lamps lit indoors for the short hour between darkness and sleep gave a glimmer of light within the rooms but didn't throw a beam through windows or doors. No one was about except the dogs. At last Chamba raised a man who told us where to plunge off the track, down a steep bank and across flooded streams. Then we saw the familiar light of our petromex lamp shining through the white canvas of Gyal Chand's tent. Hot pigeon curry and rice were waiting for us.

My first visit to Zanskar, and my last for several years, was nearly over. On the final pass, the Pensi La, there were road works; one day, buses and trucks would be grinding their way to Padam.

Out in the hills, so often too cold or too hot, subsisting on a monotonous diet and going for weeks without a bath, you dwell on the prospect of pleasures ahead – soaking in hot water; clean sheets; glasses of chilled beer; salads, toast and butter. But after the initial few hours – cleanliness is reliably a blissful indulgence – arriving at the end of a trek is always a disappointment. This time, once we had reached Kashmir, it wasn't just that I wanted to spurn indulgence and pined for the lean, harsh life in the mountains: I was also disturbed at the thought of the impending influx of visitors to Zanskar. We had met only two foreigners – two red-thighed Germans – or three counting the Memsahib from Poona. But Zanskar had only been open for two months; it could only be a few years before it would be a popular destination for adventurous tourists.

Being in Kashmir made the issue all the more poignant. Kashmir has been a tourist haven since the Moghul emperors broadcast its pleasures in the early seventeenth century. The average Kashmiri's hysterical fawning and whining greed is an indictment of tourism's effect on the local population. In Srinagar I had once attended a seminar on travel addressed by the President of the Institute of Motivational Research in New York. He maintained that the tourist of the future would be less often a holiday-maker, more often a traveller on a voyage of self-discovery, searching for anthropological experience, cultural dialogue and psychological adventure. So perhaps Zanskar's visitors would be less obnoxious than the ill-mannered French who were haggling over the price of papier-mâché on the houseboat next to ours. But I wasn't concerned to evaluate the benefits of travel to remote places for the youth of Munich or San Francisco; my disquiet was on behalf of the Zanskaris themselves.

What would be the effect of tourists with big cameras and scanty clothes, even if they were on a voyage of self-discovery and psychological adventure, on the traditional hospitality, on the relatively cashless economy, on the limited resources of food, fodder and fuel? My apprehension was fuelled by an awareness of my own acquisitiveness and lack of scruples. At Testha I had wanted a patterned cloak (the dye was set with yak's urine, they told me). When I asked a woman where I could get one she said, 'Oh I don't know, we just make them for ourselves.' I also wanted the little brass, handleless spoons everyone wore attached by a ring to the waistband of their gowns. Though I found it embarrassing to be persuading someone to hand over a personal possession in exchange for cash, I bought several of the spoons, untied by the owners from their belts, and I also bought a deep blue and orange cloak off a woman's back. The women wore magnificent coral and silver bead necklaces. I did resist the temptation to make an offer for one by imagining a visitor to my house asking if she could buy my mother's pearls. In fact it would have been worse than that, for pearls are replaceable in exchange for their cash value, while these necklaces were irreplaceable heirlooms.

My self-righteousness was short-lived. I bought a triple-row Zanskari necklace in a shop in Manali, defending myself with the dubious argument that, as it had found its way to the shop, I wasn't responsible for enticing Zanskari women to part with their inherited finery. A few years later, in Camden Market and in the boutiques round Boulevard St Michel in Paris, elegantly displayed Zanskari necklaces were being sold for hundreds of pounds.

For the moment I decided we wouldn't organize treks to Zanskar. I knew that other trek organizers wouldn't be deterred by my decision, but I was hesitant about being responsible for encouraging tourism there. Doubtless I was motivated partly by selfish interests: I didn't want Zanskar's 'unspoiltness' spoilt. Michel Peissel wrote an account of his visit a year later called *Zanskar: The Hidden Kingdom*, which expressed a similarly selfish view. And then he followed up the book with a multi-part television documentary illustrating a Zanskar with no crime, no worries, and no diseases not adequately dealt with by local shamanism. More effectively than any tour operator's promotional effort this resulted in an explosion of foreign visitors.

Within a few years thousands of tourists were visiting Zanskar every summer: large organized groups, and individual travellers who expected to live off the villagers in exchange for boxes of matches, packets of candles and tea.

It wasn't long before I had to come down off my high horse.

Everyone complained about my obstinacy: its only effect had been our company's loss of revenue. For seven or eight years we did organize treks through Zanskar. Then we had to stop because it became unpleasant. There were too many trekking parties fighting for limited camp sites, there were arguments with villagers over prices for grazing ponies, there were children and lamas begging (the lamas surreptitiously sold artefacts from the *gompas* as well), and there was too much litter. Now we made the decision because we considered the treks unpleasant for our clients, not out of concern for the Zanskaris.

Had it been in my power to choose whether or not Zanskar should be opened to tourists in 1975 I don't know what decision I would have made. With the benefit of hindsight I find it no easier. For Zanskaris the arrival of the modern world, with its radios, watches and ready-made clothes, is exciting, and brings other obvious advantages such as the prospect of antibiotics and immunizations, educational opportunities, and trucks to transport kerosene for fuel (and even solar panels) as well as foodstuffs – rice, pulses, cooking oil – to vary the diet, improving nutrition and resistance to disease.

Bhutan has taken the other option, restricting tourism and dictating that its people should adhere to the traditional way of life and even dress. It is easy for us, who know the dangers, to point out the irreversible consequences of materialism and modern life; but not one of those who have emigrated from Zanskar to settle in Manali wants to return. How many of us who might theorize about the rugged, idealistic Buddhist world of the high Himalayas would really want to spend eight-month winters huddled round a smoky yak-dung fire?

Motherhood

Rahul was born in February in Dunoon Cottage Hospital on the Firth of Clyde. Through a pethidine haze I heard the doctor shouting at me, 'Hurry up!' The baby's pulse, broadcast through a loudspeaker, was weakening. It turned out that a knot in the umbilical cord had tightened and threatened his life. I assumed that it had tangled as he twisted and bumped inside me during that bareback night ride from Chamba's village.

He was two and a half months old when he made his first spring migration to the Himalayas. When I carried him up through the orchard to Duff Dunbar the snowline was still low on the hills, the daffodils were just going over and the apple blossom was like pink and white lace over the trees. I wondered if the smell of the deodars and the evening sounds of children shouting at homecoming cattle and beating a rhythm on their pails as they made their way to the spring would become a part of Rahul's subconscious as they were of mine. We lit a fire in Garden Duff Dunbar's elegant fireplace. I sat nursing Rahul on the low chair the carpenters had made, watching the sparking pine logs, and thought it unlikely he noticed any difference between this and Scotland.

Chamba's wife had decided not to live at Duff Dunbar any more. As soon as the passes were open her brother was coming with ponies, and she was determined to take the twins and spend the summer in Zanskar. Dorze's wife didn't want to stay without her. A day or two after we arrived, Panditji, the plumber from Garhwal, came with a lanky man, taller than most Kulluis, wearing a black Nehru cap and a long black jacket. Panditji had assumed we needed a house-servant. 'This is a very good man, he comes from my village. He knows all about cooking. Oh no, he won't need much pay; he is a village man from Garhwal.'

We explained that it was a family we were looking for; a single man would be unsuitable. I looked forward to having a woman around who would wash nappies as well as rock the baby and give me the benefit of her experience. But we did need someone immediately to cook and clean and, though at last we enjoyed the luxury of running water and flushing lavatories, we also needed someone to carry drinking water from the spring. The man had a nice, open smile – we made a quick decision. 'All right, he can stay for a month, until we can find a family. Then maybe if he wants to stay on in Manali he can go out on treks.'

Boura Singh hadn't been with us for more than a day or two when he found me sitting on the bedroom floor, head in my hands, while Rahul howled inconsolably. He picked the baby out of my lap, cradled him firmly in his long arms, and instantly soothed him into silence. 'You see, I know everything about children; I have four and there are so many in our house.'

Before the month was over he had established himself as the mainstay of our household. Now, more than thirteen years later, his welcome and his presence in the house constitute home to Rahul and Tara, our daughter. Over the years he has been steadfastly loyal to our household and remained on uncontentious terms with all the men. It was he who introduced the rule that only one issue of tea would be brewed for them each morning; 'Otherwise they finish all the milk and sugar in three days'.

Boura Singh's most characteristic trait is the way he mercilessly cuts everyone down to size, from politicians like Mrs Gandhi and Charan Singh to old Gungru the *chaukidar* and any of our guests whose behaviour or dress is at variance with his ideas of propriety. His intimate knowledge of Hindu legend, practice and morality, and his lively interest in political affairs, give him a sense of worldliness; he considers the other men a little parochial but he doesn't rub it in.

Chamoli Garhwal is in the hills of Uttar Pradesh, a three-day bus journey from Manali. According to Boura Singh the jungles are full of bears and leopards, protective gods and goddesses vie with malevolent spirits in the villages, and the fields yield bountiful harvests of every crop. I never have understood why he came searching for work in Manali, for he was hardly a landless labourer; he regaled us with descriptions of the size of his family house and the quintals of rice and maize harvested from its fields. His departure may have been due to disagreements with his brother, recently returned from a military career. Ultimately the lack of harmony between the two of them led to the division of the family property, although they continued to share responsibility for their old father. 'My brother treats him so badly. When I go home Pitaji is in tears because of him and that woman, my sister-in-law.'

Whatever his domestic traumas may have been, Boura Singh continued to abandon his own family for six months every year. A daughter and then a son were born while he was in Manali; he would casually mention that a week or so earlier he had had a letter telling him that the rice was planted out and also that a baby had been born. He became fond of us and devoted to our children, and grew to depend on what became a handsome and well-deserved salary.

Just before Boura Singh came to look after us I had sent a telegram to my mother – 'Arrived safely Rahul absolutely angelic' – and followed it up with a long letter. Her anxiety, recently assuaged because I had survived so many seasons in Manali, had resurged on behalf of her grandson.

Duff Dunbar, 28 April 1976

I hope to be able to write this before R wakes. He is on the veranda under a net to keep off the flies. It's impossible to keep Chamba and Dorze from picking him up and cuddling him as soon as he is awake; in fact given the slightest excuse Chamba will pick him up while he's still asleep – 'The sun was getting on him,' or 'He was moving his head about; he wasn't comfortable.' And Sunk Ram the carpenter is the worst: he undermines any effort I make towards establishing discipline and pattern to the day. If he hears so much as a whimper he'll rush to Rahul, pick him up and admonish me, 'In our house no child is allowed to cry; my father says it brings shame on the house. Small children should be cared for.' He is making a room for Rahul, behind our room, on the enclosed veranda that has the bathrooms at either end, and putting in a window which will look out towards the kitchen. He's also making a cot, modelled on one in a Mothercare catalogue, and a swing bed in the Kangra style, with decorative knobs and slats. It will hang by chains on the veranda and there will be a cord so that you can sit and swing the baby as you read.

Now that I was a mother I was suffused with blind love for such a vulnerable creature, and in my turn I became familiar with overwhelming anxiety. Rahul once became ill with a gastric infection while Kranti was away. I had visions of rushing him to

Chandigarh in a taxi with a temperature of 115°F. What if I had left the decision to go until it was too late? If it hadn't been for Boura Singh's good cheer – 'He doesn't behave like a very ill baby; when they are ill they cry or go quiet and limp. Look at Rahul Baba: he's smiling all the time' – I wouldn't have survived.

I felt unable to deal with anything – the rats, the plumbing, the jeep . . . During the next three or four years the feeling of being out of my depth kept recurring. There were endless days, merging into each other, that had to be survived. For the first time in years I slept in the same bed for months at a time. My world had become confined.

Our clients were growing in number. Kranti couldn't be on every trip and I was tied to Manali, so we needed men who could shoulder responsibility. Taj had become less close to the household since we moved to Duff Dunbar; perhaps the atmosphere was too domestic for his roving spirit, or perhaps he felt too much had come between him and me. Soon after the Zanskar trip he moved off, and another young man joined us.

Karma was about twenty-five. He had a striking vertical dent in his forehead, from above the hairline right down through the eyebrow, where he had been kicked by a pony at the age of four. The wound must have been close to his brain but certainly hadn't damaged it in any way. He spoke some English, could read and write Hindi fluently, and had a good command of figures and accounts. He came from a Khampa trading family which for a generation had been based in Manali, where he had attended school. His background had given him a good business sense, and from an early age he had been accustomed to responsibility. He was always a little nervous, never relaxed; he didn't have Chamba's immediate warmth, nor Dorze's puckishness. Because he was reserved, more sophisticated and less familiar than the others, it was years before I knew him well. Now I know him to be one of those rare people who have the wisdom to digest what they see and to learn from it; and when I haven't seen him for a while I miss that wisdom. He became the linchpin of our organization.

Because I was spending most of my time in Manali I began to

come into closer contact with the wives and families of the men. Karma's wife was pretty and daintily built, and on formal occasions she wore expensively tailored *salwar chemises*, ornately patterned shawls and make-up. This, combined with her sophisticated manners and mannerisms, made her appear a little pretentious, but underneath it all lay a generous nature. Her children in turn were just a bit smarter than the others. There was a small-boned boy of eleven, already doing well at high school, a shy girl who had just started school, and Gikki, a girl a month or two older than Rahul. A fourth child had been sent to be looked after by her grandparents in Kinnaur. I didn't know of her existence until the day Karma received a telegram saying she was very ill. Close to tears, he told us that this almost certainly meant she had died, and he asked for leave to go to Kinnaur. He was right: like so many other children in this part of the world, she had died of measles.

A few years before Karma joined us he and his wife had been given the smaller of the two family houses by the *gompa*; his parents and the rest of the family continued to live together in the larger house nearby. At that time none of our other men owned land or houses in Kullu (although several acquired them later).

Karma's household was considerably better off than Chamba's, but the key difference between the two men lay not in the niceties of social status and family security; it was much more a question of self-esteem. Illiteracy, and more importantly innumeracy, didn't in themselves debar any one of the men from a position of authority, but they did lead to a dependence on someone else to write out the accounts, even to look after the cash – perhaps several thousand rupees – and that was a blow to pride.

None of those who suffered in this way understood or acknowledged the reason for it. Neither Chamba nor his wife could read or write. Chamba could just manage a scrawled signature in Urdu script rather than a thumbprint. The previous year, when the family was living at Duff Dunbar, we had persuaded him and his wife to allow Tsering Dolma, then about eight, to attend the little school under the deodars past the Senogi temple. We thought it would be useful to the family if she could read and write. We bought the wooden slate, bamboo pens and ink crystals, and Kranti helped her with the first letters of the Hindi alphabet. But she didn't attend school for more than four or five days all summer; she was needed at home to help look after the twins and wash pans and clothes. Now that they had moved back down to the *gompa* area, all pretence of her attending school had been abandoned.

As the business began to grow and we employed more men, a form of hierarchy began to emerge. It wasn't that we encouraged it; it simply happened, and to some extent it was associated with numeracy and being able to speak English. More clients and more groups out in the hills called for greater responsibility from our staff; some gained confidence and went from strength to strength, while others became stagnant and disgruntled.

Dorze was still under thirty. Bright and quick, he could have learnt the basics of reading and writing in a few weeks. We often suggested that we might teach him but he never wanted to try. Nor did his wife. When she first came to Manali she hardly even spoke any Hindi, but she mastered it quickly, learning purely by ear. In those early years she had been cheerful and pretty, a willing friend and helper to Chamba's family, but as time passed she became less pretty and much less cheerful. Maybe she was demoralized by the superior status of her sister – married to the *Thakur* of Testha – or by not having any children. Her shame about being childless was made worse by rumours that Dorze had fathered a child when he was a servant in Lahul. But I wondered if her lack of cheer might not also have something to do with Dorze's unfulfilled early promise. Despite his sharp eye and ingenuity on the mountainside, he increasingly lacked zest and initiative, and as he lost confidence he began to lose his enthusiasm for boyish practical jokes. Chamba likewise began to be less spontaneous, and when he and I found ourselves together our old jovial camaraderie tended to be spoilt by his readiness to ingratiate himself by telling tales on his colleagues. Their shared lack of self-esteem didn't bring Chamba and Dorze together;

sometimes they were not on speaking terms, and after one particularly bitter drunken fight they didn't talk to each other for years.

Lama Le was useful to the others as a book-keeper; he wrote immaculate accounts. He didn't threaten anyone's pride because he had no initiative and no organizational flair – he would never be in a position of authority. He lived a monastic life, in a room that was cheap because it was so far uphill from the bazaar. His winters were spent in *gompas* on the plains at Bodh Gaya or in Mysore, in free accommodation. He spent almost nothing on his food, and his frugal diet, or perhaps the short commons during his youth in the *gompa* in Ladakh, began to take their toll. He no longer treated us to demonstrations of his gymnastic prowess, but became pale and weak and preoccupied with his health. He often had himself X-rayed and, rather than buying eggs, meat and milk, as advised by me and the doctors, bought expensive courses of *takhut ki suis* (injections for health). Available from irresponsible doctors or chemists in the bazaar, these might be vials of harmless water or, more dangerously, steroids or hormones. Lama Le had always been gentle and reliable but, as he deteriorated physically, he became a moaner and incited others to make trouble.

A recent recruit was Prem. He wasn't born with great brains nor endowed with an air of authority, but over the years, through diligent and conscientious effort, he developed into someone capable of dealing with tricky clients and coping in any tight corner. His original home was in a remote Buddhist valley in the north of Pangi, but he had been rescued from an unkind stepmother by an uncle and aunt, who brought him up in Chamba and Manali and sent him to school. So he arrived with us able to read and write a little and to speak some halting English. He was presentable and unusually tall, and many a female trekker became enamoured of him.

He had married into a family of several sisters from Miyar *nala*. I first met his wife late one night as she lay moaning on a *charpoi* which was being used as a stretcher. Prem had arrived at Duff Dunbar breathless, just as we were going to bed. His wife was in labour with their first child and she was vomiting blood; would I come with the jeep and take her to the hospital?

The *charpoi* was standing beside the road; they had carried her down the track from the village by torchlight. At the hospital Sister Joan took one look, said the baby was about to be born, and whisked her into the labour room. I was allowed in too, to hold the torch if the electricity -- one dim bulb – went off. The poor girl whimpered softly, in terrible pain as her stomach tightened. Her sister, gripping her hand, was told to moisten her lips every now and then. There were no labour-ward gowns here: the expectant mother's brown corduroy Lahuli dress was hitched above her waist. In a cupboard a primus stove hissed, and on a shelf were two white enamel basins – one for sterilizing forceps, rubber gloves and scissors, the other for water to bathe mother and baby. There was no other equipment in the room.

The girl had now been in labour for over twenty-four hours. Joan put her ear to a trumpet pressed into the heaving stomach and glanced at the watch pinned to her cardigan; she tried another place and, clearly tense and worried, barked at her exhausted patient: 'If you don't push harder than this we'll be here all night. Come on, now, get on with it.'

A short while later some matted black hair appeared. The weakening girl heaved and strained, and soon Joan held a grey, slimy creature up to the dim light: it was a boy. She thumped its back, she laid it down and pressed its little chest. It was dead. The mother was hardly interested – just relieved it was all over. She sank back. Her sister began to wail. Joan was shattered with tiredness and rage: she said the baby hadn't been dead for more than an hour. It had been the poor girl's sister who had refused to let Prem go for help and bring her to the hospital earlier.

That misguided sister was married to another of the men, Kullu Lama. He was 'Lama' because he had spent a brief period in a *gompa* near his home in Ladakh, and 'Kullu' because when he first came to work for us he lived there. He was stocky, and for a Ladakhi had an unusual growth of beard; after a long trek without a shave he would be teased for looking like a hippie. He had an endearing if slightly disingenuous smile, and he was to reveal invaluable practical skills. He was a versatile cook, able effortlessly to organize the camp kitchen to serve twenty-five people. On a hearth made of five stones he would cook an excellent hot dinner, and produce it punctually and with good humour even in a thunderstorm or a blizzard. He rapidly became the organization's master tailor, making bags and pillow cases, patching tents and groundsheets, and running up pairs of pyjamas for those in need. But it was toy-making that brought out his real creative genius. When the children were older he would lavish endless care on making decorative tents, diminutive replicas of the *Deota's raths*, and horses, yaks and devil masks out of clay.

Kullu Lama's wife was the eldest of seven sisters. It was said that she had abandoned or been forced to leave her three children in Miyar *nala*. It wasn't clear whether her first husband had left her or whether passion for Kullu Lama had made her desert her home. To his disappointment she had many miscarriages but no children during her second marriage. They kept a hospitable house below the bazaar, beside the octroi post.

The last day of Dunghri *mela*, in May, had become the occasion for an annual lunch for our men and their families. The women and children straggled up through the forest dressed in their best. Karma's wife wore a pink 'terrycot' *salwar chemise*, gold earrings and a triple necklace of seed pearls. Chamba's wife had a sister visiting from Zanskar, who arrived pouring with sweat – she was wearing her Zanskari maroon tweed cloak and carried one of the twins on her back. More taken with the fizzy-orange bottle than with its contents, she poured her drink on to the lawn and tucked the bottle into the pouch of her cloak. Before lunch everyone suckled their babies; Mrs Chamba was still suckling the twins, though by now they were sturdy toddlers, and Mrs Karma fed Gikki. They were shocked that I was no longer feeding Rahul, now fifteen months old: Karma's wife was worried that my milk had dried up. When I told them I was expecting another baby they clicked their tongues in commiseration, sorry for me that it had happened so soon.

Women and children sat in lines and were served food by the men, who had cooked it. (Dorze's wife had brought her own food; a *pandit* had told her she would be more likely to conceive if she only ate food she had cooked herself.) Then we tripped off down through the forest. Babies and toddlers travelled piggy-back, tied on with shawls, while Boura Singh proudly carried Rahul in a frame. On a rock above the *mela* ground, in the shade of the deodars, we sat watching the dancing and ate hot *jelebis*. The syrup soaked through the bags made out of pages of old school-exercise books. Below the sweet-makers' temporary kitchens, where cauldrons full of boiling fat rested on hearths dug out of the ground, was a puppet show in a tent. Life-size puppets strolled in gardens full of scented flowers, or fought with threatening gods. Rahul was entranced, but his most ecstatic moment was when he persuaded old Gungru, the *chaukidar*, to let him play the *deotas'* drums.

The *nag* gods certainly sent rain that year. During July and August the road into the valley was blocked for days at a time; there would be no eggs, no butter, no petrol, no newspapers and no letters. The broody hen came off her eggs, the garden was sodden and barren, the house was untidy, and Kranti had to go to Bihar, where his father was ill. The mist and rain were relentless, and dampening in every way.

Children of Hadimba's Forest

Walking out of the light into Dunghri forest is as dramatic as entering a Gothic cathedral. Shafts of sun, like beams from the lights in a high roof, make the deodars in the contrasting shade almost black. The glades of moss and iris are emerald green, the ponds a reflected oily green, and the groves of young deodars a fresh blue-green. Looking up the trunks of the trees you are awed by the distance between you and the tops. Hadimba's three-tiered timber temple and the granite boulders which lie like primeval beasts in the glades give the forest an eerie sense of timelessness. It is easy to believe that thousands of years ago the forest trembled as the *raksha* Hadimb fought hand to hand with Bhim the Pandava.

The forest became familiar to us. We spent so much time there – walking through from the bazaar or driving the jeep up the muddy, rutted track – and Rahul's favourite evening walk was to the temple.

Our *dudhwalli* (milk-woman) and her family lived on the edge of the forest just below us, by the spring. She had six children under ten. The family was landless and poor and the children were weak and sickly. I would see the younger ones sucking fruitlessly on dry chapattis and urge her to give them gruel made from rice, maize or millet; she would say 'yes, yes' but I knew she never did. My other interference in her children's welfare was equally unsuccessful. Each of them had four thumbs, and I suggested that this would be a hindrance when they had to work, not to mention being unsightly; it would be a simple operation to remove the extra thumbs now, while they were young. The mother's retort was that if that was the way the *Devi* had created her children, it would be unwise to interfere.

Through the *dudhwalli* and Gungru the *chaukidar*, whose house was in the village on the other side of the forest, and through the villagers whom we came to know, we began to feel ourselves part of Hadimba's community. We decided to arrange a *mundan* – the cutting of a boy's first lock of hair, and the rough equivalent of a christening – for Rahul. Gungru advised, 'If Hadimba Devi comes to your house you'll need ten maunds of rice to feed all of old Manali and Dunghri villages – maybe a thousand people. If she just comes to the temple it'll be five maunds for your hundred and twenty guests. If you want the *pandit* who drew up the child's horoscope to perform the *puja* you'll have to ask him to decide on the auspicious day. If you just want a local style *puja* you must ask Hadimba's *gaur* to decide the day.' I had looked forward to a colourful ritual – to being Hadimba's hostess and having her *rath* sitting on our veranda – but we hadn't envisaged a party on this scale. We decided on the simplest

117

celebration: we would ask the *Devi* to come to the temple, not to the house, and we would ask her oracle to name the day.

In the morning Gungru came to say that the *gaur* wanted to meet us down at the temple. Would he be his everyday bazaar-lounging self or a shaking, possessed dervish? Even in the cheerful early morning the forest and its temple emanated an air of the supernatural, not sinister but powerful.

We sat cross-legged on the porch facing into the temple. The *gaur* disappeared round the back to slip off his tweed pyjamas. Bare-legged below his belted cloak, he rejoined us and the *pujari*, who proceeded to wave a ladleful of smoking juniper in the *gaur's* face. Suddenly, with a shudder, as though a goose had walked over his grave, the oracle tossed off his cap and began to shake, at first imperceptibly, then dramatically. The *pujari* rang a silver handbell and asked, 'These people, who have been living with us for the last three years, want their son's *mundan*. Oh, *Devi*, be good enough to tell us the auspicious day.'

'How can I say?' the *Devi* murmured through her oracle; she seemed to be diffident.

'Come on, now,' the *pujari* pleaded. 'Give us a day.'

The oracle said nothing, and the shakes subsided; I thought the trance might wear off before the day had been named. Then his body quivered and he looked up. 'It shall be tomorrow, the day before the first day of the festival. These people from outside shall be my children, and they shall be given headcloths from my temple.' A length of glittering purple and orange silk was wound round first Kranti's and then my head, and we hurried home.

Tomorrow! The food had to be bought, a sheep found for the sacrifice, the guests invited. Rahul and I had to have new clothes; our clothes had to be previously unworn for the ceremony.

Gungru sat on the kitchen step, thoughtful, proud to be involved. 'Well, there's the *dal* to be bought, two kinds, and mustard oil and garam masala, onions, garlic, cummin and coriander. What about the milk for the *khir*? Someone had better be sent now to wait by the path for the Gujars going back up the hill, to order the milk for tomorrow. And it will need a lot of sugar.' I suggested unrefined molasses, cheaper and tastier; he looked surprised but didn't question it. 'Then there's the sheep,' he said with a twinkle. Since the first mention of the hair-cutting, Boura Singh and he had been bargaining over the price of his two-year-old ram. 'And the rice: five maunds.' How could a hundred and twenty people eat four hundred pounds of rice? 'Hasn't the *gaur* to be paid? And the *pujari*? And the cooks? And the people who carry the cooking vessels from the village, and those who wash them? Don't they all have to be paid with rice?' His tone suggested that he considered my parsimony improper.

Was it possible that we could be ready for tomorrow? I was encouraged that Boura Singh, who fully approved of the event and took it more seriously than anyone else, showed no signs of being perturbed by the lack of time. But the preparations did not run smoothly. None of the cloth shops in the bazaar had any red silk; my blouse would have to be of humble cotton. The tailor who was to make Rahul's suit said it would be ready late in the afternoon. But at five o'clock I found him moaning on his bed, the cloth not yet cut; too much *chang*, his wife complained. She promised that her daughter would deliver the suit first thing in the morning.

The occasion had been conceived partly as a way of expressing our gratitude to people like Amar Singh of the Chandrabhaga store, Mr Sud the ration-shop owner, and the bank manager, for their help over the years. But they were hesitant about accepting our invitation. The day before the big festival they couldn't eat meat; would there be a vegetable? We had to search the bazaar for Karma and Dorze, who were buying the supplies, and add fifty kilos of peas and potatoes to their list – we couldn't offer a vegetable dish to some guests and not to others.

Sister Valerie said, 'How super, a feast!' but when she heard it was to be at Hadimba's temple she thought it would clash with the Bible-reading meeting.

We made time to drive to Katrain to invite Panditji and Raj Krishan; as our landlords and as custodians of the temple they would expect a personal invitation. They implied that it was improper not to have hired the Brahmin cooks from Jugatsukh;

it would mean that some of our guests (they didn't seem to include themselves) wouldn't be able to eat anything. But they were adamant about the impossibility of *khir* made with molasses (they must have heard about it from the *chaukidar*): 'Never in my life have I eaten *khir* made with molasses,' said Panditji. 'In the old good days, of course, it was always made with the finest Dehra Dun Basmatti rice and crystal sugar.' So, late in the evening, we had to send Lama Le with a sack and a note to the ration-shop owner, requesting him to open his shop and sell us sugar.

When Boura Singh arrived the next morning with the bed tea, Hadimba's drums were already echoing up from the forest like cantering horses. It was a grey day. The tailor's daughter brought Rahul's suit: he looked like a Hindi movie hero in a Kullui hat, vivid yellow silk *kurta* and spotless white pyjamas. My new red cotton blouse arrived crumpled from the other tailor's, and couldn't be ironed because the electricity was off. As we processed down the path Kranti was the most elegant of the party, in fluttering cream-silk *kurta* and billowing *malmal dhoti* - unremarkable in Bihar but exotic here in Himachal. Rahul followed in Chamba's proud arms, then came Boura Singh carrying a trayful of flowers for the *Devi*; he had taken on himself the role of sheep-sacrificer. The *chaukidar* joined our procession; he wore a new hat with rosebuds tucked into the brim. The men and their wives and children were dressed in their best clothes and jewellery – velvets and patterned shawls; corals, amber and turquoise.

It seemed hours that Kranti, Rahul and I had to be inside the stuffy temple. We sat in a circle round the fire, set in a pit in the rock, to the right of the massive boulder which is the shrine. The *pujari* chanted the Sanskrit mantras at a great rate, tossing rice, incense and *ghi* into the fire from time to time. When the *ghi* made the flames flare up, the silks and the gold and silver masks on Hadimba's *rath* began to glow.

As the actual hair-cutting ceremony is performed by the *gaur*, it must take place out on the porch – he isn't allowed into the temple. The ladleful of juniper was waved in his face, then three saucers were placed in front of him: one of walnuts, one of flowers, one of chapattis. We waited. Movement round the back of the temple suggested that the sacrifice was taking time (Boura Singh later blamed the bluntness of the blade); but at last a dish of steaming blood was brought round. Some was poured on to the porch steps, some offered to the *Devi* under the rock inside. Then the dish, still containing a little blood, was laid in front of the *gaur*, who began to shake and, fumbling, tied a red string round a lock of Rahul's hair. He took a miniature pair of sheep shears from his tweedy chest and prepared to cut. I held Rahul firmly and watched apprehensively; if he moved, or if the *gaur*'s hand shook, he could easily lose a slice out of one of his large and rather prominent ears. The lock was shorn without mishap. I was told to advance to the temple doorway three times, to present to the *Devi* a walnut, some flowers and juniper, and the lock of hair, held in the corner of my red scarf. She kept a share of each gift, as a token that Rahul had been accepted into her protection, and we were told to keep our share in a safe place for ever.

The men and their wives lent a Buddhist touch to the ceremony by placing white muslin scarves round our necks. They gave Rahul presents of money, biscuits and knitted socks.

The grey morning had given way to a downpour. Thunder roared down the valley and lightning shot through the deodars. 'See, Hadimba Devi is very happy with you,' the *pujari* said. I wished she had chosen to express her pleasure in some other way. Our finery was soon drenched. In the rain the food had taken longer than expected to cook; the fires and great brass cooking vessels had to be covered with umbrellas. I was short-tempered, having had to fast since the night before. When at last the meal was ready, there was an unexpected hitch: the serving ladles had been forgotten. I suggested we should fetch some from home, but Boura Singh said ours wouldn't do as they were of steel rather than of brass; what he meant was that because they belonged to a casteless kitchen they would be polluting. There was a further delay for three-quarters of an hour while the proper ladles were brought from the goddess's store.

Thirty people at a time sat in lines on the floor of the temple outhouse. Boys filled and refilled the brass *thali* in front of each person with rice, vegetables, two sorts of *dal*, sacrificial mutton and *khir*.

As we went to bed, the last of the revellers were making their way home by flaming torchlight. Rahul's feast must have fed nearer to five hundred people than to the estimated hundred and fifty. From then on, strangers we met on the forest path and in the bazaar would greet us with a *namaste*.

That winter, Tara was born in Dunoon's cottage hospital. The staff were becoming used to delivering babies who had spent their gestation period being bumped about in the Himalayas. This time the baby emerged entangled in the umbilical cord as if in a string bag.

Though by now I had been migrating to Kullu every spring for eight years I never became inured to the transition. From Delhi we sometimes flew to Chandigarh and sometimes took the Kalka Mail. Old Delhi Station at nine o'clock at night was a far cry from the signaller's fireside at Arrochar on the West Highland Line, where our journey had begun. Pushing and shoving our way up the stairs we had to cross the iron bridge over huge diesel engines and steam engines that hissed and puffed. It always seemed improbable that we would meet the red-shirted coolies who had vanished into the crowds from the taxi stand, their barrows laden with our luggage. Stepping over travellers camped on the platform, we would make our way towards the Chandigarh First Class bogie, to find our names listed on the carriage door.

We would breakfast at dawn on the lawns of the Mount View Hotel at Chandigarh – poached eggs and coffee among the roses and mynah birds. It was a respite before the heat of a ten-hour drive.

Once we were beyond Mandi and into the Beas gorge, there were only three hours to go: we were nearly home. As the road turned a corner just above the Pandoh dam we would see the first of the deodars high above, on the north-facing slope. In the gorge the vegetation is subtropical – palms, the cactus-like giant euphorbia, and trees that shed their leaves to rest dormant during the hot months of May and June. The scarlet flowers on the *Bombax ceiba* and the young leaves of the pistachio, *Pistacia chinensis*, offer the strongest splashes of colour; the large trees stand out deep red in the far distance.

As you emerge into lower Kullu your gaze is confined by mountainsides; the scale is suddenly European. On the endless plains and in the disorderly lower hills the European eye is disconcerted, but here you can orientate yourself in relation to the geographical features. No wonder the British have always felt a sense of familiarity and ease in these Himalayan valleys.

At the lower end of the valley the apple blossom was out. Higher up, the alders beside the river were only just coming into leaf, like a diaphanous green veil. And at Manali it was still winter; the orchards were colourless and bare.

During one day we had travelled backwards through an entire growing season. On the plains golden fields of wheat were being harvested; round Bilaspur and Suket the wheat was a lush green; in Manali the seedlings were no further through the earth than they had been ten days after the October sowing. It was as though everything had slept in our absence.

Our taxi couldn't go beyond the temple. I walked on ahead of the others, carrying Tara. After the commotion of the road it was quiet among the deodars. We crawled under the chain of the gate, passed the spooky gatehouse shed and made our way up the orchard track; before us, set on a convex curve of the land like Noah's Ark, was Duff Dunbar. I sat on the stone front steps, cradling Tara against the wintry chill, and gazed at the familiar view as the light grew dim. The trees and the mountains were silhouettes, the summits were white against a pale sky.

Inside, the electricity was off and I couldn't find the torch. We wandered from room to room with the only working oil lamp. Trunks and chests were opened and familiar objects emerged in the lamplight. The house was waking up from its hibernation. I had a feeling then, and also later when we had to leave it for ever, that it had a life and a presence of its own.

In the morning Boura Singh arrived with the bed tea and, murmuring smiling endearments, brought Tara from her cot in the back veranda room she shared with Rahul. I sat up to look out of the window. In the dusk of the night before, I hadn't noticed that the three large pear trees that marked the top corner of the orchard had been felled, and that Mr MacKay's tennis court had been ploughed up and drilled for potatoes.

The *chaukidar* crept up the hill, older and sadder than the year before. His wife had been ill all winter. The hippies' dogs, abandoned when they left for Goa in the autumn, had killed one of his sheep, and with his wife ill he hadn't had the time to feed the others properly; they were thin and sick. I wished I had remembered to bring him something. In London and in Scotland everything in Manali seems so remote that I doubt its reality; yet once I am here every detail of sight and sound is utterly familiar. If I didn't reawaken it by coming back, would it lie dormant for ever?

When at last we had reached Manali the night before, Karma, Chamba, Dorze and Boura Singh had been waiting for the taxi at the corner below the post office. Boura Singh had dashed off to buy vegetables, then they had all squashed into the taxi with us, jostling each other to grab Rahul and Tara.

Being met by the men at the beginning of each season was heart-warming. In later years, when the plane came into Bhunter below Kullu and I came out into the exhilarating cool air, I would see them standing behind the plate-glass of the airport shed. Karma and Prem were almost always among them, perhaps with Kullu Lama, and later Mangal Singh. Boura Singh often stayed at home, keeping the kettle on the boil in readiness for our arrival. Often he hadn't himself arrived from Garhwal, but had been delayed by the ploughing. (The children would hold a sweepstake, betting on which day and time of day he would walk up the path.) The men's welcome was never effusive. It was a courteous *namaste*, and until the next day, when we began to exchange news, there were few words. But warmth and welcome shone in their eyes.

That spring the next day's news was devastating. Bari Nomo,

the larger and more blooming of Chamba's twins, had recently died. Chamba's account was all the more poignant for its brevity. 'We were in Una. We bought a lot of medicine for her from Hamirpur, but it didn't help. Then she was very ill. We took her to Riwalsar [a Buddhist winter resort round a lake just beyond Mandi] because of the guru there, but he couldn't help. She went mad, then she died. I watched her all the time. The lamas gave prayers for her in the *gompa* by the lake.'

From the description of her final days, the mission doctor deduced that Bari Nomo must have had a TB brain tumour. He established that Choti Moti, the smaller twin, had TB too, in her case of the glands. Her neck was swollen and she still had the discharge from her ear which had begun when she had measles the previous year. All four of Chamba's children had developed TB; yet both parents looked healthy, and Mrs Chamba was a particularly efficient, organized mother. It was so unfair. And what was the point of those BCG inoculations I had persuaded them to have given to the twins born after the first TB death? The doctor told me, 'We don't understand ourselves. We are sure the inoculations do prevent some kinds of TB, particularly of the bones and chest, but not all. And of course in cases like this people lose faith.'

I often tried to analyse the practical everyday differences of attitude and expectation between me and the men. Because over the years we lived so closely together and were so much at ease with each other, I had to stop and remind myself that there *were* differences. If I were to live for ever exactly as Chamba, Prem or Kullu Lama did, what would I find most difficult? I would hanker to be able to bathe naked in privacy. A bucketful of warm water and a mug to pour it over yourself, or even a standpipe in warm weather, is fine; but to have to bathe at least semi-dressed, without seclusion, would only be bearable as a temporary solution. Lack of privacy in general, not just for bathing, would be trying. The concept of an individual's privacy doesn't exist in India, even in large houses. No one knocks as they walk into a room, rooms open into each other, and few doorways have doors which are kept shut. People dread doing anything alone, or being alone. To want to sit and read by yourself, to lie and daydream, or to have a private conversation with someone, means that you must be either peculiar or up to no good. In any case there would be no chance of ever being alone in, say, Chamba's one-room house, which is open house to neighbours.

For the men themselves the constant dread is boredom – the tedium of every day. They often make references to the problem of how to pass time. Brought up to be busy and ambitious, we are conditioned to a sense of time flying by and to there never being enough hours in the day or weeks in the year to accomplish all we should. Whereas for most people in India, working or drinking or a visitor's arrival or a game of cards is a diversion from the endless stretch of time that must be endured. If I had books and paper and pencils, was able to go out and about and had the odd kettle of *chang* or bottle of *arak*, I don't think I would fear boredom.

For me the worst thing would be having to face so much suffering. Not that we in the West can bypass suffering; on the contrary, our tendency to assume we have control over circumstances can mean that we find it all the harder to accept pain and illness. Nor is it so that Chamba and his wife can accept the death of two of their children and the illness of the other two with a fatalism that obviates pain. But the probability of accidents and illnesses here is so much greater. Facilities for diagnosis and treatment are in short supply. There are no telephones, and telegrams take days to arrive. I would feel unbearably vulnerable.

Rahul's arrival had been responsible for bringing us Boura Singh. Now Tara's arrival was the reason Sunita became part of our household. With two children and the office to run I hadn't time to wash clothes and nappies. I couldn't ask Boura Singh to do it, for it would be demeaning; I had never even suggested that he might change a nappy. Sunita's original role was to be the children's clothes-washer, but like Boura Singh she rapidly became a crucial member of the household. She was found by Chamba, and belonged to the Buddhist community; her father was from Zanskar, her mother from Pangi. When she first came to us she was a gangly eighteen-year-old. She wore glasses to cure a squint, and had a large nose and a long plait of hair. There had been a possibility of her being married to the son of the hoteliers at Murrhi but she had been turned down, considered too weak for the rigours of hotel work in the cold up at Murrhi, and her buxom younger sister had been taken in her place. Sunita would lose the squint and grow into her nose, and her plait would become a glorious mane; she would mature into a handsome and talented young woman. She spent several winters with us in London, where she rapidly learnt to speak English, with a BBC accent which would have been the envy of many a Punjabi, and where my friends and relations were impressed by her beauty and aplomb. From the beginning she had a natural talent with small children and was never harassed. Every morning Rahul and Tara would stand on a *charpoi* on the veranda, gleefully anticipating her arrival up the orchard path.

The next newcomer to our household was a cow.

A letter to my mother, Duff Dunbar, June 1977

We have bought a cross-Jersey cow (with a calf) for milk for your grandchildren. The other evening Boura Singh came up from the bazaar saying that camped by the *gompa* there were men from Kangra with cows for sale. Kranti, I and the hospital *chaukidar*, who is a Kangra man and a cow-owner, went to look. We selected a dark-brown cow, with a Jersey-looking heifer calf. The price was yet to be established. Kullu Lama and Prem were sent to spy on how much milk she was giving.

Next morning we solicited the bargaining skills of Manali's most expert cow-woman, a plump Lahuli who has a yard of four milking cows and a pure-bred Jersey bull. She disapproved of our first choice – the dark-brown cow was too old, she said – but agreed with our second choice – a fine-boned, pale cow with a bull calf. The owners were asking for 2,000 rupees; our expert said anything above 1,000 was absurd. The owners dismissed our insulting offer. Our expert advised us to jump in the jeep and drive off, and wait for the next cattle fair.

127

Rahul and I were disappointed; we had already planned where to build the cow-shed. Then two days later we met the cow-owner in the bazaar. If we wanted the pale yellow cow for 1,500 rupees we could have her – they were going home to Kangra and didn't want to walk her for four days in the heat. Half an hour later Gopali and her calf – Gopal – walked up through the orchard.

The cow-shed had to be built, and the hen-house made jackal-proof. There were white-raspberry canes that had to be kept well-watered, jams to be made and vegetables to be dried in the dehydrator. The men and their wives often wanted to air their domestic problems and expected advice and medicines; by now I had amassed a large medical store and some basic medical knowledge. Correspondence with our London office had to be attended to regularly. The store of tinned foods had to be maintained, and equipment repaired and listed. On one occasion it was discovered that one of the best-quality sleeping bags was missing; referring to the lists we were able to establish that it had come back from the last trek, so it was clear that someone had taken it. After several days Karma suggested that everyone should go down to the temple and swear on the *Devi*'s name that they were innocent. By coincidence, or perhaps in the face of such a dramatic measure, the sleeping-bag reappeared.

With so many practical responsibilities to attend to, I had little chance to worry about how to pass the time. But I felt hobbled by domesticity. Instead of detailing the distances between camp sites, or the heights of passes, or ideas for new routes, my diary now recorded nothing more eventful than the daily egg-lay from our five hens:

It has only rained once in the last six weeks. The caterpillars have finished the grass; it's yellow-brown as though it's been burnt. They lie along every blade – when you look at the ground you begin to see it moving, black and green and yellow – and they are up in the trees and inside your clothes. Last night, before going to bed, we had to sweep them off the hall floor. A lot of the day is spent watering the garden, though there's not much left in it. There's no grass for Gopali.

128

Boura Singh and I would sit in the hot June sun by an outdoor *chulha*, making jam; five kilos of apricots at a time took hours of stirring. We made pickles too – of lime, plum, onion, and the little wild apricot. But the most time-consuming job was drying vegetables. The carpenters had built a drying cabinet in which a stack of fibreglass mesh trays stood over three electric bulbs. The tomatoes, green peppers or mushrooms had to be thinly sliced and evenly laid on the mesh trays, which had to be regularly switched round so that the vegetables on the lower ones didn't burn, nor the nearly-dry ones become damp again. If the electricity went off they all went mouldy. By the end of the mushroom season we would be sick of the smell; the mushroom collectors sold us *kiltas* full of them at a good price, saving themselves the walk from the forest down to the bazaar hotels.

Monsoon

It was a busy July and August, and I sent out three parties within five days. Kranti was away again; this time it was his mother who was ill. Few people in the late twentieth century can have been so dependent on telegrams as we were. Kulluis were used to living with nineteenth-century communications, but we needed to send and receive urgent news. We used the telegraph service several times a week; and not just when members of our distant families were ill, for running a business often necessitated a swift exchange of information. I liked to think I had mastered the art of how to phrase a telegraphic message. Never heed the expense: the first essential is to ensure that the recipient has no doubts about the meaning. An added phrase, or the repetition of a crucial word, can avoid misunderstandings even if the message arrives jumbled. On this occasion Kranti's first message was so detailed and explicit that the signaller must have been shocked. The gist of it was that his mother was very ill and that he wouldn't be back for some time (six weeks, in the event).

One morning, having been up since half-past four to see a

party off, I needed something to eat before climbing home through the squelching forest. Hoping for breakfast, I decided to call on Sister Valerie (Joan was in England on furlough). She wasn't living at the hospital any longer but had a room at the bottom of our hill, which was considered more appropriate for her in her new role as a community health worker. It was some time since we had met, and she was welcoming and friendly. She had no water or sanitation in the house; only an earth closet so that she could explain its benefits to the villagers from first-hand experience. The table was laid with an embroidered tablecloth and crocheted mats, and set with butter in a dish, milk in a jug, and marmalade in a glass bowl. We had toast – which had a slight fragrance of kerosene because it had to be made on a *tawa* on an oil stove – with home-made marmalade and tea.

She was really pleased to see me, though too preoccupied with her village work to be interested in my problems. She told me that on her first visit to the village she had come across a Panchayat meeting being held on an upper veranda. She had called up: could she join the gathering and address it once they had finished? Settling herself down among the Panchayat members – all men – she had asked if they minded her coming to the village with her head uncovered. She was aware that unmarried girls covered their heads, she said, and explained that although she was herself unmarried it was difficult for her to keep a *dupatta* over her head while she worked. I thought it odd that on the one hand she could be so insensitive to other people's ways of thinking that she had unashamedly torn an amulet off a dying child, while on the other she could imagine that the village elders might bar her from the village because her head wasn't covered. It was highly improbable that they would apply the same standards of modesty to a middle-aged foreign woman as they would to one of their own young daughters. God seemed to cloud her vision rather.

During those busy weeks I would never have managed without Boura Singh and Sunita. All the men were good friends to me. It wasn't just that they were paid to be helpful; their good nature and concern went far beyond the call of duty. Boura Singh was a tower of strength. He was seldom put off his stride, and always had a restorative cup of tea at the ready – no matter what time of the night or morning it was. If ever I mentioned something that was worrying me, he would put it into perspective by citing an example from his home village or from the Hindu epics. And he was always ready for a joke. One evening old Gungru was sitting on the kitchen step when out of the blue he said he would like to have one of our stainless steel *thalis* (he ought to have known that Boura Singh would never give him anything of ours). 'What do you want that for?' Boura Singh asked, laughing at the absurdity of it. 'That *thali* will last years and years, and you're an old man about to go – you won't be able to take it with you.'

Sunita was meant to come to work from nine o'clock until two or three in the afternoon, but often she spent the night with us. I became dependent on her unobtrusive calm, and felt at ease living at close quarters with her. The children trusted her too, and knew that she wouldn't tire of entertaining them. Boura Singh took on an avuncular role, educating her about the ways of the world and often teasing her. As the years passed, and she grew in stature and beauty and had a thing or two to tell him about the ways of the world in London, his teasing became more barbed.

My memories of feeling most vulnerable and insecure are all associated with the monsoon. It was partly because of the precarious communications. It was also due to the limited horizons: being engulfed by mist, in a world where for days at a time visibility was limited to the end of the orchard, made me feel claustrophobic. The lure of this life – the sense of proportion induced by the vast landscape, the feeling of being on top of a world where anything was possible – seemed to be turned upside down. I was hemmed in by grey mist.

And I felt defenceless. In India the people immediately around you – your extended family – may care about you, but no one else does. To feel secure that in time of need there is someone both willing and able to help you, you need a relation in an important position; this is why Indian voting patterns are increasingly caste-based. There was no one in the valley in any position of authority who would care if I sank or swam.

One afternoon we went to visit our acquaintances Judge and Mrs Kapur; we needed to borrow a couple of eggs, as our hens had stopped laying and there had been none in the bazaar for days. We slithered through the wet forest, Tara on Sunita's back, bound in a shawl, Rahul on mine in a carrying frame. Mrs Kapur had no eggs to lend but she was pleased to see me; not so much because she was concerned about my welfare as because she wanted to tell someone about the saga of her friend Mrs Lal.

'You know her servant, the one she's left so much land to (she's even *told* him that), the one she makes tea for and takes it to him? Well, his wife had an affair with a Kashmiri apple-packer. After the apple-packing season she disappeared to Lahul and got murdered on a bus. Well recently Mrs Lal had to go to Delhi and she left the keys of her jeep with that servant "so that he could keep the battery ticking over". The next thing was that someone, in a jeep, went to the murdered woman's brother in Kullu and murdered *him*. Mrs Lal is terribly upset and she is refusing to let the police question her servant. She says she knows he would never have taken her jeep out. That servant has taken a new wife already, with a child, and Mrs Lal gives the child sweets and presents as if it were her daughter. Her ideas about servants are too Christian. I used to be her friend, but I can't understand her any more.'

During the monsoon Chamba's wife gave birth to a son. I had met her in the ration shop one evening and noticed that she was sitting down to do her shopping. The next morning Kullu Lama's wife said that Tsering Dolma had come for her at nine in the evening.

She had fetched the *dai*, the Chandrabhaga manager's wife, who only just had time to boil the water: by eleven o'clock the baby was born. Everyone was jubilant at the birth of a boy after four girls. Rahul, Tara and I went down to see the mother and son. She was lying on a *duri* on the floor, the baby beside her, and a *rezai* (quilt) covered them both. He was swaddled in a

Above: A thin thread of sheep above a glacier on the way to the 16,000-foot pass to Kugti

Below, left to right: Kullu Lama, Mangal Singh and Prem

Inscribed flags suspended between trees consign Buddhists' prayers to the elements.

A Gaddi shepherd and children on migration to their winter pastures

A Kullu basket for carrying hay from the hillside to the village

Stopping for *chang* with Dorze's mother and stepfather on our way through Zanskar

A family camping expedition in Hampta *nala*
Left to right: Chamba, Mangal Singh, Christina, Tara, Prem, Kranti, Rahul, Kullu Lama; *behind:* Karma, Boura Singh, Man Bahadur, Ram Bahadur, Dorze

Above: A stone-roofed village perched high on a promontory in Phojal *nala*

Opposite: Chamba's mother welcomes him to Karsha, his home village in Zanskar.

Below: A Khampa woman in her 'hotel' (tea-house)

Masks and flower offerings on a *deota's rath*

green towel (I recognized it as one we had bought from Selfridges many years before), from which he was unwrapped so that we could admire him and Rahul could press an Edwardian silver rupee into his clutched palm. He woke and turned his fat, hairy head; his face was a crumpled replica of Chamba's. Mrs Chamba squeezed a few drops of milk from her well-used breast and offered it to the little fellow, who took it with a shake of his head like a puppy. She was so proud and so happy, and he looked so robust; would he too succumb to the dreaded TB? This time I wasn't going to mention immunization and baby clinics; after Bari Nomo's death I had lost confidence in them.

As we made our way back up through the bazaar we stopped at the post office and sent a congratulatory telegram to Chamba, addressed to Major's houseboats in Kashmir: the group he was with should have emerged from Zanskar by now and be making their way there from Kargil. The gorge road had opened and mail had begun to arrive.but it wasn't yet sorted. I would have to wait until the next day for my long-expected letters.

The Accident

By the next day I had abandoned any thought of my letters: I was in the bus half-way to Chandigarh, on my way to Srinagar.

On our way home from visiting the baby we had picked up newspapers – after days without them – at Verma's, and before I went to milk Gopali that evening I had lain on my bed to read the *Tribune*. The top right-hand column on the back page was headed: 'Four foreigners among five killed in road accident'. The report was dated 25 August, and it was now 30 August. A truck had fallen into a dangerous ravine near the top of the Zoji La. Five had been killed and five others injured. Our party had been trekking from Manali and was travelling from Kargil to Srinagar. The names were garbled, but the facts were clear enough. Stunned and breathless I read and reread the report.

I went to milk Gopali. In the dark shed I pressed my head

against her flank. Perhaps it wasn't our party; perhaps I had shaped the garbled names into familiar ones – hundreds of people trekked from Manali these days. I took the pail of frothy milk to the kitchen. The children were asleep, and Boura Singh was sitting at the *chulha*, cooking; I said nothing to him. I went back up to my room and read the paper again. There could be no doubt: it was them. I lay there forcing myself to absorb the truth.

Then I called out of the bathroom window for Boura Singh and Sunita. I had to leave for Srinagar: there was no choice. It sounded as though one of our clients might be alive; and what about Chamba and Tsering, another of our regular men, and the other porters, and the son of the Mortons, guesthouse owners in Manali, who had joined the party at the last minute as an interpreter? I was worried about Tara, for I was still feeding her myself – should I take her with me? Boura Singh and Sunita were adamant: she was eight months old, she was eating solid food, and she would be fine with them. I was up at half-past four to walk down the hill and catch the first bus to Chandigarh, where I would catch a flight to Srinagar.

Looking down on the tops of the mountains from the window of the aeroplane, my eye studied the Gujars' encampments, the complicated watersheds and the forests on the north-facing slopes, but my mind was elsewhere and full of questions. Was my friendship with Chamba something that belonged now to the past? Had he died without knowing he had a son? Why had the party been in that truck when it was meant to be coming from Kargil by bus?

The plane slid over the Pir Pinjal and turned to descend into the green valley of Kashmir. Major, the owner of the houseboats where the party was to have stayed, was at the airport waiting for some clients to arrive, and by chance the headmaster of the mission school, who had buried the dead, was also there. They had sent me a telegram giving me details of the accident (when I got back I was to find it waiting for me in Manali). The headmaster gave me the name of the Ladakhi superintendent who was in charge of the case.

I took a taxi to the police station, where the superintendent told me that it seemed the party had taken a lift in the truck rather than wait for the bus, although foreigners weren't meant to travel in trucks. The driver had been killed, so no one knew what had happened – whether he had gone to sleep, or whether the brakes or the steering were at fault. The truck had failed to take a corner, gone off the road and rolled down the mountain-side; it seemed that those travelling in the back had been thrown out as it rolled. Two of our clients had been killed, as well as the Mortons' charming young son and Chamba's nephew Nawang, who must have insisted on joining the party in Padam. Chamba himself was in hospital, dangerously ill. Tsering was in hospital too, but not badly injured.

I had never been to an Indian public hospital before. There were patients in rows in the corridors and on the floors between the beds, and relations and children everywhere. Would I ever find the men or recognize them? Tsering, on a bed in the middle of a large ward, saw me and called out. His leg and back were damaged but not broken. Through his sobs he gave me an account of what had happened and then, limping, he took me to see Chamba.

I would never have found Chamba where he lay on a makeshift back veranda milling with patients; nor would I have recognized him. He and Tsering were both filthy. Neither of them had been washed or changed since they had been brought to the hospital in a truck. Chamba was huddled at the far end of his bed, tied to Heath Robinson traction equipment. He stared at me blankly for a minute or two, like a scared animal, then tried to hold on to my arm with his grubby hand. Tears rolled down his cheeks. A young Ladakhi nurse had been providing the men with food because they had had no one to look after them; a patient's relations are expected to provide food and ordinary nursing. She and the kindly police superintendent had also arranged for Nawang to be cremated according to Buddhist rites. It had been his first and last trip out of Zanskar.

I spent a long afternoon at the hospital. The ward doctor couldn't find the X-ray that had been taken when Chamba was admitted, but he did know that the patient's neck was broken and that he might be paralysed for life. No one knew much more, or cared. I refused to be brushed aside. If they couldn't find the X-ray I wanted another taken and the specialist's opinion on it. They were reluctant to take the trouble, doubtful that I would pay. At last, triumphantly clutching the X-rays, I wandered up and down corridors and in and out of dispiriting offices that smelt of socks and unemptied ashtrays. Finally I cornered the specialist. He held up the X-ray and was astonished: it showed the spinal cord almost severed. None of us could understand how it had remained unbroken while Chamba was carried up the mountainside and brought here, bumping along in the back of a truck. It was a miracle he was alive, said the doctor: he must be very tough. He ought to be in more rigid traction than he was in at present and stay in it for two weeks. After that, if he wore a wired collar for some months, there was a chance he might be saved from paralysis. But it would cost a lot of money; the collar would have to be specially made, and someone would have to nurse him in hospital. When he was discharged, he wouldn't be able to travel for some weeks. The specialist, like the doctors earlier in the afternoon, found it hard to believe that I was willing to lavish money on an ordinary Zanskari, a servant.

The headmaster's wife gave me toast and blackcurrant jam in their house in the school compound and said she thought that the school would be able to find a room for Chamba when he came out of hospital and he could eat in the Ladakhi boys' hostel. This was real Christian charity: I was so grateful.

I stayed out on Nagin Lake, on the *New Peony*, one of Major's houseboats. It was a relief to be able to sit down, to be alone, and I was thankful for Major's protection. The setting sun, the Hari Parbat hill reflected in the water, the scones and strawberry jam served on the houseboat roof, were all poignantly irrelevant to the situation. For so long I had been engulfed in the static mist at Duff Dunbar; now, suddenly catapulted into action, all my faculties and emotions were reeling.

The next morning I visited the police godown, which was like one of the hells depicted in a Buddhist Wheel of Life – a no-man's-land. It was dingy, damp and dark, its concrete floor scattered with bundles of torn, dirty luggage. By the end of a trek, sleeping-bag sheets, plastic tubs, kit bags and unwashed clothes are always ingrained with dirt; this time they had been scattered on the gritty mountainside before being bundled up. The Mortons had arrived the day before; they had motored all the way from Manali. In an extremity of grief they searched for belongings, clothes and film – all they would have left to cling to, to remind them of their son. Our battered tents, sleeping bags, pots and pans were just equipment. But I knew that on behalf of our clients' bereaved relations I must try to identify possessions – particularly rolls of exposed film and diaries that might record the last few weeks of their lives.

Tsering and I were to drive back to Manali with the Mortons. Before leaving, I went to the Nedous Hotel to book a 'lightning' telephone call to Kranti in Bihar. A trunk call is charged at the ordinary rate, an 'urgent' call at double rate, while a 'lightning' call, which is triple rate, takes precedence at every exchange along the line. I sat in the gloomy old hall, where Kashmiri stags and Marco Polo sheep heads scowled down on me as they had on generations of dramas – romances, reunions and farewells. From behind an enormous carved walnut screen I could hear the operator shouting 'Lightning, Bakhtiyarpur, going via Patna, in Bihar!' But half an hour later he came to tell me he was sorry, but 'The call is not materializing – the lines are non-functioning.'

We drove through the night and all the next day and night, miraculously without encountering a road block. It was early in the morning when we reached Manali. I went straight to Chamba's house, walking through the orchard behind the petrol pump. Mrs Chamba was sitting in the corner of the room, nursing her son. It had been generally expected that I would bring news of Chamba's death. After I had left for Srinagar the telegram sent by the kind Ladakhi nurse had arrived, saying 'Tsering OK Chamba in hospital please come', and Boura Singh had interpreted it as meaning Chamba was dead. Mrs Chamba was remarkably calm, but the rest of the Buddhist community was prepared for the ritual wailing. It was difficult to convince them that he was alive; all the more so because I had to explain that he

137

wouldn't be home for some weeks. It was assumed I was offering false reassurance to spare Mrs Chamba grief so soon after her delivery.

When I had finally succeeded I staggered up through the forest, home to my own little world, where Rahul, Tara, Boura Singh and Sunita were having breakfast in the kitchen, and cried with the relief of seeing them all.

That afternoon Kranti arrived. He walked round the side of the house and we hardly recognized him: his head had been shaved, in accordance with the mourning ritual, after his mother's death.

Chandrabhaga

Early in the summer after the accident, a botanist friend, Adam, was setting off to collect plants in Pangi. The route was to be by road to Chamba town, then over the Sach Pass and back up the Chandrabhaga valley to Lahul; the last section would complete the missing link in the route John and I had planned on our original trek to Kashmir nine years before. Tara was now a year and a half old; I decided to abandon domesticity and join the trip.

Adam trekked in style: for the two of us there were ten men. This wasn't because he indulged in fancy luxuries; on the contrary he lived off rice, *masoor dal*, chillies and garlic. (This regime was too austere even for the men; they sneaked flour for chapattis, and different varieties of *dal*, into the stores.) It was because he brought flower presses, drying paper, cameras and heavy tents, and wanted to keep the men lightly loaded so that they could cover long stages when necessary. There were seven members of our permanent staff – Karma, Lama Le, Dorze, Kullu Lama, Prem, Teshi, who was a recent recruit (married to the niece of Prem's and Kullu Lama's wives – a startlingly beautiful girl), and a Nepali called Man Bahadur. Chamba, though miraculously restored, wasn't yet fit for trekking; later he would be able to join expeditions if he wasn't weighed down by too heavy a load. Then there were three new men: blue-eyed Nawang Tsering, Sunita's uncle, who was a willowy man with a drooping moustache, and Mangal Singh, a Khampa boy who had just left school and was a protégé of Karma's.

By now Karma had been working with us for four years, but I hadn't been on a trip with him for a long time and hadn't realized how competent and authoritative he had become. As our team of men had expanded and the logistics of our expeditions had become more complex, an underlying authority was needed to hold everything together. That was what Karma managed to provide so well: he didn't do it by bossing – several of the men were older than him – but rather he set standards of what was expected by turning his own hand to whatever needed doing. He would supervise packing up camp until the last man's load was roped to his back. If one person had a particularly light load he would be given an odd kettle or lamp to carry, while another who was unfairly weighed down would be encouraged with the promise that he wouldn't have to go for wood at the next camp. Karma would dart up to the front to offer to help a client across a stream or wait for a porter lagging behind, to keep him company. He would take turns with Kullu Lama, or whomever was cook, to vary the daily menu with something tasty. And if asked for an opinion or a decision he always had a ready answer: it was this that really inspired confidence, both in the other men and in the clients.

Our first night in camp was spent in a chestnut grove below a Buddhist village. Though the villagers migrated to Kangra for the winters, the houses were well built, of stone and timber, and there was an impressive *gompa*. It was a Khampa village, but although Karma and Mangal Singh were the Khampas of our party, it was Prem who most felt at home here. When he had first escaped from home in one of the high Buddhist villages in Pangi, he had lived with his aunt and uncle in a shed by the *gompa*. These Khampas, for generations traders over the passes between Chamba and Pangi, and even beyond to Zanskar and Ladakh, had petitioned the Rajas of Chamba for land to

139

build a *gompa*, and when it was built the village had grown round it.

That afternoon everyone was up at the *gompa* preparing for a *puja*. Women and lamas were making pink statues out of *ghi* and *tsampa* and preparing hundreds of lamps – cotton wicks in oil set in brass cups. These hill-people, in their enthusiasm for distant relationships and their capacity to remember names and incidents by which to identify family connections, reminded me of people back home in the Highlands. A group of elderly women were quizzing Karma, wanting to identify him in their Khampa context, but he was being teasingly elusive.

Prem disappeared for the night with one of the lamas, to take part in the ceremony. All evening, gongs and cymbals rang out across the valley. I didn't sleep. I should have been ecstatically happy, setting off into the hills again after so long, being lulled by Himalayan sounds, but to my surprise I was consumed with worries about the children and everything at Duff Dunbar.

It was a hard slog up through the snow to the summit. I was unfit and had to count to four or five between each step. At the top we looked behind at the jagged shapes of the shadows cast by the mountains. It was only ten o'clock although we had been climbing for five hours; we had started early before the snow softened. We picked pink primulas (*rosea*) and had some boiled sweets to offer at the trident-bedecked shrine. Prem took out a piece of red cloth which he tore into strips; he tied the largest to one of the spikes of a trident, to flutter in the wind, and presented each of us with one, as a talisman to wear in buttonhole or hat. Ethnographers suggest that the high mid-Himalayan passes mark a watershed between the Hindu and Buddhist worlds. It is not so clear-cut. Here were our men, Buddhist if you asked them their religion, making offerings to shrines and icons associated with the Hindu deities – Lord Shiva and the Goddess Kali. According to Prem this shrine was nothing to do with Shivji or Kali Devi; the pass was under the protection of Mirkula, a local deity, and like all the temples and shrines in the higher hills it was venerated by everyone, be they Hindu or Buddhist. A Himalayan traveller dare not ignore a wayside shrine or any gnarled tree that shelters a local spirit; he feels himself too vulnerable.

On the way down from the pass I decided that I would go home. After several summers spent wishing I was in the hills, I now had a strong sense that I should be at Duff Dunbar. The next day I would walk straight up the Chandrabhaga valley rather than explore the side *nala* with Adam.

Having made the decision, I enjoyed the rest day, playing cards and washing, camped in a hazelnut grove beside the Chandrabhaga. Karma suggested that we should celebrate my birthday by buying a sheep; we had passed some shepherds camping not too far above. Everyone relished eating meat but the question of who was to kill or even hold the beast was always apt to be an issue – I had once had to do the holding myself. Buddhism didn't curb the men's enthusiasm for searching out a sheep for sale, or indeed for carving up the carcass, cooking and eating it, but when the chosen animal was led into camp all the men would look the other way, immediately preoccupied by some mundane task. Those who were married were always adamant. They couldn't slaughter; just suppose their wives were pregnant – it would be inauspicious for an unborn child. It wasn't the kind of issue to joke about: I didn't point out that Karma's wife had just been sterilized, nor that the chances of Dorze's wife conceiving must now be remote. On this occasion Karma successfully directed Nawang Tsering and Mangal Singh to do the deed; they were both new recruits, and perhaps young enough to be undaunted by fears of the wrath of the deity.

In the morning we all walked together up-valley for a few hours, then Adam and his team turned off to the north while Dorze, Man Bahadur, Mangal Singh and I continued on up the main valley. We estimated it would take us a week or ten days to reach home, depending on whether or not the Rothang Pass was open for traffic.

The old guide-book John and I had read while planning our original route had described the path now ahead of us (the section he and I had missed) as hazardous, because many of the 'galleries' built out along the rock faces had rotted. Adam, a veteran of many a Himalayan tight corner, had walked this way a few years before and written, 'There are many places where one has to rely on footholds alone. A slip here would put one straight into the river, from which one would not emerge alive. There is constant danger of falling stones.' '*Jhule, jhule,*' Karma waved as we parted: 'Remember about the falling stones. Don't go if it rains and start as early as you can in the morning, before the sun melts the ice that holds them. The cliffs above are high.'

For an hour or two we walked through groves of walnut, alder and ash. Then the valley narrowed. That week turned out to be the most frightening in my life. I suppose the notorious track up the Chandrabhaga might once have been an exhilarating challenge, but something had happened to me, and several times a day I felt my body stiffen with fear. Had I lost my nerve? But it wasn't just me: the hazardous track was unusually dangerous that year. Late in the winter, in March, there had been continuous days of snow, and foot after foot of loose snow had accumulated on the hard-packed winter layer. Then the warm March sun had come out and there had been devastating avalanches; villages hundreds of years old had been destroyed.

There were avalanche cones across the river, and the dammed water had covered precious fields with silt. One of these dams had burst with the force of snow-melt water behind it, and the birchtwig-rope bridge below had been whipped away, isolating the village on the far bank. It had taken the men of the village eight days to remake it. As we rested in silent awe on a narrow shelf colourful with geranium, viola and the parasitic orobanche, two hundred men squeezed past us carrying timber, saws and axes and pulling three lambs. They were on their way to repair a temple which had been destroyed by an avalanche, a thousand feet above. The lambs were to be sacrificed to the deity.

The way became worse: for hours at a time there was no track. The avalanches were not green-white banks of shimmering snow, but turrets, tunnels and caverns of filthy ice and mud. Everything was colourless and grim, like hell. I had never seen anything in the natural world on the scale of this squalor. Massive trees had been brought down, shattered and half-buried in ice and mud; their branches were entwined as though giants had been playing spillikins. It could take us half an hour to cross twenty-five yards, climbing over and crawling underneath the debris. The force of the wind ahead of the avalanches had been so great that it had torn bushes and their clods of roots out of the earth and snapped full-grown trees on the opposite bank as though they were saplings. Had it been man who had caused such devastation, ecologists would have been in an uproar.

Dorze and Mangal Singh were agile and undaunted, always in the right place at the right time, ready to heave and lower the haversacks and me. Man Bahadur was stoical: he wasn't enjoying himself but he didn't complain. I learnt to stop looking ahead (or even behind); what I saw was too frightening. I became inured to lying spread-eagled on rock faces with only toe- and fingernail-holds. I judged the horror of a stretch by whether the fall was straight into the river or whether there was a rock, tree, or snow bank that might break my fall. The prospect of being carried for ten days with a broken back left me calm: it was death, annihilation, I was frightened of.

In the late mornings rain threatened. Those terrible scree slopes – one stretch might be pieces of shale the size of peppercorns; the next, large chips which crunched out of place and slipped away as you walked. It was as if a grader had dumped banks of pre-set sizes of gravel. In conditions like these you should lean out, away from the slope, so that your sole has more of a grip, but this is the reverse of your instinct and isn't easy to remember when you are terrified. After the shale there were boulders that lurched and tilted under us. A whirling wind scuttled dust from far above. There were spatters of rain and a horrible sound of falling stones. I remembered Karma's parting exhortation, and that the Gaddi shepherds, so experienced in Himalayan dangers, fear falling stones most of all.

One afternoon we reached a meadow dancing with wild cummin, which smelt delicious after the rain, and colourful with *Euphorbia cognata*. The yellow and orange euphorbia against the lush grass was pure joy after days of colourless squalor. At the foot of the gently sloping meadow there was a hut; it was damp and dirty but it seemed a haven to us. Dorze and Mangal Singh vandalized the rotting floorboards, and the four of us slept in luxurious security round a fire.

Once we were in Lahul we were out of danger. But nature's devastating blows had struck here too. We turned one corner and found a half-blasted village; it might have been bombed. Some of the houses were mounds of rubble, while in other cases one end had been ripped off and the other stood with all three storeys intact, looking like the vertical section of a house plan. Hay that had been stacked on the roofs lay on the ground, in sodden masses half-buried in silt, and precious willow trees were upturned hulks. This year there would be no shortage of fuel in Lahul, but what of the years to come? Many people had lost relations, grain, potato seed and cattle. The avalanches had been swift and arbitrary. A man standing on his roof had had his baby torn from his arms, and never saw it again. 'It was the wind – you hardly heard its whistle, its roar, before it attacked out of nowhere.' And after the wind came the mud, snow and rocks. The industrious Lahulis were at work trying to put things back together; some of the richer ones had hired gangs of Nepalis to clear silt off their fields and rebuild walls. An old man repairing his potato field explained what had happened: 'We'd had it easy for too long. The *kuth* and the potato prices had been too good; we'd become spoilt. The young people don't give respect to the gods, don't even know about them. The gods became angry at being neglected.'

The Rothang was not open to transport, so we had to walk all the way to Koksar, twelve hours along a hot, metalled road. I felt like a tired soldier. Mangal Singh and Dorze were drawn and bad-tempered with hunger, and even Man Bahadur was silent.

At Koksar we celebrated with *arak*: come what may we would cross the Rothang and be home tomorrow. We hadn't talked much during the trip. Now relief and the *arak* revived us, and we spent a convivial evening in a corner of the scruffy hotel, gorging ourselves on platefuls of *momo* and gulping down bottle after bottle of the brownish spirit. Mangal Singh told me then that he remembered my being at his mother's death-feast up at

Hampta village; so he had been one of the sad boys in white tweed jackets. Now he was almost grown up, and was meant to be at college. I wondered if the experience of his first trek had discouraged him from venturing on any more. 'No, I like it – it's better than studying chemistry in the heat down in Bilaspur, and the money is okay. Carrying a load makes your back ache sometimes.' He laughed when I said how frightened I had been. 'I wasn't frightened. If you live in the hills what's the point of being frightened? No one can foresee the moment of death.'

That autumn Raj Krishan sold us the apple crop on four old trees. One brilliantly clear late September afternoon Boura Singh helped Rahul up into the branches to pick the Coxes and Blenheims planted by Mr MacKay, whose contemporaries relished the crisp English varieties; now only the shiny Red and Royal Delicious apples are marketable. Kranti and I filled the sackcloth-lined *kiltas* with fruit for Boura Singh and Sunita to carry. Tara, wearing a too-small T-shirt and a pair of red knickers, filled the child-sized *kilta* on her back and staggered up to the house. The sky was very blue, there was a sprinkle of new snow on the hilltops, and the leaves were beginning to turn.

Leaving Duff Dunbar

When we went to bid our autumn farewell to Pandit Balak Ram he mentioned that from next year he might want to live at Duff Dunbar himself. It seemed highly improbable that he really intended to live there, as his Katrain house was well appointed and Duff Dunbar would be a long way from his family and farm. We assumed that he wanted to assert once again the insecurity of our position as tenants. He and Raj Krishan had continually emphasized that our rent only covered eight months of each year. From time to time we resolved to buy or build a house of our own, but nothing we looked at ever matched Duff Dunbar.

During that winter in England we had a telegram from Raj

Krishan telling us that the house had been broken into. A letter followed: not much had been taken, he said, and nothing from the store of valuable trekking equipment. He had reported the incident to the police. We weren't seriously worried, and there was little we could do from London anyway.

On our arrival in April none of the men mentioned anything unusual when they met us in the bazaar. But as we came through the gates and up through the orchard I suddenly had a feeling there was something wrong. Walking up the path we saw that the doors on to the veranda were open and someone's clothes were out on the line. Old Gungru was waiting by the house, looking shifty and doleful.

His message was that we could use the ground floor – the sitting room and the dining-room store – for one month, but by 15 May we must have moved everything out. In the meantime we were allowed the shared use of our bathroom, which we could reach up the stone stairs at the back. Raj Krishan had given the front-door keys to Sheru, infamous king of Manali's drug trade, and let the house to him for a year.

Sheru and his English girlfriend were sleeping in our bedroom: we could hear them above us. One morning I met the girlfriend coming up from the garden with lettuces in her hand, and when I told her they were ours she stuck out her tongue. There was a junkie sleeping in Rahul's little bed, among the Beatrix Potter books and the hangings of clowns, and the children's postcards from their grandmother had been ripped off the wall.

After a day or two a shamefaced Gungru let slip what had happened. Raj Krishan himself had broken the upstairs lock, gone in, stolen a few of our possessions – like the children's silver *thalis* and cups – and thrown things about. Then he had gone to the police station to register a case: *his* house had been broken into and robbed. As the burglary took place during the four months not covered by our rent, the house and its contents were technically his: that was what he had wanted to establish in the eyes of the law.

We assumed he and his father had felt our continuing tenancy threatened their possession of Duff Dunbar. We had originally drawn up a contract but they had never signed it. Because we had none and because our five-year residence had not been continuous – interrupted as it was by the four vacant months each year – we had no legal standing.

To me Raj Krishan's behaviour was incomprehensible. Why had he not said plainly and clearly that he wanted us to go? He was meant to be a friend. Kranti developed a bad back and lay on the sofa in the sitting room, where all four of us had to sleep and live. Only Boura Singh shared my heated indignation. In his eyes the behaviour of Raj Krishan and his father was outrageous because they were dignitaries in the valley, because they were Brahmins, and because Raj Krishan was a politician: on every count they should have been setting an example of how to behave. None of their fellow dignitaries offered us help, or even sympathy. We were outsiders.

We sent a telegram to my mother saying that we were coming home to Scotland; at this stage of the season, and at such short notice, there were no houses available to rent in Manali. Our belongings were to be stored across the river in a policeman's room.

It took days to transport everything. We were dismantling a home, not just moving a jeep and trailer full of belongings as we had when we arrived. We had trekking equipment for over thirty people, cider casks, a walk-in cupboard full of pickles, jam and tinned food, the house and furniture the *mistri* had made for the children, the dehydrating machine, books and beds and cupboards, not to speak of the chickens, Gopali, Gopal and – our new pride and joy – a new heifer calf called Daisy.

Beautiful spring weather made the situation all the more painful. One day we took a few hours' break from packing, and picnicked up at the big rock above the house that the children called 'Indugarama'. They believed it to be a magic spot where all the good things you couldn't get in India might materialize – Weetabix, Ribena, fish fingers, strawberries and cream. Sometimes they even spotted their grandmother weeding over by the young deodars, or their cousin making a dam in the corner of the stream. Kullu Lama carried up the mundane reality of our

147

picnic – stuffed *parathas*, hard-boiled eggs and a *thali* of Boura Singh's hot *pakora* – and sat down beside us in the long grass. He said, 'Don't worry. Whatever happens, whatever they have done to you about the house, we think you are good people.'

We gave the chickens to the hospital *chaukidar* who had looked after them during the winters. Gopal was sold to a Lahuli who thought that with a specially-made yoke he could be used to plough; sooner or later he would have had to be sold. But Gopali and Daisy represented the permanence of our Manali life, in the way that dogs represent a home. Old Renu, the lead drummer in Hadimba's band, came one morning because he had heard we would be selling the cows, and named a pitiful price. I was annoyed by his presumption and offended by his paltry offer. By now Gopali was svelte and filling the brass pail with frothing milk both morning and evening; and the dish-faced, golden Daisy, being three-quarters Jersey, would be even more desirable than her mother. I had made sure that, unlike her brother Gopal, she was trained from birth to drink from a pail and received adequate milk. Renu came back the next day with a slightly higher offer; we were obliged to accept. I cried as we watched Gopali and Daisy being led off down the path.

The next morning Rahul, who had always admired Gopali and adored Daisy, came bounding into the room crying, 'They are back, they have come back home, Gopali and Daisy.' Renu wanted his money back. Intrepid *shikari* he might be, but Gopali had terrified him: she had viciously kicked him and his wife when they tried to milk her. At least Gopali understood loyalty. Joyfully we handed all Renu's money back. We decided we would give both mother and calf to Karma, who had a corner of orchard where he could keep them. If in the future we had somewhere to keep a cow, it was agreed that we could have Daisy back, but Gopali would remain his.

We left Duff Dunbar early in the morning after Hadimba's *mela*. I was angry with her too: we had honoured and respected her with enthusiasm and entrusted Rahul and Tara to her protection, but it seemed she had turned her back on us. Gungru and his old bent wife came to say goodbye, with folded palms and good wishes. There was nothing they could have done: they had worked for Raj Krishan for decades. Rahul and Boura Singh had to be called away from an early-morning game of hide-and-seek behind the hen-house. They drove down in the jeep while I walked through the forest with Karma, Gopali and Daisy, feeling that with them went my short-lived enthusiasm for domesticity.

If we hadn't felt responsible for our men and their families we might have retreated to the predictable, trusting world of Scotland and London and never returned. As it was, we resolved never again to be at the mercy of a landlord: we would acquire our own roof.

IV
THE WEB

Enmeshed

The children stayed on in Scotland. We could hardly abandon clients who had booked holidays, nor our employees, so Kranti and I came back in July and huddled for the rest of that summer and autumn in a Tourist Department 'cottage'. For the following season we rented a newly built, damp house on the developed side of the Dunghri forest – and then I found myself living once again at Gulab Das's. Twelve years had gone by since my first season as a trekking organizer, when I had lived here on the top floor. This time we rented the entire house and the kitchen, which was a separate building at the front, on a three-year contract. Gulab Das's property now belonged to his brothers and his two widows. The whining old man himself had taken a new wife, a twenty-year old girl from Sial village, fathered a child, sunk into a gloomy madness, and died.

Although he was dead the house continued to be known as 'Gulab Das's'. The public road still ended at its orchard gate but it was no longer as secluded as it used to be. Gulab Das's brothers had sold a plot of land to a Punjabi. Dozens of labourers from Bihar were constructing a five-storey hotel just below the gate, and our privacy was often invaded by tourists strolling up our track from other burgeoning new hotels round the log huts.

The place was adequate. The veranda was only a passage, too narrow to sit on, so instead we sat out on the paved yard by the kitchen, on *charpois* shaded by the apple trees. There was no feeling of space round the house and no garden, for the land fell steeply through the orchard down to the Manalsu *nala*. Our bedroom and the visitors' room ran the breadth of the house at

151

either end. Because the house was built into a steep bank, the back of each of these two rooms was at ground level – you could almost reach out to the tufts of rice – while the front was on an upper storey. The children slept in a tiny inner room off ours, and the inner room off the visitors' room was my office. Downstairs were a low-ceilinged sitting room and some poky, damp store rooms. The house was built into a rock which jutted into the downstairs bathroom; when you sat on the lavatory you could rest your feet on it. The cramped rooms leading off from each other, separated only by wooden partitions, didn't allow for privacy. The house was a far cry from Duff Dunbar. I didn't think of it as our home: it was merely useful as an interim dwelling.

The three years we spent at Gulab Das's saw the business flourish and make a real profit. The seeds sown in the early years had been carefully nurtured, and we now had our own office in London; we were a success. But I felt like a spider enmeshed in the web that I had spun myself. The organization didn't depend entirely on me, but if I vanished it would jeopardize holidays, some booked a year in advance, and undermine the security of our employees and all their families. If I tore my way out of the web I would destroy what I had spent all these years creating.

On crisp autumn evenings I would escape to the big southeast-facing rock below the Lahuli cow-expert's orchard and sit there clenching my fists in an effort to summon self-control. I determined to buckle down and do what had to be done for the benefit of the whole – as a good Hindu should. I would be a cheerful mother and a tolerant wife, I would count tins of sardines and list tents that needed new zips with a good grace, and I would listen with concerned patience to clients' questions and criticisms.

I wasn't consistently successful. I would be caught unawares: the sounds of echoing *mela* trumpets and drums turned me into a melting jelly of sobs.

Sunita had spent two winters with us in London when her mother came to say that this year she wanted her to spend the winter learning to weave. 'When she marries and has children it will be good for her to have something she can do at home, so she can earn money for herself; you can't see into the future.'

When we were back at Gulab Das's the following spring she was meant to come every morning. The children would wait for her but some mornings she never appeared or, without offering any explanation, her mother came in her place (she was embarrassed, and I knew it meant that she lost a day's wages on a building site). Boura Singh sniggered and said that Sunita had strayed from 'the proper path'. I was upset. We had paid her well, appreciated her considerable talent, given her responsibilities and opportunities, and become very fond of her. In India you are always being warned that if you are too good to servants 'they'll only take advantage of you'. I didn't want to think that of Sunita. We were baffled. A few months passed and then her mother sheepishly explained what had happened: during the winter in the weaving shed Sunita had fallen in love with a Kullui weaver. The family had done its best to divert her, to arrange a marriage for her with someone from her own community; even a rich Khampa family down at Bajaura had been willing to take her because she had been abroad and was 'smart'. But she had refused. The Kullui boy's family was not pleased either, but ultimately both sides agreed to honour the 'love marriage' with a formal ceremony.

We had just acquired a telephone; a ping of its bell had us all running. A few days after Sunita's mother had delivered her news Kullu Lama rang from the petrol pump. He shouted so loudly that I might have heard him without the telephone: would we come to Sunita's marriage at ten o'clock tomorrow morning? Boura Singh considered it too informal an invitation; he said there should have been a printed card with coloured edges.

The wedding was held at Sunita's home, across the river below Vashist village. In front of the house was a low-roofed tent made of dazzling white parachute material. Here sat the women and children and a few shabby Zanskari men with vacant expressions. The men and the more important women sat round an open-ended room at the back of the house, where the party was in full swing. Sunita's mother and sister were filling glasses with beer and whisky as well as *chang*. The bridegroom was slumped at the far end of the circle. He and his pale-blue 'terrycot' trousers both looked the worse for wear. I hoped he might be more prepossessing when sober.

Mrs Karma, these days a teetotaller (because her children complained that after a wedding she couldn't do any work, not even milk Gopali), sat demure and slightly disapproving in her sobriety. But the rest of the women were determinedly having a good time; their shiny brocade suits were splattered with the white stains of *chang*. Mrs Dorze, by now matronly and definitely a *barri memsahib*, was handsomely bejewelled. Mrs Chamba was being thwarted in her efforts to enjoy herself by the antics of her second son, already an active toddler. Kullu Lama took over as *chang*-pourer and made slow and increasingly unsteady progress. All our men were helping as cooks, servers or organizers; in their red tartan shirts they might have been uniformed attendants from a catering company.

We found Sunita secluded in the kitchen. Cool, calm and self-assured as always, she was demurely made-up and had a *sindur* in the parting of her hair. She wore a discreetly patterned 'terrycot' *salwar chemise* and a necklace made of corals and pearls; she had bought it with her weaving wages, she said. Surrounded by bundles of babies, she seemed to be the baby-sitter, rewinding their swaddling cloths and rocking them to sleep while their mothers enjoyed themselves. Against the wall stood a shiny new attaché case. Tara went through the bride's trousseau: neatly folded new *salwar chemises*, a needle case we had once given her, eau de cologne, Bromley Fern soap and a box of lemon-shaped soaps which she must have saved from her visits to London, a silk scarf my sister had given her at Christmas in Scotland, and a pair of china candlesticks she had bought in the post office in Camden. Tara volunteered to help look after the babies; she wanted to stay close to Sunita.

The bride's mother insisted we should sit in the bedroom. Like the kitchen it was papered with newspapers for winter insulation, and for today it had been turned into a shrine room. Two lamas sat on a *charpoi*, intermittently mumbling prayers. The shrine was decorated with flowers and *tsampa* figures, and there was a tinted photograph of the Dalai Lama with a garland of marigolds round the frame. There were silver bowls of holy water, *agarbatti* sticks, burning juniper, and a sheep's leg standing upright with its sharp end wedged in a tin of rice. This was decorated with a swastika (the symbol of good luck) in *ghi* and *tsampa* 'icing', and a flagpole with red, white and green prayer flags was stuck in the top end of it.

Sunita's mother came to escort us to the feast. She looked weary and anxious; her husband, an unusually tall and rather taciturn Ladakhi, left all the running of household and family to her. The feast was served outside. The guests sat in rows that ran parallel to the valley; my eye ran along the line of colourful people and on up towards the Solang range, where recently fallen snow shone as white as the parachute tent. My appetite for mixed *dal*, cabbage, noodles, meat and rice had been dulled by much too much *chang*; I had had more than a cupful with every group and from every server's kettle.

Sunita, faceless under shawls, was escorted to the parachute tent to sit between her husband and her parents. Two *thalis* of rice were set down, one in front of each couple, and we queued up to present our gifts. Karma was the clerk, noting down the givers and their gifts. Kullu Lama was meant to be the master of ceremonies, but *chang* had got the better of him and Prem had to take over. 'One "cotswool" suit and twenty-one rupees from Rigzin, *jhule*; one pressure cooker, Prestige, and fifty-one rupees from Sahib and Memsahib, *jhule*; one shawl merino, one shawl *pashmina* and a sewing machine to arrive next week from the bride's parents, *jhule*.' A white scarf was given to the happy couple with each present. When they began to look stifled Sunita's mother would take off a handful and pass them back to Prem to be used again. Half of each sum of money given was placed on the *thali* of rice in front of Sunita and her husband, and half on her parents' *thali*. When the last guest had made his offering, Sunita and her mother counted their money and Karma

155

presented a tally of his accounts: 'If I have made any mistake I ask you to forgive me; too much *chang* in the hot sun.'

I too was beginning to feel the worse for wear, and Boura Singh had passed out – he was found lying beside the jeep on the road. But we weren't allowed to leave. We were led back into the shrine room with the lamas, the bride, the groom, their parents and an old Zanskari. The lamas began to chant. One of them clashed the cymbals while the other beat a gong hanging from the ceiling by a wire. The oldest lama held a bell in one hand and the leg of mutton in the other and waved each three times in front of the bride, three times in front of the groom. Next he took a kettle of *chang* and filled Sunita's cup, then her husband's, three times. Each time the bride and the groom had to 'say something nice' before they drank; I had a feeling we were meant to add an appropriate homily. The lama concluded the ceremony by addressing the now very woebegone groom: 'We have reared and cherished this girl; you must look after her with love and care.'

We moved outside. A brazier of smoking juniper was carried in front of the newly married couple. The groom was crumpled and unsteady on his feet. Sunita (still faceless) and her mother and father were all sobbing. Tara clutched a corner of Sunita's shawl as we made our way down the steep path to the waiting taxi. Before she squeezed in with her parents-in-law, Sunita lifted a corner of the shawl and pressed her face to Tara's. Then the car sped off to the groom's village down the valley. Tara was disconcerted by the sobs. In her view a girl's wedding day was meant to be the happiest in her life, and she was unconvinced by the suggestion that maybe Sunita wasn't really unhappy, but her tears were a way of showing gratitude and respect to her parents. 'Well I'll never leave home and I won't get married in India.'

Rahul and Tara were upset that Sunita had left but her role in our household was soon filled.

Man Bahadur, the elderly Nepali, washed their clothes and doggedly obeyed their commands. He had become attached to us through his adoration for Tara. Although for years he was only paid a daily wage while out on a trek, he chose to turn up at the house every day rather than sit on the kerb in the bazaar with the other Nepalis waiting for coolie work. Even Boura Singh seldom ridiculed him; everyone was softened by his loyal stoicism and sweet nature.

The Manali branch of the DAV (Dayanand Arya Vhikash) had just opened. It was a fee-paying, 'English Medium' school, meaning that all subjects were taught in English. The children began to attend, but they were unimpressed by the teachers. Tara complained that 'The Mams tell you to copy out this and copy out that and then they go away for tea for ages and when they do come back they never look at what you've copied.' Few of the teachers had mastered even conversational English, let alone a standard that might be expected of a teacher. For us the teachers' and pupils' lack of English meant that our children's Hindi benefited. But other parents – shopkeepers, minor Government servants and people like the Garhwali plumber – believed that the considerable financial sacrifice involved in paying for fees, books and formal uniforms was an investment; they assumed they were buying a privileged and English-speaking education which would help to secure employment for their children in the future. In fact the ill-trained and uninterested teachers taught mediocrity, from books that disparaged village life and rustic ways. To her embarrassment Tara found herself to be a teachers' pet; not because she was brilliant or diligent, but because she was pale-skinned, foreign and enviably sophisticated. Sadly, the DAV Manali is not unusual. There is a proliferation of such schools bleeding unfortunate parents all over India.

For Rahul and Tara it was a different world from their Camden primary school, which was dedicated to 'caring and equal opportunities'. The DAV gave them their first taste of moral outrage. While their fellow pupils lived in fear of being caned, Rahul and Tara knew they were safe because the Principal Mam was in awe of us. For the same reason they escaped the 'monkey punishment'. Anyone talking during prayers or failing to wear the regulation handkerchief pinned to his chest was pulled out of the lines at assembly to spend the rest of the morning squatting out in the sun with his arms through his legs, holding on to his ears. But it is lunchtime that lives most vividly in their memories. All the children took tiffin boxes, and before lunch each day the Mams would open them to look for tasty titbits. Rahul's Mam, the wife of the bank manager, was fond of sweets. Luckily for our children none of the teachers wanted the butterless Marmite sandwiches they always chose. If they did have treats – a piece of mango or a biscuit – they soon learnt to hide them in the second levels of their boxes.

Mangal Singh was a help with homework. He was now a part of the household, sharing Boura Singh's room behind the kitchen. We had offered him a permanent job at the end of his first season, after the trip up the Chandrabhaga, but he hadn't turned up in the spring – 'gambling in Kalka' was the rumour. One evening a month or so later, Boura Singh came down to the garden at Duff Dunbar to say, 'That schoolboy has come. He wants to borrow seventy-five rupees. He says he'll go out with the next trek, and have the loan deducted from his pay. He says he's sorry.' Kranti shared Boura Singh's predictable opinion: the boy had failed to keep his word, and they weren't interested in his apologies or promises for the future. I persuaded them both that 75 rupees was not a large amount for us, and that we should give him a chance. Boura Singh was won over and was soon to assume the role of Mangal Singh's moral guardian. For though he painstakingly instructed Rahul and Tara in the pen strokes of the Hindi alphabet and listened to their tables, Mangal Singh had wasted his own educational opportunity, running away from home and abandoning a college scholarship. From time to time his father would appear, urging us to hand over his son's pay lest it should be squandered.

As well as helping with the homework Mangal Singh provided entertainment. He taught Tara to dance round the kitchen *chulha* while he sang, and showed Rahul how to play *sip*, a card game that entailed intricate arithmetic.

But it was Boura Singh who was the underpinning presence in the children's and all our lives. At Gulab Das's we woke as the wire-mesh doors from the veranda swung shut and he arrived with the bed-tea tray. If Rahul's hot milk wasn't frothy enough Boura Singh would pour it from glass to glass to make it frothier. It was he who made sure the children ate their chapatti-and-milk breakfast and who packed their Marmite sandwiches. And in the evening round the *chulha* it was he who teased them as he cooked their supper, rocking back on his stool as he anticipated the joke. Rahul was developing a fondness for money, and often frequented a shop in Manu market which sold comic books recounting the stories of Hindu heroes. Boura Singh had only to make a veiled reference to the Punjabi shopkeeper's daughter in 'Money' market to have Rahul running round the *chulha* scarlet with rage. Another of his recurring teases was the question of Rahul's marriage prospects. If it was to be an arranged marriage in Bihar, within the proper caste, how much money could he expect as a dowry? If he agreed to take on a well-to-do bride with some disability then the dowry price would escalate. Boura Singh suggested he might get 25 lakh rupees for a midget, and wondered how much he would get for one with no legs? Then he would double up with laughter while the pancake on the *tawa* burnt.

I had never quite forgiven Hadimba Devi for our eviction from Duff Dunbar, and at Gulab Das's we were some way away from her temple and the Dunghri forest. But we did still think of ourselves as belonging to her parish; it would have been odd suddenly to sever all contact with a world that had been so familiar.

During our first season at Gulab Das's we were kept in touch with Dunghri through Gungru, the old *chaukidar*, who came every day with our milk. I never discovered how the purchase had been funded but he had acquired a Jersey heifer. His visit filled a regular time after breakfast and before morning coffee, when he would sit on the kitchen doorstep (he never came into the kitchen lest his untouchability should pollute it) and tell Boura Singh, and us, the Dunghri gossip.

When the Jersey heifer had calved, Gungru's pleasure had

been marred by a cruel blow. The *chaukidarin*, proud and excited about the happiest event in their lives for many years, had gone down to milk the cow for the first time. The old woman was later found where she had fallen in the cow shed, and from then on she couldn't get up. Gungru called in the lamas (the Harijans did sometimes go to the Buddhist lamas for help) but, though they chanted prayers for several days, and though she also had medicine from the Lahuli *vaidya*, her condition didn't improve.

One day he accepted my offer to take her to the mission hospital. It seemed unlikely that much could be done for her but I was pleased to be able to try and help. Dunghri forest was velvety in the sun after rain. Every bend and rut in the track was familiar and I enjoyed the challenge of driving the jeep at the steep banks. The *chaukidar* and his three sheep and the cow were standing at the Duff Dunbar gate with the evening sun behind them, as I had seen them so many times before, on their way home from the orchard. The *chaukidarin* was dressed up for the occasion in a pair of new pale-pink pyjamas under her *pattu*.

The doctor at the hospital confirmed that she had had a stroke, and that there was nothing to be done, and I took her home. The old man helped her up on to the veranda, wrapped her in blankets against the chill of the evening, and lowered her on to the veranda floor, propped up against the wall. He himself huddled in a shabby, woman's coat, bought from a second-hand stall in the Tibetan market, and slumped down. A niece brought tea. The old couple didn't rage or moan against their fate; they simply sat there on the veranda and waited for the end with equanimity.

Gungru continued to supply our milk, but by the following year Man Bahadur had to collect it every morning for the old man was housebound; his niece took the cow and sheep to graze in the orchard. One morning Man Bahadur arrived saying that Gungru had died in the night and we should go to his house now for they were about to take the body to the *ghat*. As Kranti, Boura Singh and I made our way through the forest I realized how much I would miss the *chaukidar*; he had been a constant if undramatic character in our lives for so long.

On several of the Dunghri houses the yellow patterns round the doors and above the windows had recently been painted (with deodar pollen and yoghurt), but not on Gungru's. A few sombre-faced people crouched outside. Three dishevelled women were struggling to change the *chaukidarin*'s clothes: two held her up while the third tried to disentangle her grimy feet from her pyjama legs. At last she was ready. The men helped her towards the bier, where she sank to the ground and had to be supported again to place a cone of *dhup* (incense) on a coconut and light it. 'There should be three,' someone murmured, 'but it won't matter.' She was heaved towards her husband's body, and her withered old hands touched his feet. She barely had the strength to scatter the ritual coins. The women wailed and shouted directions to the corpse for a safe journey. Then the widow was bundled up and carried back to the house, while the village boys scrambled for the scattered money.

The bier, covered with an orange cloth, set off soundlessly through the forest. There were no drums or trumpets, nor hardly a procession; the few mourners, each carrying a log of wood, made their way behind the temple and down towards the *ghat*.

By now we had fifteen regular employees. They were expected to turn up at the house at nine o'clock to spend the morning repairing the tents, washing sleeping bags, cutting vegetables for drying, and attending to the various maintenance tasks. Apart from Boura Singh, the only non-Buddhists among them were Man Bahadur and Bihari Lal, who was from Kangra.

No Kullui ever joined our permanent staff. There was one bright young boy who said at the end of a season that he wanted to join us, but the following spring he told us he had been married, so it wouldn't be suitable for him to go into the mountains any more. Few Kulluis relish the adventure of trekking – 'What if the weather is bad when we're up on the pass?' – and their desire for a regular pay packet isn't a strong enough incentive for them to go in search of work, or to keep to it once found. The majority of those in the valley who were becoming increasingly prosperous – shopkeepers, hoteliers, or-

161

chard owners and contractors, skilled craftsmen like plumbers and masons – were not Kulluis but incomers – Lahulis, Khampas, Tibetans, Punjabis and Kangris. Inevitably the Kulluis feel resentful, but they are unwilling to make the connection between endeavour and success.

In our second season at Gulab Das's we took on two more men: Nawang and Panchok, both Zanskaris. Nawang was methodical and sturdy, a middle-aged man of few words; he was the Zanskari equivalent of Man Bahadur. Panchok was a cousin of Chamba's, though physically they had nothing in common; in contrast to Chamba, with his round face and rolling gait, Panchok was aquiline-featured, skinny and agile. He was another bright young man whom we encouraged, with an absolute lack of success, to learn the rudiments of reading and writing.

We first met him in Zanskar. I had recovered from my loss of nerve on the Chandrabhaga trip, and to escape the monsoon the children and I had accompanied a party as far as Testha; from there we were to turn back home while the trek went on to Leh. The two days in Testha turned out to be traumatic. Kullu Lama had been found lying immobile in the shade of a willow. It was not, as we all assumed, the result of overindulging in Testha's hospitality: the trek doctor diagnosed a slipped disc. The patient had to be abandoned lying flat on his back at Mrs Dorze's father's house. He sobbed like a child, convinced he would never see us again. 'Poor fellow,' Dorze commented disparagingly, 'he has a very small heart.'

I would have liked to have been going on north, over the high passes, and my homeward-bound party didn't inspire confidence. It consisted of Boura Singh, never at his best at high altitudes; Sunita's mother, standing in for her daughter and not enjoying her first trekking experience; and a timorous, fussy old pony man.

That evening a traveller strolled into camp, alone, on his way from Padam back to Manali: Panchok. When I asked him to join us, he readily agreed, and from the beginning conveyed an air of cheerful confidence.

The Shingo La, the main route into Zanskar from Lahul, is an unpleasant pass. It isn't particularly high, at just under 17,000 feet, but it is squalid and sordid and lacks grandeur. Michel Peissel described it as '. . . a frigid hell rather than the abode of the gods; the only beauty was the eerie silence in which one could hear, as it were, the creeping of nature and feel the slow formation of the mountains, the primeval thrust of creation.'[5] Tara must have been less impressed. None of us noticed that she had fallen asleep in the saddle, and when her pony stumbled on the rocky debris of the glacier she fell. Panchok, just ahead, turned with a lightning reflex and caught the three-year-old bundle as she tumbled headfirst towards a raw-edged rock. 'It was lucky I fell just there,' she commented, 'because as I was falling I saw a blue poppy among the rocks.'

Without Panchok we would never have persuaded the timorous pony man to attempt the river crossings. All the way from Testha he had frightened Boura Singh and Sunita's mother with hair-raising warnings of how dangerous the rivers were, and when we reached the first one he pointed out the spot where two French girls had drowned the week before. Panchok, stripped to his underpants, leapt into the stream to steady the bridle of my pony. Tara sat on the pommel of my saddle, and Rahul's reliable mount plunged in behind us: the children hung on to the ponies' manes and squealed with excitement as their steeds lurched and the glacial water lapped their feet. Boura Singh and Sunita's mother, shamed into having to let their pony follow the others, clutched each other on their shared saddle and shut their eyes.

During my first years as an employer I had paid the four permanent men the same small monthly salary for eight months of the year and fifteen rupees a day when they were out on a trip. Later the daily payment was dropped; it was hardly fair, as it was we who decided who went on a long trek through Zanskar and who went on a short saunter up Jugatsukh *nala*. Instead we increased everyone's monthly wage. When a year or two later there were seven or eight permanent employees, their salaries still remained equal, on the egalitarian basis that they all in their various capacities worked equally hard. Then, when trekking organizers from Delhi and Nepal began to come to Manali looking for guides and porters, it was obvious that the bright young English-speakers like Karma, Prem and Mangal Singh could demand a higher rate in the marketplace than the Man Bahadurs or the Nawangs. We felt obliged to reward those who had organizational skills and who shouldered responsibility; indeed, Panchok would only agree to join us if he was paid more than old Nawang, recruited at the same time.

Kranti explained what we expected of the team. 'We think of everyone as part of a family, and anything might be expected of you at any time. We expect the more responsible members [meaning those who were paid more] to be more conscientious and to look after others as an older brother might.' Karma and Boura Singh (who bore responsibility for the household) were to be paid the highest salaries; the rest were to be paid on a decreasing scale. Egalitarianism was over.

The men had developed a pride in the organization and were anxious that clients should have a good time. They weren't obsequious or sweet-talking; they showed their concern in the way they cheerfully served food in pouring rain, willingly helped an ungainly woman across a single-log bridge, and made bed tea in the freezing pre-dawn before a party crossed a high pass. Their unforced attention to the clients' welfare sprang from their innate sense of good manners rather than from our directives. We were aware that the team was the organization's most vital asset and that it was essential to retain it. The men must be well paid. Soon their salaries were on a scale rarely equalled outside the big cities. If any one of them should become disgruntled and feel inclined to look for alternative employment it was highly unlikely that he would find another job at a comparable wage. We bound them to us.

I could remember, but only just, how when I first stayed at Gulab Das's I had had so much time that I sat about waiting for something to happen. Nowadays, every moment of the day was apportioned. Letters to my mother became short accounts of the antics of her grandchildren and my occasional diary entries took the form of brief notes:

The apricot blossom is a vivid pink on bare branches. Strips of green winter wheat emerge between the snowdrifts, but higher up, the snow is still deep enough to soften the sharp edges of the hills towards the Rothang. There are piles and piles of building stones on the flat ground on the far side of the Manalsu river, where the new 'motor' bridge is to be built: everyone is building guesthouses and hotels.

Gyal Chand, the pony man, came through the kitchen door at breakfast this morning, his Lahuli coat slung rakishly over one shoulder. He had been married during the winter, he said (until then he had been sharing his brothers' wife), and is building a house. He wants a loan against what his ponies will earn from us this season. He brought three eggs for the children, warm from the chest-pouch of his coat.

Boura Singh says that his cousin Raju's wife has died in childbirth. 'It was her mother's doing. She's the one who is a witch. It was her doing that our buffaloes were killed, and she got one to gore Raju's mother. Raju has had to go home to get the evil spells destroyed. It won't be easy. Even people who quarrel with ordinary neighbours or relations often go mad because the enemy hides a dangerous potion somewhere in their house – bat's claws, maybe. But a real witch, like this one, is much cleverer and more dangerous. Even the *deotas* can't help; they don't know where to look for the hidden spells.'

The old loony, who has been around here for years, gets increasingly decrepit. If you didn't know about him and met him in the dark he would scare the wits out of you – long black tresses, a long, greasy, colourless coat tied at the waist with a piece of cord which has rags hanging from it. He wanders through the forest and round the village. People usually ignore him, though occasionally boys jeer and throw pebbles, but Gulab Das's old dog goes berserk when he comes up our path. Boura Singh is delighted by it: 'Dogs know who is who. We used to have a dog that could tell a Harijan by the smell. Even if the man was well dressed the dog barked because it knew that he was a Harijan underneath.

Karma told me that at the end of the autumn, when we've left Manali and the men have their pay, they all contribute towards a party. If during the past season any one of them has crossed a new pass, he has to give an extra twenty or twenty-five rupees. There's whisky, beer, a whole sheep, salad and *chutni*, and everyone cooks. Last year it went on for two days and nights.

When we left Duff Dunbar we abandoned our tradition of a Dunghri *mela*-day lunch. This year, inspired by Karma's description of the end-of-season festivities, we decided to have a picnic instead. We chose a grassy *maidan* partly shaded by prickly oak, *Quercus glauca*; it was a ten-minute scramble up the hill behind the house.

The morning of the party dawned sparkling blue and snowy white; whistling thrushes and cuckoos sang loud and clear, and orange-spotted butterflies hovered over the gentians. An axe and a chopper, *dekchis*, kettles, oil, vegetables, glasses, *thalis*, rice, *dal* and Tara's dolls were all carried up the hill in *kiltas*. Kullu Lama and Nawang dug troughs for three *chulhas* in a connecting row, so that fire could pass from one to the other. Dorze engineered a water supply by diverting the stream in an irrigation ditch into a concave piece of wood which formed a spout. Chamba and Tara collected twigs and fir cones to make a fire for the first cup of tea; and soon afterwards Man Bahadur and Panchok, who had set off at half-past five that morning, arrived carrying loads of firewood from high up in the forest.

Below the *maidan* a ploughman was coaxing and shouting at a pair of bullocks hock-deep in mud, preparing a rice seedbed. On the south-facing slopes above the Hampta *nala*, rocks and black promontories were beginning to emerge from the snow. The light was so strong that I could see the scars where rocks had rolled down the snow-slopes four or five miles away and had to blink once or twice to refocus on the violet beside me.

Lama Le and Panchok sat on the grass peeling potatoes and shelling peas. Karma arrived with fifteen kilos of meat and two twenty-litre jerry cans of *chang* which he had brought to the road end in a jeep. He and Kullu Lama found two logs to use as butcher's boards and hewed a stirring spoon from a willow branch. A vat of salt tea was brewed to sustain us as we worked. Bihari Lal, cross-legged in front of a flat rock, spent hours grinding spices, garlic, ginger and chillies. Chamba and Nawang sieved the *chang* through a striped nylon shopping bag to remove the worst of the lumps and debris. Tara and I hid Easter eggs. We had hard-boiled eggs, some dyed bright blue with a powder bought in the bazaar, others dyed orange and yellow with onion skins, and little chocolate ones, speckled like real birds' eggs, which I had brought from London. We hid them in nests among the spiky oak leaves and the clumps of berberis.

At about midday the women and children began to arrive. Kullu Lama's wife and Mrs Nawang the Gaddini were first; Mrs Nawang brought morel mushrooms she had found in the forest on the way. Dorze's wife came with her nephew, the son of the *Thakur* of Testha. Prem escorted his wife and son, born soon after the stillborn baby and now a tubby two-year-old, and the ravishing Mrs Teshi, with her six-week-old daughter swaddled on her back.

We had met Sunita in the bazaar a day or two before; she had been spending a few days at her parents' home and agreed to stay on to attend the picnic. She brought her brothers, Tsampal and little Dorze, presents of mangoes and cakes and a jug filled with pink-striped wild tulips. She looked blooming and elegant in a grey Tibetan tunic. Karma's wife, even more elegant, was dressed in a green brocade *salwar chemise*, and her children too were immaculate. They brought a bottle of beer for Kranti and a bunch of bananas for the children.

Chamba's family, making slow progress up the hill, was the last to arrive. Boura Singh commented, 'By next year you'll need a taxi to get here, or maybe a Tourist Department bus.' By now Tsering Dolma, the pot-bellied toddler of my early years in India, was an almost grown-up girl of fifteen, prettier than the surviving twin, who was still scarred from her TB. Chamba Tanjin, the first-born son, was an exact replica of his father, and the fourth child was an energetic boy of two and a half. Mrs Chamba, despite all her trials, looked as blossoming, full-cheeked and handsome as she had done ten years before.

The women and children spread themselves out at the far end of the *maidan*, away from the kitchen. We served both sweet and salt tea and shared out the cakes, mangoes, bananas and biscuits. Chamba suggested we begin on the *chang*. He filled the kettle and put blobs of butter on the lid and spout, then he and I, soon joined by Boura Singh, settled under an oak below the women and children. Initially they were too bashful to come down, but a few drops of rain provided an excuse for them to join our circle in the shelter of the tree. Kullu Lama's wife and Nawang's accepted glasses of their own; the rest pretended they weren't drinking but took sips from other people's. Panchok or Kullu Lama would bring us snacks of 'half-fried' liver, potatoes and peas, served on scraps of newspaper, and join us for a few minutes and a quick glass of *chang*. Everyone was determined Boura Singh should be well looked after; '*Suka suka pio!*' they urged, and refilled his glass to the brim.

The children wanted to eat in the red mess tent which had been brought up when rain threatened. They scuttled to form a cross-legged line round three sides of it and tucked into *thalis* piled with rice, meat in a rich dark gravy, salad, vegetables and *chutni*. Everyone else, except for the chief cooks and waiters and Kranti, who was drinking his beer, made a wide circle on the grass and gorged themselves. Then Karma's wife and I had the easy job of serving the cooks and waiters while the other women washed dishes and laid out gleaming, neat rows of *thalis*, glasses, lids, *dekchis* and spoons.

The children were playing with Tara's dolls in a pink-striped toy tent made by Kullu Lama. Rahul, Panchok, Mangal Singh and Dorze's nephew settled to a serious game of cards. The rest of us formed a large circle round the *chang*. An empty jerry can was handed to Sunita to use as a drum. On the grassy bank behind us bundles of sleeping babies wrapped in patterned shawls lay scattered round the vase of striped tulips. There were calls for a song: who would be the first to perform? At last Chamba, complaining, staggered to his feet and pulled a shawl off Kullu

Lama's wife. Binding it into a bedraggled turban round his head he began a Punjabi act, crouching and jumping and gesticulating angrily. Then Boura Singh, suffering from everyone's attentions with the *chang* kettle, was prevailed upon to sing a Garhwali song, on condition that we promise not to laugh. (Tara, who had nestled in beside Sunita and the drum, was unable to keep her word.) Karma's children sang a Hindi movie song and Tara 'You Are My Sunshine'.

Karma and Prem began to dance, breaking into a Zanskari song as they twirled their arms to the sky, and the women gustily provided the answering chorus to the verses. Then the women themselves were pulled on to their feet and led into intricate dances by Dorze's and Kullu Lama's wives. Men and women held each other's hands without embarrassment; all except for Boura Singh. He tried to avoid being next to a woman, and he had an anxious moment when he thought he might have to hold my hand. Even when everyone was as relaxed as they were now, there was a difference between the relatively easy-going Buddhists and the touch-me-not fear of the caste Hindu. Chamba was now brimful of party spirit: he made each of the men take a shawl, and led them into complicated movements to a slow beat, twisting and wafting the shawls high above their heads.

The card-players joined us and Mangal Singh took over from a tired Sunita as the drummer. Prem sang a romantic solo, and then Kullu Lama, with a sudden burst of energy, took to the floor and became alternately a ferocious snake and an enraged bull. We were beside ourselves with laughter, rolling about among the sleeping babies.

The sun began to slip behind the hill at our backs and the shadows on the hill opposite were turning a deep blue. Kullu Lama, no longer a charging bull, had collapsed on a lower terrace. The mothers began to bind their children on to their backs. In moments everything was packed into the *kiltas* and all that was left after a day of pleasure for fifty people were the remains of the *chulhas*, a few burst balloons, the odd *biri* stub and some bruised grass and gentians; the crows had long ago flown off with any remaining scraps of food.

I staggered down the hill, contentedly numbed by timeless hours of slow, steady drinking. I hadn't heard anyone giving orders and there hadn't been an acrimonious word, hardly even a tear, all day. The idea of holding a picnic had been mine, but I hadn't envisaged anything on this scale: this was a kind of picnicking that belonged to the Buddhist-Himalayan world and outclassed any I was familiar with. On the way down Chamba kissed me 'for such a good party; I cannot eat for three days.'

I wrote a letter to my mother describing the picnic and was later thankful that I had made the time to do so, for it turned out to be the last proper letter I wrote her. As the trekking season gathered momentum I wrote only short bulletins in reply to her increasingly frail, spidery notes. And that autumn, soon after we reached home, she died.

Land

Our need for land to build on was becoming urgent. Kranti's view was that sooner or later, since everyone knew we wanted to buy, we would be told of a suitable plot, but I thought we should go and search. Until the children went to school, one day had been like any other; now weekends began to exist and we had Sunday outings. We would take a picnic – a humble conventional one of hard-boiled eggs, Marmite sandwiches, *alu parathas*, cucumbers and beer – and drive down-valley, exploring the area and asking passers-by if there was any land for sale. The question never roused an enthusiastic answer. No one wants to sell land in India: those who must, to raise cash for marriages or to pay off crippling debts, are reluctant to admit it.

In upper Kullu there are few large landholdings and few tenant farmers; most cultivators farm their own land, in small strips. When the British took over the administration of Kullu after the first Sikh war in 1846, they showed a British concern for exactitude and fair play (as well as an interest in who would pay the tax on the crop) as they set about establishing who owned every strip and corner. In this way, they reasoned, justice could be seen to be done and future arguments could be settled against recorded facts. The fields were measured chain-length by chain-length and detailed on a map kept by the *patwari*. Any change in ownership had to be approved by the *kanundar*, registered by the *tehsildar* and recorded on the map. This system is still in force today.

Though Kulluis have long lived and tilled their land on a 'joint family' system, an original holding may have been subdivided over several generations; one terraced strip, for instance, may now be owned by several brothers. The precipitous mountain-sides allow little opportunity for new cultivation. Recently there has been a growing tendency for the 'joint family' to break up and divide its land into individual holdings. One brother may decide he wants to sell his share but the *patwari*'s map may still record the entire field in his father's, or even his grandfather's, name. The land cannot be apportioned or sold without the agreement of all the brothers in the family, and the *patwari*, the *kanundar* and the *tehsildar* will require time (and persuasion) before alterations to the records are complete; it can take years.

If we had tried to buy land round Manali during the 1970s, it would have been easier; if we had left it until a few years later, it would have been almost impossible.

During the hundred years that Manali had been marked on the map as 'Duff Dunbar'–1870–1970 – the incoming traders had established themselves in more permanent buildings, but the scale and style of the bazaar hadn't altered dramatically. When I arrived in 1970 tourist accommodation was by and large government-owned – rest-houses, tourist bungalows and 'log' huts. The few privately owned guesthouses were run by descendants of early British settlers or their erstwhile cooks and bearers who had set up on their own. In the vicinity of Manali some well-to-do city dwellers from the plains built themselves holiday houses or bought old houses from British orchard-owners who left after Independence. In recent decades a number of Lahulis had searched out available land to use as winter quarters in the

171

comparatively mild climate of Kullu; grasping opportunity, they invested savings made from *kuth* and seed-potato sales in land for orchards. Then the early 1980s saw an unprecedented demand for fruit, potatoes, timber and holidays. Enterprising locals (but seldom Kulluis themselves) became preoccupied by money, mastering the idea that it can be invested and made to work for you; land remained a popular choice. Encouraged by the tourist boom, and by the government's generous loans for hotel-building, developers from the cities began to acquire whatever land they could.

As the months passed we did see a few available plots; some without access, some without a reliable source of water. We found one stony bank in a good position with an adequate right of way. The man who showed it to us was keen to sell – he wanted money to buy irrigated land for rice elsewhere – but it turned out that the division of land between him and his brother hadn't been registered and the brother had no intention of selling. Next we found a wide swath across the Beas, up beyond Manali. A chilly wind would sweep down from the Solang *nala* but a windbreak could be built or grown; and there was undisputed access along an old mule track. The land belonged to three brothers. Two of them wanted to sell but the third was mad – too mad to sign his name. No one else had the right to sign for him.

I had begun to lose hope when suddenly it seemed that Kranti's theory was to be proved right: we were told that a Mrs Lal (the friend of Mrs Kapur's whose over-familiar servant had been involved in a murder case) wanted to sell some of her large orchard, and that she was only interested in selling to 'the right sort of people'. The orchard was some way down the valley, near Nagar.

We went to look at it and to present ourselves to her. It was a well-established orchard of apples, pears, plums, apricots, cherries and persimmons, spread over wide terraces planted in the 1930s. The valley here is broad and open: you can see away up to the Rothang, even to the holy peaks of Mount Geyphang in Lahul. We sat on the veranda and the notorious servant

172

brought us coffee and biscuits as we discussed contemporary literature. Mrs Lal was a cultured woman of Christian upbringing. She had dressed up for the occasion in a beige toque, dangling earrings, scarlet lipstick and what had once been smart beige trousers. She was bitter that these days, now that she lived alone with her white Alsatians and her out-of-the-ordinary ideas, the Kullui establishment neither visited her nor treated her with the respect to which she had been accustomed. That was partly why she wanted to travel. She wanted to sell some of the orchard so that she could go abroad to her daughter in America, visit London and Paris, and go to the theatre and the opera again. We felt we were a success – she considered us appropriate neighbours. She particularly took to Tara: 'I would like to think of this lovely little girl having half my orchard and living close to me.'

The land was on a different scale from anything we had envisaged. It would be an ambitious investment – we would have to interest others to help finance it – but the orchard, even as Mrs Lal ran it, with minimal maintenance, yielded a handsome revenue. We weighed up the pros and cons. It was twenty-five kilometres from Manali – a long distance to run a business from, and quite a way to expect the men to travel every day. Karma, who was enthusiastic, approving of the investment and the idea of a grand estate, suggested we might build 'quarters' for them. It was a dream-like place; owning it would elevate us to the status of respectable landowners, and when we were too old to trek we could still cultivate our orchard. Yet it was just what I didn't want. I envisaged myself seeing the children off to boarding school because I was tied to the place. I knew I would be responsible for yet more employees, and I thought I might become like Mrs Lal – slightly squalid and bitter, incarcerated in the peaceful beauty of the orchard. But I knew that it was a chance unlikely to come our way again and that it would be madness to let it go.

We decided to raise the money to buy it, and went to tell Mrs Lal just before we left the valley for a week or two. Ten days later we read in the newspaper that she had been found murdered in her orchard. Were we somehow responsible? Had the murderer been motivated by jealousy over the sale agreement? Had the servant felt our presence would interfere with his inheritance? Or was it that the murderer was after cash which he assumed, mistakenly, we had paid as a deposit? I don't know whether the murderer was ever caught, but it was rumoured that one of the contractor's men was responsible for the crime – wanting a large sum of money that the contractor had paid Mrs Lal for the apple crop. The incident dashed our enthusiasm for land-searching, and for a while afterwards any plots we did look at seemed too modest.

Long before, we had asked Mangal Singh's father, who was *pradhan* of Prini village, on the opposite side of the river and a little way down-valley from Manali, to tell us if he heard of land for sale. I had been unenthusiastic about the 'left bank', having always lived on the 'right bank' and enjoyed the benefit of the early-morning sun, but when he sent a message, some time after Mrs Lal's death, that he knew of a possible plot for us, we could no longer afford to be fussy about morning sun; our lease at Gulab Das's was soon to expire.

The plot turned out to be in a perfect position. We sat on a narrow rim between the terraces and admired the view up the Solang *nala* and all the way down the main valley. Though only three kilometres from the bazaar, it was spacious and peaceful here, away from the increasing congestion of buildings and tourists in Manali. Rice terraces stretched down from the foot of the hillside in a gentle slope half a mile wide. The higher fields belonged to Prini village, while much of the lower land was owned by farmers from some distance away – from Manali village and as far up-valley as Palchan, where there was little land that could be irrigated for paddy.

The plot consisted of three narrow strips running with the terraced contour. The only buildings in sight were a Lahuli house just beyond it, Prini village houses a kilometre above, and two Khampa houses on the corner. My anxiety about the morning sun was allayed. The Hampta *nala* to the left and the Prini *nala* to the right cut through the mountains, and the peak in the middle was set back so that the sun would rise over its right shoulder and warm a veranda here just as early as at Sial or Duff Dunbar.

The strip for sale was said to be about twenty *biswas*. It belonged to a Garhwali shop-owner and money-lender who had been settled in Manali for many years. Boura Singh knew him and confirmed our suspicion – that he had accepted the land in lieu of a bad debt. Now he wanted to sell it to raise a dowry for his daughter; but even in these circumstances he was so reluctant for it to be known that he was selling land that we never met. A stream ran past the upper end of the land, so water for bathrooms was assured; drinking water would have to be carried from a spring. The plot was fifty yards above the road, and the *nala* would provide legitimate access (where there is permanently running water there is always a right of way), but there was no verge between the stream and the rice terraces, no room for a path. How would we wade home on a monsoon night, and how would we carry building materials up through a rushing stream? Karma suggested constructing a wooden platform over it; it seemed a promising idea. Once again our hopes were raised.

A few weeks later, on a clear autumn day, Kranti, Rahul, Tara, I, Mangal Singh's father and the *patwari* measured out the land, chain-length by chain-length. It wasn't easy. The drop between each terrace had to be taken into account, the heights of the dividing ridges were all different, and rocks and irregular wedges jutted out of the banks. We spread the *patwari*'s well-worn cloth map on the hump of fallow land beside the stream. Its numbered strips seemed to match those on the ground, and we calculated the area to be twenty-one *biswas*, a fraction more than the estimate. The price agreed was 3,500 rupees a *biswa*.

The following spring, donkey trains began to empty loads of sand and gravel beside the road. A contractor had agreed to deliver stones of a given size, extracted from the river bed, and these too arrived by the truck-load. We had had a wooden platform built over the stream, and initially it was our own men who carried the stones. Each man could only carry two or three at a time, stacked on a piece of sacking on one shoulder or on a wooden back frame made for stone-carrying. Mounds of stones accumulated at the site.

Time passed. We had asked an architect to draw up a plan and budget for a house built in the local style, of stone and timber with a traditional veranda on all four sides; mortar, concrete and plate glass were to be kept to a minimum. Our concessions to modern comfort were an indoor staircase and three bathrooms with 'flush'. In due course the architect had written to say that a model of the projected house was ready for our approval. On a steamy August day I went to a workshop in Old Delhi to be shown the model of a green-roofed villa with split level glazed balconies and flights of angled steps that ran up to suburban, concrete-pillared porches. The plans had to be redone.

The architect was to have sent a clerk of works who would advise, assess estimates, and evaluate completed work, but he didn't appear. Local contractors promised their attention but never turned up. Manali's building boom was gathering momentum, and they were stretched beyond their resources. If we were to hope that the roof would be on before the winter snow it was essential that foundations should be dug before the monsoon began.

We couldn't afford to go on waiting for experts. We pulled up the remains of the winter wheat (to be fed to Gopali) and dug the first clod out of a terrace bank with a pick. The men had summoned a lama and bought a bag of *laddus* (orange balls made of lentil flour and sugar). Karma explained that I should crumble one and scatter it to the north, south, east and west, then offer one to the head mason and some to the rest of us. Once our strip of terracing had been levelled, Karma, the mason and I pegged out the lines of the walls with lengths of taut string. The mason supervised the measuring of the foundations and the work of his stone-chisellers, but he lacked organization or any sense of urgency. It was Karma who initially ran the show; without his energy and competence the house wouldn't have been built that year.

Digging down took weeks. The men dug in pairs, and the further down they dug the more awkward it became to work.

The clay soil, compacted by centuries of rice irrigation, held fast round ancient boulders. We had to summon a professional stone-splitter, who stroked the rock with callused fingers to feel which way the grain went, then unhesitatingly chose the right pick to split it with perfect accuracy down the fault. Before the rains arrived (and before our men had to abandon the site for a trek) the foundations were pronounced deep enough. Now it was Rahul's and Tara's turn to perform the *puja* for the laying of the first stone. This time we used *halwa* rather than *laddus*. Their heads deferentially covered with handkerchiefs, the children stood at the bottom of the trench, obeying the instructions of a very tall, maroon-cloaked lama.

Soon afterwards Karma and I and most of the men were to set off on a trek, but before we left we had lengthy discussions about how we might try to prevent the seeping damp which had been a feature of all the houses we had lived in since Duff Dunbar. We suggested a deep trench along the upper edge of the ground to drain off the water running through the rice terracing, and also a dampcourse, but the mason wasn't convinced that a layer of plastic sheeting would last the life of the house, or prevent rising damp. For the moment we set the problem aside.

A three-week trek to Barabangahal was a relaxing prospect after our day-to-day preoccupation with the building.

Sitting on a rock above the first camp site I thought of how our trekking style had changed over the years. The sun was slipping fast. As it began to dip behind the shoulder of the hill opposite, its horizontal beams became as clearly defined as a searchlight's, throwing the rest of the landscape into obscurity. Half an hour earlier the hillside had been a ruddy ochre; now it was flat and colourless. On the saucer below me, among rank docks and nettles, there were seven neatly pitched yellow tents and a red mess tent. The clients were settling themselves, and the men were purposefully moving round the camp, inflating mattresses, clearing away the tea, polishing stainless steel *thalis* and bringing jerry cans full of water. In the beginning I had had no idea how I would react to whatever challenge might lie ahead, nor what to expect of the men. Now there was a routine, an underlying feeling of confidence; out in the hills we were in our stride.

From clients' appreciative remarks and from their letters it was clear that for most of them the men's trustworthiness, conviviality and natural manners were among the most valued memories of the holiday. Any one of the men would meticulously cut an apple into as many slivers as were needed to make sure that everyone sitting nearby had a mouthful. And they attended to everyone's well-being with the same degree of concern; whether it was a potentially tip-giving client, a relation, or the humblest Nepali.

Karma in particular set exemplary standards of behaviour. When we reached the top of the Thamsar Pass, later on this trip, the wind was bitter and we knew the way down wouldn't be easy. We were preparing to move on straight away when we saw that one old Kullui was still struggling up – or rather had taken his pack off and was sitting amongst the scree some way below. 'Why did you leave him by himself so far behind?' Karma admonished the other Kulluis. 'He's too slow, he's not well,' was the reply. Calling three of the stoutest Kulluis, Karma told them to get down the hill and help him. They didn't move, but sat sullenly looking the other way. 'All right, then,' said Karma, slipping off his own haversack, 'I'll go myself.' This shamed the younger men into action and they scampered downhill. For the rest of the trip Karma made sure that the old man had a light load.

We were confident in our routine, but no trek, particularly a high one, is ever predictable. At any moment bad weather, illness or an accident might force my freewheeling brain into adrenalin-soaring activity. On this trip the first ten days were fine. There had been no real dramas, though there had been a lot of snow on the northern side and one of the women had fallen. She hadn't seemed to suffer anything worse than bruises, but as we descended towards Barabangahal she became unwell. During the rest day at the village her condition worsened; although the trek doctor could diagnose nothing more serious than slight anaemia.

178

The next day I was trundling along in my usual place at the back of the party when I began to notice just how slowly she was moving. After a mere ten steps she would stop for breath; and we were only at just over 10,000 feet. By the afternoon she was having to be helped by Prem and Mangal Singh, taking a few steps at a time and then sitting down. It would have been crazy to continue on up with a woman whose condition was deteriorating from an unknown cause and was therefore untreatable. She didn't have the obvious symptoms of altitude sickness and had in fact become more ill when we were at our lowest altitude. We pitched camp on the steep banks of an uncomfortable *nala*.

Karma and I climbed up and sat on the ridge above. We agreed that there was no hope of getting her up over the pass, 5,000 feet ahead. She was large, so it would be impossible to carry her up or down the steep, slippery snow. There was no easy route out, as the Ravi gorge path is too narrow for anything but sheep and goats and men without a load. The only hope was to send for help to Manali; in fifteen trekking seasons it was the first time I had had to do it.

We called Prem and Teshi: were they willing to set off for Manali now (it was five in the evening)? Neither so much as murmured a hesitation. Travelling in a group we were still five days away, but walking fast without loads they calculated they might reach Manali the next evening, certainly by the following morning. I wrote a note to Kranti to ask him to try for a helicopter, enclosing a map on which I had marked the alp a couple of miles ahead where I planned we should camp and adding that as there wouldn't be much landing space the helicopter would need skids rather than wheels. I didn't know if a helicopter was a real possibility; nor, even if it was, how long it might take to arrange. I suggested that as soon as he received my letter he should send men on foot with a proper stretcher. Prem and Teshi set off with their sleeping bags, a pocketful of chapattis, an onion and some chillies.

The next day the patient, the doctor, Man Bahadur, Mangal Singh and I pitched camp at the appointed alp, and the rest of the party moved on. Mangal Singh and Man Bahadur passed the days helping a neighbouring Gaddi shepherd dip his flock, hurling the sheep into the fast-flowing stream, while the three of us played cards. The patient didn't seem to be getting any worse, nor any better.

I explained that I had no idea whether or not a helicopter would actually arrive, and that though I was certain help would come, I couldn't say when. She accepted the situation stoically. In the evenings I lay watching the flocks trail down to the shepherds' camp on the opposite alp and the moon rise above the plume of smoke from their stone shelter. Anxiously I studied the movement of the clouds up-valley in the cleft in the mountains to the north-east: were they dispersing or building up?

On the morning of the third day I was taking a walk in the scrub juniper on the crest above the camp when suddenly a helicopter appeared just in front of me. It hovered above me and then, to my rage and despair, circled and disappeared down-valley, the way it had come. I catapulted myself down to the camp, and the helicopter roared round the corner again, lower now, and hovered like an indecisive insect. I scrambled, panting, to the plateau above the far side of the camp, waving my scarf and screeching for the patient to come – as if she couldn't hear that the helicopter had arrived. The whirling blades sent blinding dust and decades of sheep droppings flying into the air. Still the machine hovered above the ground, afraid to land on its useless little wheels – skids had been too much to ask for. Then, through the stinging dust, we saw the pilot hold up two fingers – for the patient and the doctor? We pulled them towards the hovering helicopter and the pilot helped to heave them up while we pushed them from below. Away they whirled. We lay back on the hillside, drained by the noise and the excitement.

Though their entire flock had scattered in panic across the hillside, the Gaddis on the ridge above sat staring. I'm sure they considered themselves fortunate to have watched the spectacle, and that for years to come they would relish describing it to others. I doubt if they considered it in relation to their own lives, but I thought about the man our shocked young doctor had been asked to visit in Barabangahal, whose dead (and stinking) toes had been tied to the stump of his foot in the misplaced hope that they might regrow. The previous autumn, on his way out of Barabangahal, he had been caught in early blizzards and forced to turn back home suffering from severe frostbite. Had he had a helicopter-lift, he wouldn't now be a one-footed cripple and a burden to his dependent family.

One of the clients on that trek was a chartered surveyor and knew about dampcourses. He confirmed that to lay sheets of plastic under a house was a standard practice. Heavyweight white sheets were unavailable until the apple-packing season and we could hardly delay the building until then, but our helpful trekker assured us that the thin black plastic strips we could obtain would be adequate. So there they lie now, black ends peeping out above the house's plinth, a souvenir of the helicopter-rescue trek.

To my relief, Sunk Ram and his brother, our old friends the carpenters from Kangra, had arrived at the site while we were away. They immediately assumed control: they had the confidence of real professionals, and an aptitude which combined traditional skills with an interest in new ideas. They could also interpret a plan, assess the practicality of an idea and adapt it to something they knew would work. We began to make free improvisations from the architect's drawings. Sunk Ram would study a particular section and a few hours later, his brow furrowed in concentration, he would say he had been thinking: those beams would never work that way – they should be like this. Soon the site was scattered with ends of wood on which, taking a stub of pencil from behind his ear, he had drawn a joist, a vertical section or a window frame. Their usual work was to fit out a shop, or make an extension to a school, or build a new ward in the hospital; they saw our house as an opportunity to exercise their craftsmanship to the full. They knew it was appreciated. Sunk Ram and I minded about every finish and trim – and he minded even more than I did.

The *mistris* complained that the timber they had to use was unseasoned; we had had a small stock of seasoned deodar but it was soon finished. Acquiring timber wasn't easy. The Forest Department permits a landowner to fell one or two deodar trees for his own use at a concessionary rate.[6] We had been issued with a permit for two trees but we required two more. It was an accepted procedure to give the Forest Ranger presents – a chicken, bottles of foreign liquor or even a wad of bank notes – so that he would look the other way while several extra trees were felled. Instead, and to the Forest Ranger's surprise and annoyance, we chose the seldom-used official channel, which entailed applying to the Forest Office for a permit to fell additional trees and paying the market rate. It also entailed endless journeys to Kullu and endless delays.

When at last we received the permit we contacted a family of lumberjacks (many such families come to Kullu for the summer from Barot in the Uhl valley). The men leant out from the trunk of each 200–foot tree against ropes which were tied to their waists; they lopped off the heavier branches to lighten the tree and ease its fall. It then took them a day to saw a cross-cut through the trunk and prepare for the final crash with wedges and guiding ropes. Once the trees were on the ground (and only then did you appreciate their height), the women of the family helped with the trimming and barking and sawing into ten-foot sections. Then, with a blade set into a frame to steady it, they sawed lengthways down the sections. Nepali labourers carried the ten-foot sleepers down to the roadside, to be transported by tractor to the sawmill and cut into planks according to the *mistris'* specifications.

The stone masons were from Kangra. A few of the labourers on the site were Nepali men, but the majority were women, mostly Zanskaris or Ladakhis. These included Sunita's mother, Chamba's wife and their eldest daughter Tsering Dolma, sometimes Teshi's beautiful wife, and a regular gaggle of robust, hard-working women from the growing Buddhist community round the *gompa*. Grasping babies and toddlers and bundles of food for the midday break, they poured out of the bus each morning. They sat under umbrellas, breaking stones, mixing cement, and passing stones along a human chain that stretched from the piles on the ground up the ladders and on to the bamboo scaffolding. It was hard, dirty work but they created a jovial picnic atmosphere, taking time off to settle in a corner and suckle their babies, often making jokes at the expense of one of the men, and always exuding an air of having a good time.

To thank him for his help with buying the land, we asked Mangal Singh's father to dinner. We also asked Karma's father, assuming that as they were both Khampas it would be appropriate. Mangal Singh's father, the younger of the two, clean-shaven and trim, arrived first, swathed in a fine, white shawl. He drank beer. 'I don't drink whisky or *arak* any more, not even *chang*. Otherwise everywhere you go you have to drink, and then if you refuse to drink in someone's house they become offended. Few people have beer to offer so it's easier this way.' Before he took a sip he dexterously flicked three drops over the rim of the glass in different directions – an offering to the presiding spirits.

Karma's father arrived wearing a natural-brown *pashmina* shawl. He accepted whisky, served in a silver cup made by the one-eyed Kinnauri silversmith; it was easier to flick from than the beer glass. He tossed the drink down his gullet but it didn't loosen his dignified reserve; his narrow eyes and imperturbable demeanour remained aloof.

We sat in the kitchen, which was one of the best things about Gulab Das's establishment – large but cosy, with room for a circle of people to sit round the *chulha*. Karma, who also joined us, was not subdued in the presence of the two older men; he freely contradicted their opinions and told his own stories, and to my surprise he openly smoked and drank in front of his father.[7] The older men reminisced about the grandeur of marriages in the past, when the *barat* was a procession of men mounted on fine ponies with embossed saddles, and the feasting lasted for a week. 'In those days we really enjoyed ourselves. Nowadays it's all over in a day or two and all anyone thinks about is whether the young couple have a sofa set and a scooter: it's money, money, money.' Karma argued that the weddings of the past just burnt up the family's savings; at least today's bride and groom had the use of their sofa sets. But all three of them agreed that an obsession with money was eroding the old standards and styles of behaviour, and they were unanimous in their condemnation of the pernicious custom of dowry. 'It is only recently that it has crept into our Buddhist community from the Hindu plains. We used to despise those Punjabis for selling their daughters, but now it happens in our community too. What can you do? Everyone wants his daughter to be married into a good family.'

The conversation turned to the impending marriages of daughters in their own families. 'There are more Khampas in Kullu than in any other part of India; we have been settling here because nowadays we can't move around so much. We used to be in Tibet, in China and in Lahore – we would travel wherever there was trade. There are some of us scattered in Bombay and Delhi, big businessmen maybe, and they come here to ask us for our daughters, but we don't like to send them down there; it's so hot and you can't tell if they will be happily settled.'

It was nearly eleven when we ate: in India the serving of food means the end of drinking and conversation. It had been a lively evening. The old men were worldly and articulate; I was impressed by their wisdom and their astute interpretation of events. They, like Boura Singh, were used to thinking within a moral and religious framework, as perhaps our grandparents in the West might have done but as we rarely do today. Their wisdom will stand the community in good stead if it is to grapple successfully with the influx of Western materialism and the escalation of cash-based power in Kullu.

Professional Trekkers

We had decided to give a party because four groups of clients were to be in Manali on the same evening – two just back from the hills and two about to set off – but when the day came, with all its hectic demands of equipment to be listed 'in' and 'out', sleeping-bag sheets to be express-laundered and medicine boxes to be checked, we began to regret that we had ever contemplated such an idea. We were just dashing back home after one of many trips to the bazaar when we were flagged to a halt by Dorze and Lama Le, who handed us a letter.

It was an unfriendly petition, couched in a formal style, and the gist of it was that it was unfair that some employees who had recently joined us received large salaries while 'we who have worked for you since the first years receive less. If the situation is not redressed without delay we will leave your service immediately.' It was signed by Dorze and Lama Le but hinted that Chamba was also involved. Our relationship with Chamba had become increasingly strained of late. Often he didn't turn up for work, and Boura Singh told us that recently, after asking for leave to go home to Zanskar, he had joined a Japanese trekking group instead. Kranti considered his behaviour ungrateful and I was upset to see my old friend, with whom I had shared so much, following such an ill-advised course and looking so dejected.

It wasn't surprising that petty jealousies had built up among the men, but we felt that after so many years of familiarity and friendship they could surely have come and aired their grievances at a more appropriate moment. We felt hurt and indignant that their strategy had been to present a formal ultimatum when our resources were stretched and every man was needed for the trips setting off the following morning. I wanted to bury my head and pretend it hadn't happened.

After getting up at four o'clock to see off the parties who were leaving for home, we bent our minds to devising at least a temporary solution to satisfy the troublemakers and ensure that they set off with the two outgoing groups. We summoned Karma, Prem, Panchok and Mangal Singh, assuming that they were the focus of resentment, and explained that the higher monthly salary they received for shouldering responsibility would now be made up in a lump sum, as a bonus at the end of each season. Then at breakfast everyone squatted round the kitchen *chulha* while Kranti delivered a diplomatic homily on how members of a team had to control personal grievances for the benefit of the whole. He cited the example of how the elder statesmen had stifled their indignation and accepted with a good grace the young Mrs Gandhi as Prime Minister, and he quoted from the Bhagavad-Gita, explaining Lord Krishna's admonishments to Arjun about 'duty'. All this was greeted with admiring nods and murmurs of approval from Boura Singh.

After breakfast I set off in the bus with Rahul, Tara, Prem, Kullu Lama, Mangal Singh, Nawang Tsering, his younger brother Madan, Man Bahadur, Gyal Chand the pony man and fifteen clients, to drive over the Rothang into Lahul and trek up Miyar *nala*. The petition was never referred to.

Jagdish was at the wheel. He was a Department of Tourism bus driver who regularly drove our groups and considered himself part of the team, wearing a red-tartan flannel shirt like the rest of the men. When he wasn't driving he was seldom sober, but once on the road he inspired absolute confidence. A protective image of Jawalaji Devi dangled from the driver's mirror in front of him, and before he set off on a journey he would always fold his hands, touch his enormous steering wheel and make obeisance to the road ahead and to Jawalaji. Now Rahul sat on the bench alongside him, seldom admiring the majestic Himalayas, totally absorbed in a game of *sip*.

Miyar *nala* had become a regular low-altitude summer trek for our groups. We were familiar visitors and received a convivial welcome in the valley; partly because it was seldom visited by other tourists, partly because some of the men – like Nawang Tsering and Madan – lived there and many had relations there. Once we had come through the gorge and into the upper villages there wasn't a hamlet where we weren't tugged indoors and offered hospitality. One of Kullu Lama's and Prem's many sisters-in-law seemed to live in each village; they all looked so alike that for several years I was never sure whether I was being welcomed by a different sister from the one we had met the previous day or whether the same sister had moved ahead to prepare for our arrival. Kullu Lama was warmly welcomed everywhere; once he began on the well-matured *arak* it wasn't easy to move him on towards the camp site, and someone else would have to take his place as cook for the evening. But he wasn't the only one to receive hospitality. Many households invited the trekkers in to sit round the iron stoves in large living rooms, and went to considerable trouble organizing the numerous cups and glasses required to serve tea, *tsampa*, yoghurt, *arak* and *chang*.

The experience certainly made an impact on the trekkers, and I think our hosts felt some benefits in return. Some of the wages we paid found their way into the valley through the local men we employed and their wives, and we were instrumental in setting up a community health clinic there. In the houses we visited, framed photographs of smiling families, sent from abroad by our trekkers, were on proud display. Sooner or later, without our involvement, money from those who went away to work, health clinics and even photographs would have come into the valley, but I like to think that we may have helped to establish good will and civil relations between local people and visitors. From the earliest days of taking trekkers into the hills I fiercely forbade clients to give anything to people along the way. Begging children, and even lamas, may be a common sight in Zanskar, but so far I haven't seen anyone begging in Miyar *nala*. Tourists who have been made welcome here have had their eyes opened: they have been able to appreciate that their poorly dressed hosts, living at subsistence level in a remote valley, cannot be dismissed as simple rustics; on the contrary, they are people with high standards of courtesy and hospitality.

Beyond the highest villages the valley opens out; clean white peaks and massive glaciers tower above but they don't bear down on you. The camp sites at the head of the valley are some of the finest in the Western Himalayas. Tents can be pitched far apart from one another on the spacious swaths of grass, which are intersected by trickling streams. There are irises, gentians, potentillas and geraniums, and clumps of blue poppies jut out of clefts in the rocks. Distant sounds drift over the camp – bells from the ponies that graze among the yaks on the steppe-like plateau; a shepherd's flute from the high slopes where the Gaddis graze their goats and sheep.

In the evening, when everyone had gradually dispersed to

their tents, Mangal Singh, Prem and I sat round the fire. Fuel was precious up here. The ponies had had to carry up loads of wood and it was used sparingly, mixed with yak dung; Kullu Lama moaned that the smoke stung his eyes. There was no moon, but the snows were a pale-green moon colour. A canopy of yellow stars seemed quite close, and the brilliance of the Milky Way was perfectly reflected in the little lake between us and the tents. Animism creeps over you at moments like this: the mountains seem a fit part of everything and yet aloof, looking on with detachment.

On our way down-valley we were told there had been an accident and a boy was hurt; would our doctor go and help? The young trek doctor had already been disconcerted by the standard of local hygiene she had seen, overwhelmed by the children's fly-encrusted eyes and infected wounds, but she agreed to go. As we approached the house we could hear chanting and the clash of cymbals: it sounded ominous to me, as though the child might already be dead. We were led upstairs into a low-ceilinged, dark room jammed with people. The windows were tightly shut, the air fetid. In front of an elaborately decorated altar, two lamas sat chanting prayers and women sobbed round a bundle which I assumed was the dead child. A grieving man stood over it, unsuccessfully waving a yak's tail at the swarms of flies.

The child wasn't dead. We asked the family to carry the bundle through to another room where we could shut out some of the onlookers and open the window for light and air, then unwrapped the blankets to find a boy of about twelve, his head bound with a scarf. His parents told us that he had fallen off a rock the day before. He hadn't been unconscious at the time and they had taken him to the dispensary, where the wound had been dressed. He was now semi-conscious and delirious. We unwound the scarf and found wads of cotton wool stuffed into his skull. The doctor became courageous, dexterous and decisive. With boiled water, Swiss army-knife tweezers and a pair of nail scissors she removed the cotton wool; I heard her gasp as, by the beam of the torch I was holding, she saw that part of the boy's brain was exposed. She stitched the taut skin over the gaping hole, gave him an injection, and explained to the parents the dosage for various powerful antibiotics which we provided from our stores.

I should tell them, she said, that because the brain was exposed there was a high risk of infection; it was improbable that the boy would survive. I didn't pass this information on; it would have been considered inauspicious. The grieving father drew bank notes from his pocket: '*Please* give the best medicine, the most expensive.' I thought he was disappointed that we refused payment; he might have felt there was a better chance of his son's recovering if the medicine cost him money. I was relieved, though, that he seemed to understand how to administer the drugs, and that it was essential the dressing should not be opened for a week. The women of the house wouldn't listen. People in isolated communities, who over the centuries have had to accept suffering, may use prayers and potions as palliatives to pain and illness but they are inclined to regard medical action as a hazardous, even impertinent, interference in the workings of destiny. They are afraid that whatever is done might be seen later as instrumental in a death. A complete lack of attention or effort, on the other hand – what might seem to us to be careless indifference – isn't considered in any way reprehensible. All too often they are right: fate does have to be accepted. But on this occasion the doctor's skill and the antibiotics worked. The next summer I saw the boy running across the fields, the scar on the side of his head very visible but well healed.

On our way down through the gorge we found that sections of the precarious track had become a morass of rubble, mud and ice, impassable for the ponies. Worse lay ahead: we were told that there had been cloudbursts, and that thirty kilometres beyond Udaipur a bridge on the main road had been washed away. It wouldn't be repaired in less than a week. Jagdish and his bus would be waiting on the other side of the broken bridge. How would we get there?

Prem went to search for Nepali labourers to help clear the gorge track for the ponies, while I went to see if we might hire a truck from the military road-builders. On the way I met the major in charge, a plump, well-groomed Sikh. 'I am very sorry – I am having to move on foot myself. One of my trucks has broken down and another has met with an accident. There is one public bus plying this side of the breach; you could try and book that.' I found the bus inspector in the bazaar, playing cards. 'No, you cannot hire the bus and I cannot accommodate your party. I am giving the same answer to the Italian party who have been wanting transport for three days. Bus is booked.'

The trekkers and ponies emerged from the gorge hot, dishevelled and frightened. Gyal Chand was spitting and red-eyed with rage: he said he would never take his ponies to Miyar *nala* again. Late that night the public bus stopped in front of the rest-house and Jagdish came swaying round the corner. 'Do not worry, Memsahib, my bus is ready waiting at the breach and the driver of the bus here will take us to it; he is my brother's friend.' I told him what the inspector had said to me. 'What does the inspector know? I have told my friend the driver we will give him something, so he will definitely be here at six in the morning. But you must have everyone ready, he will not like waiting.'

In the morning, at about seven o'clock, a battered Jagdish turned up on foot. 'The bus will not be going until maybe eight or nine; it has gone to the workshop for the steering – not a big job.' These are awkward moments for a tour leader. You don't know whether to keep your clients abreast of information – inconclusive, changeable and sometimes downright disconcerting – as you receive it, or to give them your own idea of what is likely to happen, or to embark on the uphill struggle of persuading them to learn to take it easy and wait and see. Some time after nine we saw the bus careering out of the bazaar, past the group of angry Italians, and screeching to a stop outside our door. It was already full, and extra passengers were travelling on the roof. Jagdish's brother's good friend became impatient as we loaded pack after pack of equipment on top and pushed the clients inside.

After a short while on the road the driver stopped at a hotel – I assumed for tea. An hour later there was still no sign of him or of Jagdish. I found them up a rickety ladder, in a room above the hotel. 'Oh Memsahib, come in, come in.' Jagdish's eyes were rolling. 'Have a glass.' They were merrily drinking an orange-coloured spirit. 'You see, the trouble is this: there were no spares in the workshop so now the steering is loose.' The driver swung his hands, demonstrating a freely turning wheel: 'Quite free.' 'Well,' I said, 'we'd better get the luggage down, find some porters and walk to the bridge.' We were still fifteen kilometres away and it was now midday. 'No, no, we do not want you inconvenienced,' Jagdish protested. 'He will drive on. Normally he would not without any steering, but my friend the driver says for you he will go.' I balked at the prospect of being in an overloaded, top-heavy bus without any steering, driven round hairpin bends by a driver merry on orange spirit, but Jagdish and the driver were convinced they were doing us a favour and would brook no argument.

I told no one what I knew. By the time we reached the breach my fingers, clutching the bar of the seat in front of me, were white and stiff. I had to prise them off one by one. When all of us had successfully crossed the river – using planks and jumping from rock to rock – Jagdish tucked himself in behind his own steering wheel and drove for nine hours, perched on his seat like a tiny bird with huge red eyes. We reached Manali at two in the morning.

Before the onset of winter the *mistris* had the roof on our new house to protect it from the winter's snow; floors and staircases would have to be finished in the spring.

When we arrived back early the following April for our last few months at Gulab Das's, the winter weather still wasn't over. It was so cold and bleak – there were snowdrifts up to the front steps – that I decided to take the children and Boura Singh on trek with me; Kranti had already left to meet a party in Simla.

The route was from Kangra over a spur of the Dhaula Dhar into lower Kullu. The clients had been anticipating a holiday as described (by me) in the brochure: 'You will enjoy the exhilaration of walking along high ridges, not knowing whether to turn to the south for a view of crest after crest of verdant Kangra valley or to the north to gaze at shining white peaks against an azure sky.' As it turned out, the sky was grey, and in the driving rain you didn't dare lift your head to look up at the 'vivid scarlet blooms on the magnificent *Rhododendron arboreum*'. At Parasher – 'a jewel of the Himalayas where, cradled in a tranquil green saucer of turf, a sixteenth-century, three-tiered temple is reflected in the still waters of a turquoise lake' – a whirlwind churned the water into white horses. We watched two of the tents blow down, and the unfortunate clients had to spend an uncomfortable night on the floor of the temple shelter.

There was worse to come. A blizzard began soon after the clients and I – ahead of the others – left Parasher to traverse a ridge high above Kullu. When the snow began to settle and to drive into our faces we took shelter in a Gujars' hut and lit a warming fire. We ate lunch, and shortly afterwards I saw something red approaching out of the whiteness: it was Bihari Lal, in a red coat, carrying Rahul wrapped in a red sweater. Rahul had been so perished on his pony that they had taken him off and rubbed him all over; even so he was numb and speechless when he arrived. Bihari Lal said that the ponies weren't very far behind. Where was Tara? I asked. He was surprised. 'Isn't she here? She and Boura Singh set off long before us, soon after you. We thought they had caught up with you, but maybe they're sheltering somewhere on the way and they'll come with the ponies.'

Rahul, in dry clothes and shawls, began to come to life as Mangal Singh and Bihari Lal rubbed his hands, feet and legs with their warmed palms. The ponies arrived, their baggage covered in slushy sleet, but there was no sign of Boura Singh and Tara. It wasn't possible to pitch tents in the driving snow, so Kullu Lama built an efficient kitchen *chulha* at the far end of the hut and we huddled round our original fire for warmth. The atmosphere was soon very smoky. The clients stoically tried to settle down and read or write by the guttering candles perched on the buffalo stalls, but their eyes were red and streaming. Water dripped in from the flat, sodden roof and mud squelched underfoot.

At half-past three I gave Bihari Lal and Mangal Singh a whistle each and they set off into the whiteness. I knew Tara was wearing hers; I had put it round her neck before I left in the morning. I had tucked a packet of glucose biscuits into her pink anorak pocket, too, in case she was hungry before lunch. But I remembered now, with anguish, that when she had called 'Ma, Ma!' as I set off up the path from the lake I hadn't even turned round.

We bashed a hole through the roof of the unfortunate Gujars' hut to let the smoke out, not that it helped. I hung Tara's clothes to warm on the line and put up the sleeping bags to dry; they were steaming in the smoke. It was still snowing. Rahul had revived. 'Where's Tara?' he kept asking. He wanted to play bridge and, since there was nothing else to do, he and I played a rubber with two of the trekkers – a general and a young dentist. We won.

I remember thinking that I must blot out my anxiety and apologize to the clients for the weather and their discomfort. This wasn't what they had paid £1,500 for. It was getting dark and the snow was still falling, though less densely. The General, perhaps smarting from his defeat at bridge, was suddenly on a short fuse: I should do something, he said. Like what?

We heard whistles through the opaque mist. I strained to make out grey figures in the greyness. 'Not found,' was all the searchers said. Soaked and doleful, they sat at the far side of the fire, their hands in front of their faces – either to protect themselves from the smoke or to hide their despair. I packed away Tara's clothes. No one talked and no one wanted to eat the kedgeree and *rajma* beans Kullu Lama had painstakingly prepared. Mist billowed in through the open door, pushing the smoke back in. All sixteen of us would have to sleep in this dripping hut. The dentist suddenly began to rail: it was unbearable, he was going to take his sleeping bag and sleep outside, he wanted a tent pitched. I told him that in the dark and the mud and the snow it was impossible, and gave him two sleeping pills. We laid our sleeping bags on top of the mess tent, which lay in turn on top of all the plastic bags we had. Even at ground level it was smoky.

As I shifted the sleeping Rahul he murmured, 'Where is Tara?' Where was she? Would I ever see her again? I lay and imagined Boura Singh falling, somersaulting down a *nala* through the scrub, lying immobile with a broken leg, and Tara blowing her whistle for me until quite quickly, for she was so small and thin, she sank into unconsciousness and hypothermia. I got up to stoke the fire, and I could just make out Man Bahadur. He hadn't even laid out his sleeping bag; stony-faced, his back against the wall, he was sitting by the *chulha*. I wished Karma was there. There was nothing he could have done, but his wisdom would have been reassuring. From the shivering ponies who munched at the midden by the door there was a tinkling of bells all night.

It was a soaking dawn. Mangal Singh and Man Bahadur set off to search along the ridge again, and Dorze and Bihari Lal went to search the far side (all the men wanted to go but some had to accompany the clients). They took dry clothes for Tara, and biscuits and a flask of tea. I went on with the party, up to the pass and then down to Bajaura. There was just a chance that Boura Singh had made his way down there, and in any case I didn't know what else to do.

As we reached the jeep track to Bajaura we saw an umbrella approaching round a corner; even from the far distance we recognized the unmistakable figure of Boura Singh. Confused in the white-out he had crossed to the wrong side of the ridge, where he and Tara had found a lone house; the people who lived there had offered them a fire, food and blankets. Tara hadn't cried much though she had kept asking where I was. 'Memsahib, I knew you would know that I would rather be dead than let anything happen to Tara Devi.' I sped on and found her in Prem's arms on the rest-house veranda, where he'd arrived from another trek. She was a little indignant: where had I been all this time?

The searchers didn't arrive until after dark. They looked half-dead with exhaustion and despair until they saw Tara alive and smiling. She was surprised by the fuss everyone made over her – from Bihari Lal's hugs to Mangal Singh's kisses and Man

Bahadur's murmurings of adoration — and wasn't sure why a night by the fire with Boura Singh was something to make such a to-do about.

Prini

After the dreary greyness and squalor of snow and rain, the claustrophobia of being hemmed in by the cold and the mist, it is dazzling to wake up one morning and find the world suddenly green and shining, with each distant peak and each sprig of unfurling apple-leaf minutely defined. At such a moment the Himalayas humiliate the eye: we don't have the optical agility to absorb the vast backdrop and the detail at the same time. Sounds too are released — no longer muffled by the mist — and the valley is filled with movement and energy.

The sound of a *deota*'s band and the sight of a *rath* glinting in the sunlight are irresistible. When I heard that the Aleo *Deota* was on its way to Prini *mela* I left the house, where I had been discussing the panelling on the doors with the *mistris*, and followed the procession up through the terraces to the village. The *rath* was set down in a pink and white apple orchard, where women offered flowers, anointed the forehead of each burnished mask with a *ghi tika*, and hung lengths of yellow and pink silk from the *chattri*.

With clashing cymbals and an excited roll on the drums the procession then left the village and the apple orchard and made its way up a boulder-strewn path. At the foot of the steep flight of steps that leads through the deodar and elm grove to the Prini temple, we were welcomed by trumpeters.

The little *mela* ground is quite open, visible from the path going on up to Hampta village, but the temple is secluded; you could pass it without noticing. Hidden by ancient deodars and by the steep stone roofs of its outbuildings, it is set on a narrow shelf: the land falls away two hundred feet to the village and terraces below. In front of the temple there is a paved area with a low pedestal of black stone, for sacrifices, set into it. The doorway is decorated with entwined snakes and there are ibex heads under the overhanging roof; there are white muslin scarves, too, hung there by Buddhist devotees, for this is a temple to Jamlu. Originally from Spiti, Jamlu is a relation of the powerful deity at Malana and of the wild god who presides on Mount Geyphang in Lahul. Here in Prini, Jamlu is revered by both Hindus and Buddhists, and particularly by all those on their way up the Hampta *nala* and on towards Spiti.

Having made our obeisance at the temple we processed on to the *mela* ground to be welcomed by two *deotas*. One had a small, conventional *rath* while the other had no *rath* at all – no masks, no *chattri*, no jewellery, no flowers; it looked more like a bundle of cloth set down on a low wooden stool. The cloths were undone a little to reveal a single very small image, half-mask, half-head. This was Jamlu, the god reputed to have a taste for virgins' blood and human milk. On the ground in front of him were a mace, a simple, elegant silver water kettle, two silver-handled yak's-tail fly whisks, four thin copper horns, and two upturned cymbals to collect the offerings.

Women offered money, bunches of primulas, scarlet rhododendron blooms and sprigs of opaque white seed-pods from the tree that grows round the holy lake at Riwalsar near Mandi. Several more *deotas* arrived. The *shehnai* player began a loose, tentative tune, and white-cloaked, marigold-wreathed dancers began to test their limbs. The stone-terraced seats here are built against the upper bank, so the spectators looked out past the colourful dancers to the snow peaks and the darkening valley. Two of the *deotas* joined the dancing, the men struggling under the heavy *raths* as they swayed and jigged enthusiastically.

I wanted to stay until midnight when, so I was told, the *deotas* would race one another down across the terraces in the moonlight. But we weren't Prini Deota's parishioners quite yet, and I had to get back to Gulab Das's.

The day of the next full moon was Lord Buddha's birthday. In front of the Lahuli *gompa* there was a thirty-foot prayer flag

capped with a multicoloured cloth *chattri*, and a crowd of Manali's
Buddhists had assembled in the garden there. On the ground
there were *thalis* piled high with rice, barley, fried cakes, dried
curd and sugar crystal. We formed ourselves into a wide circle
round a fire fragrant with the smoke from incense gathered in
the mountains, and threw our offerings into the air. Then the
head lamas processed out of the garden followed by banners and
flags. The prayer books, carefully wrapped in maroon and yellow
cloths, were also taken out in procession; a 'book' being a stack
of long prayer sheets tied between two leaves of wood. Among
the bearers there were many familiar faces, including Karma and
Dorze. People lined the path and bowed their heads to be touched
by the holy books as they passed. Then came an image of
Lord Buddha in a yellow and gold palanquin, followed by its
ornamental parasol, and musicians with cymbals, long copper
horns, conch shells and hand drums. The dignified procession
made its way round the *chortens* to the Zanskari temple and then
out into the main bazaar.

That evening Rahul, Tara, Boura Singh and Mangal Singh
went to see *E.T.* at the Funtime video parlour. As I waited to
collect them I saw a dozen young maroon-cloaked lamas emerge
– they had treated themselves to a show on their god's birthday.
Rahul had helped the audience with a running translation but
the lamas were still a bit confused. 'It was odd. Where was it? Is
the creature a god there?'

It wasn't many weeks before we moved to Prini. The house was
to be called 'Prini Ropa', which was a description of where it
stood; *ropa* means 'rice terraces'. The *mistris* were still at work,
the plaster (not the traditional dung and mud but an expensive
smooth cement mixture) was damp, and the wooden staircase
lacked banisters. The veranda had no rail, let alone a balustrade,
and there was no glass in the windows; the pre-monsoon mist
billowed into the rooms like stage smoke.

The house is built on a square and stands on a stone-flagged
plinth, like Duff Dunbar, but unlike Duff Dunbar it is higher
than it is long. Its veranda juts out under the roof on all four

sides. The ground floor is almost windowless; timber-framed vents let in air and a little light. The front of the house faces north, up-valley. A double front door leads into the entrance hall: on the right is the capacious, shelved trekking store, and on the left Boura Singh's room and bathroom. The first floor has two bedrooms and two bathrooms, with running hot water and lavatories that flush at a flick of the wrist. The views from the bedroom windows are half-framed by the struts supporting the veranda. On the second floor, to the right and the left of a little landing, are two studies. The middle doorway leads into the sitting room, which runs the full breadth of the house. Upstairs again, under the sloping roof, is a long attic bedroom with dormer windows, one looking across the valley, the other to Prini peak and the rising sun.

We unpacked with zest. Familiar, long-forgotten possessions emerged, stored since Duff Dunbar days: cider barrels, Gopali's brass milking pail, chicken coops, playpens and swing cradles. Boura Singh turned the site hut into a kitchen which immediately assumed his customary disarray; not for him an attempt at orderly lines of jars and plates and *dekchis*.

He was pleased that we had become property-owners and could no longer be humiliated by a landlord, but moving to Prini, to the left bank, disoriented him a little. He had spent so many years around Dunghri, above the bazaar, that he was known by everyone there and felt familiar; over here he didn't know who was who. From Duff Dunbar and Gulab Das's a visit to the bazaar had been almost a daily habit for him, but for some reason, although Prini was hardly any further, he seldom went after we moved.

At the end of the first day we sat out on the veranda, on *charpois* covered with the checked blankets and cushions we had had at Duff Dunbar, and admired the view up-valley. The fallow terraces, dun-coloured with wheat and stubble, were patterned with cones of manure. Lines of women had begun to hack at the compacted earth with broad-bladed pick-like tools; sometimes three together attacked a particularly stubborn clod. Below us a ploughman grunted at his black bullocks, and round him the earth, flooded before ploughing for the rice seedbed, was moist and glinting: in places the emerald-green seedlings were already showing through. On a patch above, a man was scattering seed. Ahead of him a woman, her yellow-checked *pattu* hitched up to her thighs, stuck willow twigs into the mud. For years I had wondered why seedbeds bristled with willow twigs – were they thought to be auspicious symbols, to encourage the seedlings to grow upwards? Now at last I understood. The twigs marked the span of the falling seed, so that the sower could see where to direct the next handful. If I sat on the veranda every day and looked carefully enough, there would always be something new to learn.

Afterword: Today

I often walk up through the terraces (it isn't easy when they are flooded and you have to balance on the slippery dividing strips) through Prini village and on up the steep path and flagstone steps to the temple. On the far side of it, partly shaded by deodar, there is a private spot where you can sit on the moss undisturbed, for passers-by take the path across the *mela* ground. From here I can look down on the *ropa* and our house standing alone; its days on its own are numbered, though, for a luxury hotel is being built just fifty yards away.

Agriculture is changing. Apple trees are being planted in the *ropa* – easy money and less work to cultivate than rice. The stone huts, lived in by the villagers during planting and harvest times for hundreds of years, are falling into disrepair; building labourers are camping in some of them.

A pony train meanders along the road, carrying seed potatoes down from Hampta village. Recently several muleteers have sold their animals, bought sawmills or established themselves as apple contractors, and then used the resulting profit to buy taxis or build guesthouses and hotels. New buildings straggle along the main road on the far side, the 'right bank'; they are beginning to spring up along the 'left bank' too. Lack of access to plots off the road encourages this ribbon development. The massive rocks that are such a feature of the landscape are being demolished and used for building stone; forests can regenerate or be re-planted, but rocks are irreplaceable.

Rahul and his friends from the village, the Prini Cricket Club, are playing on the fallow terraces below the house; their pitch is where the hotel will be. A few years ago a Sikh from Simla bought that land for 15,000 rupees a *biswa* – and recently a developer from Delhi bought some adjacent land for 32,000 rupees a *biswa*, nearly ten times what we had paid six years

200

before.[8] At dusk the boys will run into our house to watch a Hindi movie on the video, hired by Rahul and Boura Singh.

What has really upset Boura Singh about the move to Prini is the coincidental fact that the household is rarely now the bustling place it used to be. Rahul and Tara (and I) have to be away in London and spend only all-too-short holidays in Manali. For Boura Singh, time hangs heavily. He tries to 'eat it', sitting outside the kitchen and watching passers-by on the road, or listening to Garhwali songs on the tape recorder which Rahul insisted we should buy him, but 'when Rahul Baba and Tara Devi leave the place it's too quiet. You need children round a house. All I hear is air whistling in my ears – I don't like it.'

Sitting in my mossy corner by the temple I am aware of an undramatic flooding of pleasure. It isn't so much that I crave Kullu when I am away; rather that when I'm back I'm aware I have been missing something. It's like feeling well again when you have been ill.

I can see across to Prem's well-established house at Rangri, and beyond it to Sial – no longer the separate village it was when I lived there but part of Manali's sprawl. I can see Kullu Lama's house too, next door to the Ladakhi artist who painted the murals in the Zanskari *gompa*; now he sells his *thankas* to Japanese collectors for tens of thousands of rupees. Kullu Lama himself runs a prosperous household and boasts a fat stomach.

I'm looking out on a world where I have seen a new generation grow up. Tsering Dolma, Chamba's eldest daughter – a toddler herself when I first arrived – now has a sturdy son of her own. Chamba's wife and the surviving twin both work on building sites or sort potatoes, while the two boys attend school. Chamba himself is still on our regular payroll, though these days he isn't fit for trekking. In relative terms, despite nearly twenty years of continuous employment and the opportunities of Manali, his family's position has deteriorated rather than improved, and he still rents the hut beyond the petrol pump. He is seldom his merry self these days; he wears a hangdog look and makes endless requests for money.

Karma is an established and respected citizen in the Buddhist community. His wife runs a shop in the Tibetan market and his son is working for an MA in economics at Chandigarh University. Karma himself is a little over-burdened by responsibility and the tedium of organizing easy treks for the elderly; I can see that sometimes he thirsts for the challenge of the unknown.

Sunita has an impeccably neat room, with a television and large plate-glass windows, behind the *gompa*. Her husband works in a shawl shop and has good connections with a video parlour; Rahul often negotiates the rent for a sought-after film through him. They have two unusually mischievous children (somehow the result of our influence?) who attend the recently opened school at the mission hospital.

I can see part of the bazaar; the rest is hidden by the 'protected' deodar forest that runs beside the river. Manali is a boom town, changed almost unrecognizably from the messy single street it was when I arrived. It is true that it has burnt down twice since then, and that much of it has had to be rebuilt. After the second time, when the fire engine from Kullu was driven with such excitement that it ran into a tree (and the one from Mandi didn't reach Manali until the next day), the Notified Area Committee decided it was time to build a temple to Kali in the bazaar and buy its own fire engine. The town bristles with television aerials and satellite dishes, and banging and hammering ring out everywhere; these are the sounds of new construction, of everything from butchers' shops to luxury hotels. There are 150 hotels, restaurants where diners are entertained by colour television, a dozen video parlours with their own generators, 80 private taxis (there used to be just one jeep run by the Tourist Department), and numerous vans, trucks and tractors with trailers. The new bus station stands back from a wide dual carriageway; even so there are noisy traffic jams in the potato and apple seasons.

The legless beggar on a trolley has gone. For years he used to sit below the old post office. I never gave him anything until the last time I saw him, when he looked so ill that I gave him 100 rupees. Now gaudily dressed Rajasthani women and children have arrived; they scavenge along the *nalas* and beg off bazaar tourists.

Drug manufacturers are enjoying booming sales. There are at

least half a dozen chemists' shops and several private doctors, one of whom has just opened an amniocentesis clinic here. Women who want to abort a foetus if it is found to be female no longer have to travel to Chandigarh.

Verma sells ice cream, Fanta and Thumbs Up from a fridge, and so many newspapers and even books that he doesn't need to bother with tea and *puris* any more. There is the three-storey Tibetan market where you can buy anything from foreign – smuggled – down sleeping-bags and Sony stereo systems to Levi jeans, lengths of Chinese brocade and porcelain bowls. There are numerous bakeries. Gone are the days when there was no bread if the grumpy deaf baker decided not to bake: you can buy large loaves or small, brown or white, as well as buns, vegetable patties and macaroons. And in Manu market frozen broiler chickens, ready-made kebabs and stacked trays full of eggs are readily available.

New values alter traditional relationships; a man may envy his brother's imported jeans and his nephew's 'English Medium' education. Prosperity, opportunity and a cash economy mean that some people are crushed by a sense of diminishing status and lack of self-esteem while others thrive.

I can see the dark swirl of the Dunghri forest. Duff Dunbar itself is hidden by the lie of the land but I can see up to Lumbadukh, to the alps below the Kali Hind Pass, and away up Solang valley where, to avoid the long winter snow on the Rothang, they are tunnelling a road under the mountains to Lahul.

Notes

1. Major N. Hamilton Fletcher, H and F Enterprises, 24 November 1986
2. Although in theory Buddhists are casteless, in practice the *lohars* (originally blacksmiths) are the menial caste in Lahul and Zanskar.
3. The path forks: you must always walk so that *chortens* and *mane* walls are on your right.
4. Polyandry has always been customary among Buddhists in the West Himalayas. A girl married all the brothers of a family and any children born would be ascribed to the eldest brother. This system limited the number of children born and ensured that valuable land wouldn't be split up. The Indian government has declared polyandry illegal but the tradition persists – although people tend to be embarrassed when outsiders learn of it.
5. Michel Peissel, *Zanskar: The Hidden Kingdom*
6. In some parts of Himachal, particularly around Simla and in the hills of Uttar Pradesh to the east, the deodar forests have been decimated; partly to supply wood for local buildings and villagers' fuel, but mostly by unscrupulous contractors for profit. In spite of this the Forest Department in Himachal, which has existed for over a hundred years, seems to have been efficient and effective overall – felling, replanting, and fencing off areas for natural regeneration with prolific success. Since 1987 the Department has prohibited the commercial felling of deodar in Kullu and its transport out of the valley.
7. In India it is unusual for a son to smoke or drink in front of his father (although some do drink in front of their fathers in Himachal); this restraint is a sign of respect.
8. The price for which we bought the land worked out at roughly £17,500 an acre. The 1990 price translates at roughly £160,000 an acre.

Glossary

agarbatti incense
alu paratha chapatti stuffed with potato and fried
amma mother
arak distilled liquor
barat bridegroom's procession
barri large
behin(ji) sister (the *-ji* suffix denotes respect)
Bhagwan God
bhang hemp, cannabis
bhatti bar selling local liquor
biri small cigarette, rolled in a leaf
biswa a measurement of land approximately equal to one-hundredth
of an acre
chang locally brewed beer
chapatti flat bread
charas hemp; cannabis
charpoi bed made of webbing woven across a wooden frame
chattri umbrella or parasol
chaukidar caretaker, watchman
chemise long shirt worn by a woman
chena chickpeas
chogtse a long low stool, used as a table when one is sitting on the floor
chomo Buddhist nun
chorten Buddhist *stupa*, often marking the path to a village
chulha stove or hearth for cooking
chutni a freshly made, concentrated sauce, often hot and spicy
dai midwife, or sometimes maid
dal many kinds of pulses
dekchi handleless saucepan
deota (devta) male deity, or the image of him
deshi local (often slightly pejorative)

devi(ji) female deity or the image of her

dharma life's duty or purpose

dhoti length of cotton cloth wound up through the legs, as worn by Gandhiji

dhup incense or light

dudhwalli milkwoman

dupatta a length of cloth worn by a woman, covering the shoulders, chest and head

durbar public audience

duri cotton carpet

dush spirit, curse or power

galu a pass or a neck between rocks or crags

gaur the oracle of a deity

ghat cremation area by a river

ghi clarified butter

gompa Buddhist monastery and temple

got grazing ground

gur unrefined sugar

guru religious teacher and leader

halwa a sweetmeat made of fried semolina

Harijan: the name in the plural means 'children of God' and was given to the untouchables by Gandhi

jelebi sweet, made of coils of butter soaked in syrup

jhule Buddhist greeting

-ji a suffix denoting respect; e.g. *behinji, deviji, mataji*

jogini local spirits or fairies – sometimes mischievous

jot saddle-shaped pass

kanundar an officer above the *patwari* in local administration

khadi hand-spun cloth

khir sweet rice pudding

kilta large conical basket carried on the back

kurta long shirt worn by a man

kuth root crop sold for medicinal use

laddu a sweet: orange balls made with lentil flour

lassi a drink made with yoghurt or buttermilk

lathi stout stick, often bamboo

lohar iron, and hence a caste that is associated with metalwork

maidan large flat ground
makki ka roti chapattis made with maize flour
malmal muslin
mane loosely built walls made up of stones which have been placed as offerings and inscribed with Buddhist prayers
masoor dal a *dal* made with the finest type of lentil
mata(ji) mother; also used when referring to a female deity.
mela a fair
mistri artisan; for instance a mechanic, carpenter or mason
momo dumpling
mundan the ceremony of a boy's first hair-cutting
nag snake
nala valley, stream or river
namaste a greeting made with folded palms (both the spoken greeting and the action)
nomo girl
pahari of the hills
pakora a batter and vegetable snack
pandit(ji) priest; can also refer to any Brahmin
paratha fried chapatti
pattu length of tweed worn by Kullui women as everyday dress
patwari village accountant and record-keeper
pilau rice dish
pio 'drink up' – a familiar rather than a respectful invitation
pradhan the head man of a village
prasad offering
puja worship
pujari officiating priest
puri deep-fried bread, like a pancake
raitha a yoghurt dish
rajma large, dark-red beans
raksha demon
rath the decorated frame on which the masks of Kullui *deotas* are carried
rezai quilt
ropa rice terraces
sadhu wandering holy man
sag panir spinach and cheese

salwar a woman's baggy pyjamas
samadhi state of trance
sawan one of the monsoon months – approximately the same as August
sawan purnima the full moon during *sawan*
serai camping site or shelter
shehnai a wind instrument
sherab liquor; usually spirits rather than beer
shikari hunter
sindur the mark worn by a married woman in the parting of her hair
sip a card game
stupa a mound commemorating the Buddha's death
subji vegetable
suka dry
tach grazing ground
tawa iron griddle used for making chapattis
tehsildar an officer in local administration, above the *patwari* and the *kanundar*
thakur a feudal title originally used by Rajputs
thali metal plate with a raised lip
thanka Buddhist religious painting mounted on a scroll
thuppa broth
thurka the fried ingredients added to *dal* just before serving
tika the mark a woman wears on her forehead
tsampa parched barley flour
vaidya one who has knowledge of and practises Ayurvedic medicine
zenana women's quarters